# THE LOST HALL OF RECORDS

## Edgar Cayce's Forgotten Record of Human History in the Ancient Yucatan

John Van Auken
Lora Little, Ed.D.

Memphis, Tennessee
Eagle Wing Books, Inc.

Published by
Eagle Wing Books, Inc.
P. O. Box 9972
Memphis, TN 38190

ISBN 10: 0-940829-66-5
ISBN 13: 978-0-940829-66-4

Retail Price: $16.95

First U.S.A. Printing: August 2000
Reissued & Revised: May 2020

# Dedication

This book is dedicated to our spouses
without whom it would not have been possible:

**Doris Van Auken**
**Greg Little**

# Acknowledgments

*John Van Auken:* I would like to thank Doug Richards, Ahmed Fayed, Ann Jaffin, Joan Hanley, William Fix, Richard Cavendish, David Hatcher Childress, Howard Church, and Edgar Cayce for instilling me with the wonders of mythology, archaeology, and adventure. And I want to extend a special thanks to Gregory Little for help above and beyond the call of duty.

*Lora Little:* I would like to express appreciation to the many people and organizations who made substantial contributions to this work. The libraries and staff at Vanderbilt University, Emory University, and the University of Memphis were very helpful resources. To the University of Pennsylvania Museum of Anthropology and Archaeology I extend a special thanks. The efforts of Allessandro Pezzati, Charles Kline, and Melissa Wagner are much appreciated. John Montgomery is also acknowledged for his illustration and photos as is The National Geographic Society for the cover photograph. I also want to thank John and Doris Van Auken for their patience and support for this project. Finally, a special thanks is expressed to my husband Greg for his patience and support.

## Illustration/Copyright Acknowledgments

Sources for photos and illustrations are cited in the text. Every effort has been made to identify and contact the owners of copyrighted photos and illustrations used in this book. Any omissions or errors are purely unintentional and will be rectified at the earliest opportunity. Readings from the Edgar Cayce materials are reproduced by permission of the Edgar Cayce Foundation as are several illustrations from the A.R.E. Other photographs are used with permission from The National Geographic Society, John Montgomery, and the University of Pennsylvania Anthropology Museum. Additional photographs and illustrations are by the authors, from the Corel Gallery©, DigitalVision®, Dover, Gramercy, the Carnegie Institution, clip art books, and uncopyrighted internet sources.

# Table Of Contents

## Section I
## Edgar Cayce & the Mysterious Hall of Records

## Section II
## Archaeological Evidence at Piedras Negras

## Section III
## The Akasha & the Archaeological Record

# Section I

# Edgar Cayce
# &
# the Mysterious
# Hall of Records

## Chapter 1

# Introduction:
# The Mysterious Maya
# & Cayce's Yucatan
# Hall of Records

The archaeological world continues to marvel at the mysterious splendor that was the Maya civilization. Scientific investigation begun in earnest in the mid-19th century has only scratched the surface as to the origin of these intelligent and highly evolved people. In fact most texts admit that the Maya seem to have appeared almost magically as an organized society around 2000 B.C. in parts of Mexico, Guatemala, Belize, and Honduras, an area collectively known as the Yucatan.

Maya civilization had complex astronomical, architectural, artistic, and mathematical abilities as well as a calendar system with an accuracy we are only now able to duplicate. The Maya also had a complex written language which only very recently has begun to be interpreted. Attempts to locate the remains of the ancestral cultures of the Maya have been largely unsuccessful. Some have theorized that the Maya evolved from the Olmecs, another highly developed ancient Yucatan culture that itself cannot be traced to a formative stage.[1] The mystery of the origin of the Olmec and the Maya civilizations remains unsolved in archaeology.

The Olmec culture, which also has been dated as originating around 2000 B.C., is noted for its unusual sculptured monuments which depict people with Asian, African, and Caucasian features. The most well known are the colossal heads which appear to be portraits of Africans wearing the helmets of ball players. The smallest of these heads weighs 8.5 tons.[2] Even more astounding is that the boulders from which they were carved are made of basalt which had to be quarried and transported from a site located 80 miles away! (See *figures 1 & 2*.) Other sculptures include Caucasian looking men (*figures 3, 5-7*) with beards (Native Americans are generally unable to grow beards). The Olmec settlements, located on the Mexican Gulf Coast, were discovered originally in 1926, but were not excavated until the National Geographic Society sponsored expeditions beginning in 1939.[3] Once their antiquity was confirmed, these settlements were thought to predate the Maya. In fact, due to the number of similarities between the Maya and the Olmec cultures, some scientists believed that the Olmecs were precursors of the Maya. But discoveries of complex Preclassic city structures at El Mirador and Nakbe in Guatemala and at sites in Belize have pushed the Maya Preclassic era back to around 2000 B.C. making the Maya likely contemporaries with the Olmecs. (See timeline chart on following pages.) As a result, it is still not understood how these groups emerged so successfully from the cave dwellers, hunter-gatherers and small farming groups of the so-called Archaic Period.[4]

*Figures 1, 2*

Right: Helmeted head from Veracruz (from Corel Gallery). Left: Helmeted head at La Venta (by Lora Little). Both of these figures — as well as many others at Olmec sites — show African and Polynesian features.

## Linguistic & Written Clues

Descendants of the ancient Maya currently live in parts of Mexico and Guatemala. Linquists and ethnologists have traced their modern languages (which now include around 30 different dialects) to one common language they call proto-Mayan. This language appears to date back prior to 2000 B.C. putting it in the Archaic period.

Much of the history of the ancient Maya was lost during the Spanish colonization in the 1600s. When the Spanish arrived in the New World, the Maya culture had regressed to primarily an agricultural society of small villages. The great Maya cities were already overgrown ruins. The Aztecs, centered at the current location of Mexico City, were the dominant culture, and had custody of not

Figure 3
Bearded man on relief at La Venta (from Drucker, 1952).

| Table 1 | | |
| --- | --- | --- |
| **Mesoamerican Cultures: Timeline and Locations** | | |
| (Dates reflect periods when cultures were at their height and are still being revised for some groups. Source: Richard W. Adams, *Prehistoric Mesoamerica*, 1991) | | |
| CULTURE | TIMEFRAME | GEOGRAPHIC AREA |
| **Olmec** | 1500-400 B.C. | Gulf Coast of Mexico/Tabasco |
| **Maya** | A.D. 50 - 1000 | Yucatan, Guatemala, Belize, Honduras |
| **Toltec** | A.D. 500 - 1162 | Central Mexican Basin and Yucatan |
| **Aztec** | A.D. 1000 - 1580 | Central Mexican Basin |

only their own sacred manuscripts, but those of the Maya as well. At that time, hundreds of Aztec and Maya books (called a *codex* or codices for plural) were destroyed by the Spanish Catholic hierarchy in an attempt to stamp out the pagan religions of the native groups. At the same time, ironically, some of the very same clergy who destroyed the Maya books provided historical descriptions of the Maya culture that are widely used in archaeological research today. Also, for-tunately, a few Maya priests secretly copied some of the sacred books. These were preserved in libraries and museums primarily in Europe. Much of what is known about the ancient Maya belief system comes from these remaining copies. Some of these, including the Madrid,

*Figure 4*

Maya Codex on deerskin at Natl. Museum of Anthropology in Mexico City (photo — Lora Little).

*Table 2*

# Maya Developmental Timeline

(Source: Robert Sharer, *The Ancient Maya*, 1994)

| CULTURE | TIMEFRAME |
|---|---|
| **Lithic Period** | **25,000 - 7000 B.C.** |
| **Archaic Period** | **7000 - 2000 B.C.** |
| **Preclassic Period** | **2000 B.C. to A.D. 50** |
| Early Preclassic | 2000 - 1000 B.C. |
| Middle Preclassic | 1000 - 400 B.C. |
| Late Preclassic | 400 B.C. - A.D. 50 |
| **Classic Period** | **A.D. 50 - 1000** |
| Protoclassic | A.D. 50 - 250 |
| Early Classic | A.D. 250-600 |
| Late Classic | A.D. 600-800 |
| Terminal Classic | A.D. 800-1000 |
| **Postclassic Period A.D. 900 - 1500** | |
| Early Postclassic | A.D. 900 - 1200 |
| Late Postclassic | A.D. 1200 - 1500 |

*Figure 5*
Bearded mask with Oriental features at
Mexico City museum (photo — Lora Little).

*Figure 6*
Bearded man on stela at Monte
Alban (from Corel Gallery).

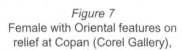

*Figure 7*
Female with Oriental features on
relief at Copan (Corel Gallery),

Paris, and Dresden Codices, are named for the cities in which they are stored.[5]

Other information has come from collections of ancient sacred writings preserved by two different modern Maya groups. One is the *Popol Vuh*, from the Quiche (pronounced Key-chay) Maya and the other, the books of the *Chilam Balam*, are from the Yucatec Maya. In addition, over the past 20 years, ethnologists, linguists, and archaeologists have collaborated to begin deciphering the hieroglyphic writings found on the many Maya monuments discovered throughout Mesoamerica. From these writings and the work of explorers and archaeologists over the past 150 years, the complexity of the Maya social, spiritual, and political culture is beginning to be understood. How they came to this level of complexity so quickly and why they seemed to decline just as suddenly remain a mystery.[6] This mystery was just as puzzling to people in

the 1930s. As a result, in 1933, the famous psychic Edgar Cayce was asked to explain the origins of the Maya culture. His response was very detailed and included references to a lost Hall of Records which he said was located in the Yucatan near where archaeologists were digging at that time. In this book we will examine the fascinating information Edgar Cayce supplied in view of modern archaeological knowledge in an attempt to shed some light on the origins of the Maya and the location of this mysterious Hall of Records. But, first, who was Edgar Cayce?

## The Edgar Cayce Connection: About Edgar Cayce

Edgar Cayce (pronounced, KAY-see) was born on a farm near Hopkinsville, Kentucky, on March 18, 1877. As a child, he displayed unusual powers of perception. At the age of six, he told his parents that he could see and talk with "visions," sometimes of relatives who had recently died, and even angels. He could also sleep with his head on his schoolbooks and awaken with a photographic recall of their contents, even sighting the page upon which the answer appeared. However, after completing seventh grade, he left school – which was not unusual for boys at that time.

When he was twenty-one, he developed a paralysis of the throat muscles which caused him to lose his voice. When doctors were unable to find a physical cause for this condition, Edgar Cayce asked a friend to help him re-enter the same kind of hypnotic sleep that had enabled him to memorize his schoolbooks as a child. The friend gave him the necessary suggestions and, once he was in this trance state, Cayce spoke clearly and directly without any difficulty. He instructed the "hypnotist" to give him a suggestion to increase the bloodflow to his throat; when the suggestion was given, Cayce's throat turned blood red. Then, while still under hypnosis, Cayce recommended some specific medication and manipulative therapy which would aid in restoring his voice completely.

On subsequent occasions, Cayce would go into the hypnotic state to diagnose and prescribe healing for others, with much success. Doctors around Hopkinsville and Bowling Green, Kentucky, took advantage of Cayce's unique talent to diagnose their patients. They soon discovered that all Cayce needed was the name and address of a patient to "tune in" telepathically to that individual's mind and body. The patient didn't have to be near Cayce, he could tune-in to them wherever they were.

*Figure 8*
Edgar Cayce

When one of the young M.D.s working with Cayce submitted a report on his strange abilities to a clinical research society in Boston, the reactions were amazing. On October 9, 1910, *The New York Times* carried two pages of headlines and pictures. From then on, people from all over the country sought the "sleeping prophet," as he was to become known.

The routine he used for conducting a trance-diagnosis was to recline on a couch, hands folded across his solar-plexus, and breathe deeply. Eventually, his eyelids would begin fluttering and his breathing would become deep and rhythmical. This was the signal to the conductor (usually his wife, Gertrude) to make verbal contact with Cayce's subconscious by giving a suggestion. Unless this procedure was timed to synchronize with his fluttering eyelids and the change in his breathing, Cayce would proceed beyond his trance state and simply fall fast asleep. However, once the suggestion was made, Cayce would proceed to describe the patient as though he or she were sitting right next to him, his mind functioning much as an x-ray scanner, seeing into every organ of their body. When he was finished, he would say, "Ready for questions." However, in many cases his mind would have already anticipated the patient's questions, answering them during the main session. Eventually, he would say, "We are through for the present," whereupon the conductor would give the suggestion to return to normal consciousness.

If this procedure were in any way violated, Cayce would be in serious personal danger. On one occasion, he remained in a trance state for three days and had actually been given up for dead by the attending doctors.

At each session, a stenographer (usually Gladys Davis Turner, his personal secretary) would record everything Cayce said. Sometimes, during a trance session, Cayce would even correct the stenographer's spelling. It was as though his mind were in touch with everything around him and beyond.

Each client was identified with a number to keep their names private. For example, hypnotic material for Edgar Cayce is filed under the number 294. His first "reading," as they were called, would be numbered 294-1, and each subsequent reading would increase the dash number (294-2, 294-3, and so on). Some numbers refer to groups of people, such as the Study Group, 262; and some numbers refer to specific research or guidance readings, such as the 254 series, containing the Work readings dealing with the overall work of the organization that grew up around him, and the 364 and 996 series containing the readings on Atlantis.

## The Scope of Cayce's Readings Expands

It was August 10, 1923 before anyone thought to ask the "sleeping" Cayce for insights beyond physical health – questions about life, death, and human destiny. In a small hotel room in Dayton, Ohio, Arthur Lammers asked the first set of philosophical questions that were to lead to an entirely new way of using Cayce's strange abilities. It was during this line of questioning that Cayce first began to talk about reincarnation as though it were as real and natural as the functionings of a physical body. This shocked and challenged Cayce and his family. They were deeply religious people, doing this work to help others because that's what their Christian faith taught. As a child, Cayce began to read the Bible from front to back, and did so for every year of his life. Reincarnation was not part of the Cayce family's reality. Yet, the healings and help continued to come. So, the Cayce family continued with the physical material, but cautiously reflected on the strange philosophical material. Ultimately, the Cayce's began to accept the ideas, though not as "reincarnation," per se. Edgar Cayce preferred to call it, "The Continuity of Life." He felt that the Bible did contain much evidence that life, the true life in the Spirit, is continual.

Eventually, Edgar Cayce, following advice from his own readings, moved to Virginia Beach, Virginia, and set up a hospital where he continued to conduct his "Physical Readings" for the health of others. But he also continued this new line of readings called "Life Readings." From 1925 through 1944, he conducted some 2,500 of these Life Readings, describing the past lives of individuals as casually as if everyone understood reincarnation were a reality. Such subjects as deep-seated fears, mental blocks, vocational talents, innate urges and abilities, marriage difficulties, child training, etc., were examined in the light of what the readings called the "karmic patterns" resulting from previous lives experienced by the individual's soul on the earth plane.

When he died on January 3, 1945, in Virginia Beach, he left 14,256 documented stenographic records of the telepathic-clairvoyant readings he had given for more than 6,000 different people over a period of forty-three years, consisting of 49,135 pages.

The readings constitute one of the largest and most impressive records of psychic perception. Together with their relevant records, correspondence and reports, they have been cross-indexed under thousands of subject headings and placed at the disposal of doctors, psychologists, students, writers, and investigators who still come to examine them. Of course, they are also available to the general public in books or complete volumes of the readings, as well as on CD ROM for DOS, Windows, and Macintosh computers.

A foundation known as the Association for Research and Enlightenment (A.R.E.) was founded in 1932 to preserve these readings. As an open-membership research society, it continues to index and catalog the information, initiate investigation and experiments, and conduct conferences, seminars and lectures. The A.R.E. also has the largest and finest library of parapsychological and metaphysical books in the world.[*]

## Problems Interpreting His Readings

Edgar Cayce's readings do present some difficulties in interpretation and understanding. First, they are somewhat difficult to read, mostly due to their syntax and the presence of archaic or biblical terms and style. They are *written* records of a *verbal* presentation, a process that occasionally does not carry the full intent that was expressed, and punctuation can significantly change the meaning or intent of the voiced statement. Also, most of the readings were given to specific people with uniquely personal perspectives and prejudices on the topics being discussed, and therefore, the responses were slanted to fit the seeker's perspective. For example, in a reading for one person, Cayce recommends one marriage for life, to another he recommends never getting married, and to a third he encourages him to marry at least twice. In the few cases where a reading was purposefully for broader presentation to

[*] Their address and phone number are: A.R.E., 215 67th St., Virginia Beach, VA 23451, (757) 428-3588.

many people, even the masses, the "sleeping" Cayce was still somewhat at the mercy and wisdom of the those directing the session and asking the questions. Nevertheless, Cayce and his wife Gertrude and their assistant Gladys were very conscientious people, always seeking to be exact and true to the original intent of the reading. As indicated earlier, the "sleeping" Cayce would occasionally stop his direct discourse to give an aside to Gladys about the way she was recording the material, correcting spelling or giving a clarifying explanation of something he had just said. Finally, because some of Cayce's readings cover so many points or issues within the text, it can be difficult to determine which one he is referring to when the paragraphs are so complex. Despite all of this, with sufficient practice, one can become familiar enough with the syntax, terms and "thys," "thees," and "thous"; a repetitive use of the word "that"; and the complex thought pattern, so that one can learn to read and understand the Cayce readings fairly easily.

On the topics of Yucatan, Maya, Aztec, Mu, Atlantis, and the Hall of Records he mentioned these in 397 of his readings. He gave 68 people readings in which he said that they had previously incarnated in Yucatan. That is not many when you consider that he gave 581 people prior incarnations in Egypt. For his readings on the ancient Hall of Records, see the section on The Lost Hall of Records.

## Cayce's Story of the Maya Civilization

As speculation regarding the origin of large numbers of ancient ruins built by a mysterious people in the Yucatan began to reach the United States in the early part of this century, some of those who were obtaining readings from Edgar Cayce decided to see if he could shed any light on the subject. In November of 1933 a reading was given in the New York home of an active A.R.E. (Association for Research and Enlightenment - the organization that studies and researches the Cayce readings) member in which Cayce was asked to "give an historical treatise on the origin and development of the Maya civilization..." His response was surprisingly detailed and linked the Maya culture to several different influences occurring over many thousands of years. Of even greater significance, Cayce found it necessary in the reading to clarify that the Maya culture is only one of many civilizations that have been present in "this *particular portion of the world*" and that these other civilizations will be discovered "*as research progresses.*" As it focused on the Maya culture, the reading began by describing an influx of immigrants fleeing the third and final destruction of the legendary continent of Atlantis "*10,600 years before the Prince of Peace came into the land of*

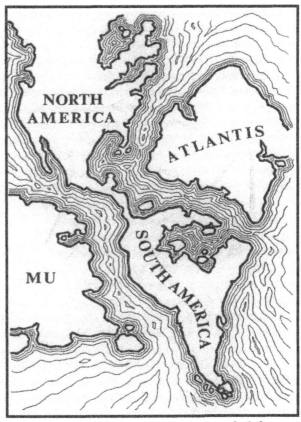

*Figure 9*
Map of Edgar Cayce's description of the migration of various groups into the Yucatan. Reprinted from *The Great Migration* by Vada Carlson (1970) A.R.E. Press — by permission.

*promise."* By the time the reading ended, Cayce had identified three additional major cultural influences in the Yucatan.[7]

First, were settlers from the legendary southern Pacific continent of Mu (Lemuria), who had fled to Yucatan (and elsewhere) during its destruction. This occurred sometime before the final destruction of Atlantis (between 28,000 and 10,000 B.C.). Second, he mentioned a people he called "the Incal." These people descended from a mixture of Lemurian immigrants and a group of earlier Atlantean immigrants who had left during the second major destruction of Atlantis around 28,000 BC. (See *figure* 9.) And thirdly, he identified the arrival by boat of remnants from the Lost Tribes of Israel around 3,000 B.C. Cayce also indicated an indirect Egyptian influence stemming largely from the parallel migration of Atlanteans to Egypt shortly before the final Atlantean destruction. In addition, the readings indicated that a primitive native presence pre-existed in the area prior to the coming of these outside groups. Cayce's historical timeline of these events is summarized on pages 264-265.

## Other Theories That Agree With Cayce

Well, leave it to the Cayce readings to come up with a fascinating and difficult-to-prove theory. Interestingly, Cayce was not the first or the only one to propose that the Maya culture was the result of outside influences. James Churchward in his 1931 book, *The Lost Continent of Mu*, claimed to have found inscriptions on buildings in the Yucatan that contain references to ancient Mu dynasties.[8] At least two sixteenth century Spanish historians (Oviedo & Valdes, 1535 and Gomara, 1552) proposed that Atlanteans migrated to Mesoamerica. It was popular during the 18th and 19th centuries to believe that the overwhelming evidence for ancient complex civilizations being found throughout the Americas could not possibly have been related to the indigenous "savage" Indian populations currently in existence. Theories of migrations from outside cultures were numerous and included almost every known historically established culture from Phoenicians to Irish to Norwegians to Chinese to Africans to Hindus to Romans and many others. Abbe' Brasseur de Bourbourg and Augustus Le Plongeon, the former a respected 19th century Maya historian and the latter considered a crackpot, both, after years of study, came to the conclusion that the Maya were descended from Atlantis. Edward Thompson, who was in charge of the reconstruction of the famous Maya ruins at Chichen Itza, also came to believe that the Maya were descended from the Atlanteans.[9] It is the official belief of the Mormon church that the Maya are descendants of the Lost Tribes of Israel.[10] As a result, even today Brigham Young University has a very active archaeological field program in the Yucatan (more about that later).

These theories fell out of favor politically as the new countries within the Americas developed their own national identities. In addition, scientific archaeological methodology came to provide evidence that seemed to support the theory that the Americas were populated by Asian immigrants who evolved gradually after crossing the Bering Straits at the end of the last great ice age 11,000 years ago. Since this theory was more politically correct, it helped to cement the relationship between mainstream archaeological research and the various national interests. This relationship has resulted in much fruitful, although relatively close-minded, scientific investigation.

## Support From Current Investigations

Fortunately, both scientific and popular interest in the Maya mystery continues to grow as does the abundance of archaeological information. In the fifth edition (1994) of *The Ancient Maya*, Robert J. Sharer, Professor of Anthropology, and Curator of the American Section of the University Museum of Archaeology at the University of Pennsylvania, required almost 900 pages to provide a comprehensive update of the current scientific findings on the Maya culture. In the introduction he noted that, since the fourth edition was published in 1983..."the accelerating pace of research and the explosive growth in information have already rendered important sections of that edition woefully out-of-date."[11]

## Pre-Clovis Sites Now Confirm Genetic Evidence

During the late 1990s the field of archaeology was rocked by the discovery of several pre-Bering Strait era settlements in both North and South America. Prior to this discovery most archaeologists assumed that the first Americans walked over the Bering Straits near the end of the last ice age - around 9,000 B.C. This group left a particular style of spear point, called the Clovis point, throughout North and South America as evidence of their occupation. (See *figure* 10.) Most archaeologists refer to this as the "Clovis First" theory. Mysteriously, however, these Clovis points were not found in the open, ice free corridor through which they were said to have migrated. Also, the archaeological evidence indicated that they would have had to have spread throughout the two continents within an unbelievably short span of 500 years.[12] Archaeologists have now uncovered many pre-Clovis sites in the Americas indicating that the accepted American occupation chronology goes back far further in time than 9,000 B.C. Sites are now being routinely reported indicating settlement in the Americas at 12,000 B.C. and even earlier. At some controversial sites it is speculated that occupation may have occurred earlier than 30,000 B.C.

Genetic studies have only deepened the mystery. Siberians and Alaskans were found to be genetically different from their Native American cousins to the South and East. Certain genetic subtypes which were present in the southern natives were not present in the northern groups who, according to the Bering Strait theory, should be the forbearers of the southern groups. This difference indicated that the southern natives may have had contact with groups from some other areas or that not all of the first Americans came over the Bering Straits.

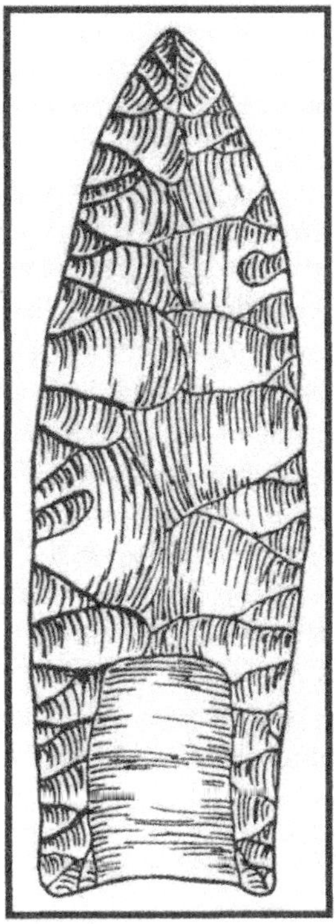

*Figure 10*
Typical Clovis point. From *Tellico Archaeology* (1985) TVA.

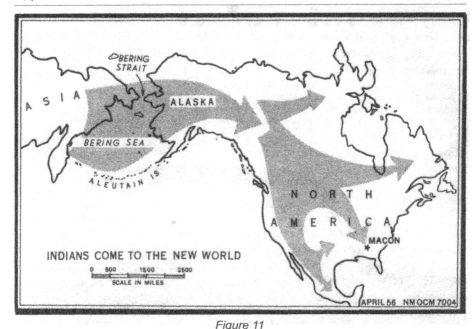

*Figure 11*

The "Clovis First" Theory, asserting that the first Americans crossed Beringia about 9000 B.C., is collapsing as evidence from linguistics, genetics, and new archaeological finds mounts. Reprinted from *Ocmulgee* by G. Pope (1956), Natl. Park Service.

Linguists had already noted that the languages of the North American natives in the eastern sections were not from the same root as those of the western groups. Some theorized, and have found evidence, that Asian groups migrated down the western coast of the America by boat. However, genetic study has also revealed the presence of Eurasian, possibly Middle Eastern, subtypes among some Native Americans which is not accounted for by the Spanish colonization. Even more amazing is that, through genetics, scientists have been able to determine the amount of time which has elapsed since the first Asians migrated to America. They compared the genetic makeup of modern Asian and Native American groups and determined that a period of 30,000 years would need to have elapsed in order for the genetic differences they found to occur. Needless to say, the archaeological community is still reeling from these challenges to their dogmatic, and seemingly ironclad, Bering Strait migration theory. As a result, some scientists are conceding that Native Americans could have been settled by more than one group and by more than one route.[13, 14, 15] The "Clovis First" theory is falling apart.

## Atlantean Hall of Records in the Yucatan

Another area of interest in the Cayce readings with regards to the Maya is his identification of the Yucatan as one of the three places where an Atlantean Hall of Records can still be found. As will be discussed in the next chapter, these records are said to contain a history of the origins of humanity up to Atlantean times. The A.R.E. has started monitoring archaeological excavations that appear to be very near a site in Guatemala which Cayce identified as the location of the Yucatan Hall of Records. Since 1997 archaeologists from Brigham Young University have been excavating at the site. So far they do not appear to have found the Yucatan Hall of Records, but it does seem interesting that a Mormon university is the one doing work at this very remote Maya site. (More on that later.) Even more interesting is that Cayce indicated that scientists working in the Yucatan in the 1930s had already unknowingly unearthed artifacts containing carvings that describe the Atlantean power-producing device Cayce termed "the firestone." Cayce also stated that manmade circular stones that were in existence at the time of the last Atlantean migrations could still be found in the Yucatan.

## Blueprints for the Atlantean Firestone Already Discovered?

Several of the Yucatan readings stated that the Atlantean records contain information regarding the construction of the Atlantean firestone. Cayce even specified that certain stones which contained the *emblem* of the firestone were uncovered in the Yucatan and may have been placed in museums in Pennsylvania, Chicago, and Washington during the 1930s. "In Yucatan there is the emblem (of the firestone). Let's clarify this, for it may be the more easily found - for they *(these stones)* will be brought to this America, these United States. A portion is to be carried, as we find, to the Pennsylvania State Museum. A portion is to be carried to the Washington preservations of such findings, or to Chicago. The stones that are set in front of the temple..."[16] When asked to be more specific as to which Yucatan temple, Cayce referred back to a reading given in November of 1933. "Also the records that were carried to what is now Yucatan in America, where these stones (that they know so little about) **are now during the last few months being uncovered.**"[17]

Inquiries were then made to the Pennsylvania State Museum which ultimately led to the Archaeology Museum of the University of

Pennsylvania (Penn) as to the specific sites they were working on in the Yucatan in 1933. The answer was none in the Yucatan, but they were doing work at Piedras Negras, Guatemala during 1933. Although Cayce never named Piedras Negras or any other specific site in the Yucatan as *the* location of the Yucatan Hall of Records, a follow-up question was asked that linked Penn to the firestone emblem and the Hall of Records. A question was asked during a Cayce reading as to whether "it would be wise to write the Pennsylvania State Museum, or called University of Pennsylvania" regarding this information. Cayce agreed that it would be prudent to do so.[18] Since the questioner's reference to the two institutions as being one and the same was not corrected by Cayce, it was assumed that he meant that Piedras Negras was most likely the site. Although Guatemala is not in the Yucatan per se, Cayce researchers believe that Cayce used the term Yucatan broadly to indicate a much larger area of Mesoamerica than is currently identified by the archaeological community.[19, 20] It should also be noted that, in common usage, the term Yucatan generally encompasses a broader area than the archaeological community recognizes as Yucatan. Piedras Negras is, in fact, very close to the area that is today considered the Yucatan and is known to have played an important role as one of several Maya cities that interconnected with what is now the Yucatan and Central Mexico.[21]

## Piedras Negras — Location of the Hall of Records?

So, is Piedras Negras really the location of one of the Atlantean Hall of Records? Was the firestone blueprint or emblem found by Penn during the 1930s? What was sent to the Pennsylvania State Museum and to museums in Washington and Chicago? Is there any evidence from archaeological research for the possibility that other cultures migrated into Mesoamerica? What information may be found in the Hall of Records? How do the Maya and Aztec creation stories relate to the Atlantean migrations and the search for the Hall of Records? How do these creation stories relate to those from other cultures such as the Hebrews and the Egyptians?

In this book we will attempt to answer these questions. In order to do so, we will take you on a journey through the jungles of Guatemala and into the mysteries of the origin of humanity as detailed through hundreds of Cayce readings. We will begin with Cayce's description of the lost Atlantean Halls of Records in the Yucatan and elsewhere. From there we will move on to the archaeological data from Piedras Negras and other ancient Maya sites which, amazingly, confirm much of Cayce's story! In fact, it appears that the firestone emblem was indeed found during the 1930s at Piedras Negras. In addition, we will show how the ancient creation stories of the Maya and the Aztecs closely parallel the Cayce readings.

Perhaps the great interest shown by an amazingly large number of people in the hunt for the better known Egyptian Hall of Records is fueled by a deep desire to know —exactly — what is in the Hall. Many people seem to want some form of deeper understanding of their ultimate "roots" and a historical confirmation of their origin. The Egyptian Hall of Records appears to hold the promise of this confirmation, but uncovering the Hall in Egypt has been far more complicated than expected. The records in the Yucatan may be more accessible and closer to discovery. Cayce stated that the Yucatan Hall of Records stored essentially the same information as in Egypt. So the long-hidden mystery of our true history may soon be revealed. Somewhat less well-known is that Cayce has already told us what is recorded in the records. In his thousands of readings Cayce specifically outlined how and why the Hall of Records was established. It's an astonishing story of the ultimate history of humanity — who and what we are — and where we are going. This fascinating story of the unfolding of human existence as given through the Cayce readings is the conclusion of this book. It takes us through creation up to and including the migration of the Atlanteans to the Americas and the establishment of the Hall of Records.

## References

1. Sharer, Robert (1994) *The Ancient Maya*. Stanford, California: Stanford University Press.

2. Adams, Richard (1991) *Prehistoric Mesoamerica*. Norman Oklahoma: University of Oklahoma Press, p. 66.

3. Coe, Michael (1981) Matthew Williams Stirling, 1896-1975. In Elizabeth Benson (Ed.) *The Olmecs and their Neighbors*. Washington, D.C.: Dumbarton Oaks Research Library and Collections.

4. *Prehistoric Mesoamerica*, op. cit.

5. Coe, Michael (1992) *Breaking the Maya Code*. New York: Thames and Hudson.

6. Freidel, D, Schele, L. and Parker, J. (1993) *Maya Cosmos*. New York: William Morrow.

7. Reading 5750-1

8. Churchward, James (1968) The Lost Continent of Mu. New York: Paperback Library, Inc.

9. *Breaking the Maya Code*, op. cit.

10. *The Book of Mormon*, (1963) Salt Lake City, Utah: The Church of Jesus of Latter-day Saints.

11. The Ancient Maya, óp. cit., p. viii.

12. Begley, Sharon and Murr, Andrew (1999) The First Americans. *Newsweek Magazine*, April 26, p. 50- 57.

13. Torroni, A. et al (1993) mtDNA Variation of Aboriginal Siberians Reveals Distinct Genetic Affinities with Native Americans. *American Journal of Human Genetics*. 53 (3), pp. 591-608.

14. Callegari-Jacques, S.M. et al (1993) GM Haplotype Distribution in Amerindians - Relationship with Geography and Language. American *Journal of Physical Anthropology:* 90 (4), pp. 427-444.

15. Horai, S. et al (1993) Peopling of the Americas, Founded by 4 Major Lineages of Mitochondrial DNA. *Molecular Biology and Evolution*, 10 (1), pp. 23-47.

16. Reading 440-5.

17. Reading 5750-1.

18. Reading 440-12.

19. Hatt, Carolyn (1972) *The Maya: Based on the Edgar Cayce Readings*. Virginia Beach, VA: A.R.E. Press.

20. Cayce, Edgar Evans, Richards, Doug and Cayce, Gail (1997) *Mysteries of Atlantis Revisited*. New York: St. Martin's Press.

21. The Ancient Maya, op. cit.

## Chapter 2

# The Lost
# Hall of Records

O ne of the most interesting pieces of information to come through
Edgar Cayce's visions is the existence of an ancient Hall of Records.
In this Hall are stored the records of a prehistoric descent into matter of
the souls who inhabit the Earth today. The records record millions of
years of activity in the mythological lands of Mu, Lemuria, Atlantis, Og,
Oz, Zu, and others. Actually, Cayce says there are three Halls.  One is
under the waters near the Bahamian island of Bimini, another is underground near the Sphinx in Giza, Egypt, and the one we are most interested in is beneath a temple in the Mayan lands. The records in this
temple are "overshadowed" by another temple that "overhangs" or is
built over it. But Cayce says that the Record Hall will "rise again." He
says the records are in the remains of "the temple by Iltar." Iltar, according to Cayce, was a high priest migrating with his people from the legendary lands of Atlantis to the new "Aryan or Yucatan land" and there
built this temple of records. (See *figures 12 & 13*)

### The Bimini Records

Records in the waters off Bimini Island in the Bahamas are in a
submerged temple, but Cayce says this temple also "will rise and is
rising again." These records are in the temple of "Atlan." Like Iltar, Atlan
was a high priest who attempted to preserve the records of Atlantis, but
his temple sunk during a series of earthquakes that destroyed Atlantis.

*Figure 13*

The journey from Aztlan as depicted in the *Codex Boturini* shows one individual leading the way. The island of Aztlan, depicted as a pyramid, may have had vocanic eruptions causing the residents to flee. (Note the material coming from the top of the pyramid.) Other depictions of this event show an island sinking in a volcanic eruption with many people drowning with one male leading the way in a boat. This man may represent Iltar and the island may be the mythical Atlantis.

*Figure 12*

The Aztecs reported that their origin was an island called "Aztlan." It was an island as depicted in this drawing from the *Historia mexicana* (1576)

## The Egypt Records

The temple of records in Egypt is entered by a hall or passageway that begins at or near the Sphinx, according to Cayce. He is inconsistent in his description of it, sometimes referring to it as a "pyramid of records," other times calling it a "temple or hall of records," and on one occasion calling it a "tomb of records." In some discourses Cayce describes its location as being off the right front paw of the Sphinx in line with the Great Pyramid, which would locate it somewhere east-southeast of the Sphinx. He also references the Temple of Isis as a key to locating this hall or pyramid of records. Remnants of the Isis temple still stand between the Sphinx and the Great Pyramid. In another discourse he clearly states that the Egyptian record cache is between the Nile and the Sphinx, off its right front paw in line with the Great Pyramid. On one occasion he said the shadow of the Sphinx points to the cache. But it seems impossible to cast a shadow across the right front paw when the sun never gets behind the Sphinx's head from the northwest. However, Cayce also said that the poles of the Earth were reversed during the ancient times. In which case, the Sphinx would indeed throw a shadow over its own right paw. A mystery yet to be understood.

He also said that the base of the sphinx was "laid out in channels," and in the left rear corner of the Sphinx, which is facing the Great Pyramid, one can find the wording of how the Sphinx was "founded, giving the history of the first invading ruler, Arart, and the ascension of Araaraart to pharaoh." According to Cayce, Arart was the first dynasty not Menes, as we have it today. Araaraart was the second pharaoh. Arart and his people invaded Egypt from Mt. Ararat. It will be an amazing confirmation of Cayce's gift as a seer if these two names are recorded in a corner of the Sphinx.

## The Yucatan Records

The Hall of Records in Yucatan may also be laid out in underground channels because both Mayan and Aztec complexes are known to have underground tunnels, chambers, and passage ways.

Cayce clearly says, "as time draws nigh when changes are to come about, there may be the opening of those three places where the records are one, to those that are the initiates in the knowledge of the One God..."

Figure 14
The Sphinx. From Corel Gallery.

*Figure 15*

In another codex, an " immigration" across the ocean from a country lying to the east is depicted. People emerge from a cave and ride upon the back of turtles to Veracruz. As we will see later, the cave and the turtles both play a significant role in unraveling the mystery.

## What Is In The Hall of Records

According to Cayce, the three record caches contain stone tablets, linens, gold, and artifacts of import to the cultures that created them. He indicates that mummified bodies are buried with the records. As to the question about what language the records may be in, Cayce did not answer directly, only saying that this was a time when the world spoke one language, a time prior to the Tower of Babel legend in the Bible. Therefore, we could assume that the records in these three locations will be in the same language. Although, in one reading he did indicate that the Atlanteans had a slightly different dialect or perhaps pronunciation of the worldwide language then the rest of the world. In another reading he actually stated that there are exactly "thirty-two tablets or plates" in the Egyptian hall of records. These tablets will require interpretation, and this interpretation will take some time. Let's hope it does not take as long as the interpretation of the Dead Sea Scrolls of the Qumran caves.

Cayce says that the records tell the story of the beginnings "when the Spirit took form or began the encasements" in physical bodies in the ancient lands of Mu and Atlantis. They also contain information about the ancient practice of building pyramids. As you may know, pyramids are found all around the globe, from China to America.

When people would ask Edgar Cayce if they could be a part of the discovery and interpretation of these records, he would answer yes, but not necessarily the physical records. As strange as this may seem, according to Cayce, the records are also recorded in consciousness, in the collective mind, and therefore one could open and study the records anytime! Here is an excerpt from one of these strange readings:

"(Q) How may I now find those records, or should I wait - or must I wait?

"(A) You will find the records by that channel as indicated, as these may be obtained MENTALLY. As for the physical records, - it will be necessary to wait until the full time has come for the breaking up of much that has been in the nature of selfish motives in the world. For, remember, these records were made from the angle of WORLD movements. So must thy activities be in the present of the universal approach, but as applied to the individual.

"Keep the faith. Know that the ability lies within self."

From the perspective that Cayce gained in his deep, hypnotic "sleep," all time is one. There is no space, no time. These are only characteristics of the limited dimension of physical, terrestrial life. Within us is a gateway to oneness, timelessness. The records may be reached by journeying within consciousness and through dimensions of consciousness, as Cayce did. He never physically went to Egypt, Bimini, or Yucatan. But he so set aside his terrestrial, outer self, that he could journey through dimensions of consciousness to the *Akasha*, the mental hall of records. In this book we have devoted a major portion to the Akashic records and what Cayce read from them concerning the ancient times leading up to the sealing of these stone records.

But for now, let's get back to the physical records. Here is one of the most detailed of Cayce's readings on the Atlantis migration to other continents and the setting up of temples and record caches. His syntax can be difficult, so take your time, read slowly, deliberately.

**TEXT OF READING 5750-1**

This psychic reading given by Edgar Cayce at the home of Mr. and Mrs. Ernest W. Zentgraf, 400 St. Paul's Ave,, Stapleton, Staten Island, N.Y., this 12th day of November, 1933, in accordance with request made by Mrs. Ernest W. Zentgraf, Active Member of the Ass'n for Research & Enlightenment, Inc.

PRESENT

Edgar Cayce; Hugh Lynn Cayce, Conductor; Gladys Davis, Steno.

Zentgraf Family, Mr. and Mrs. MacBeth, Mr. and Mrs. Clark, and Mr. and Mrs. Wilson.

READING

Time of Reading 4:40 to 5:15 P. M. Eastern Standard Time.

1. HLC: You will give an historical treatise on the origin and development of the Mayan civilization, answering questions.

2. EC: Yes. In giving a record of the civilization in this particular portion of the world, it should be remembered that more than one has been and will be found as research progresses.

3. That which we find would be of particular interest would be that which superseded the Aztec civilization, that was so ruthlessly destroyed or interrupted by Cortez.

4. In that preceding this we had rather a combination of sources, or a high civilization that was influenced by injection of forces from other channels, other sources, as will be seen or may be determined by that which may be given.

5. From time as counted in the present we would turn back to 10,600 years before the Prince of Peace came into the land of promise, and find a civilization being disturbed by corruption from within to such measures that the elements join in bringing devastation to a stiffnecked and adulterous people.

6. With the second and third upheavals in Atlantis, there were individuals who left those lands and came to this particular portion then visible.

7. But, understand, the surface [of Yucatan] was quite different from that which would be viewed in the present. For, rather than being a tropical area it was more of the temperate, and quite varied in the conditions and positions of the face of the areas themselves.

8. In following such a civilization as a historical presentation, it may be better understood by taking into consideration the activities of an individual or group - or their contribution to such a civilization. This of necessity, then, would not make for a complete historical fact, but rather the activities of an individual and the followers, or those that chose one of their own as leader.

9. Then, with the leavings of the civilization in Atlantis (in Poseidia, more specific), Iltar - with a group of followers that had been of the household of Atlan, the followers of the worship of the ONE with some ten individuals - left this land Poseidia, and came westward, entering what would now be a portion of Yucatan. And there began, with the activities of the peoples there, the development into a civilization that rose much in the same matter as that which had been in the Atlantean land. Others had left the land later. Others had left earlier. There had been the upheavals

also from the land of Mu, or Lemuria, [in the Pacific] and these had their part in the changing, or there was the injection of their tenets in the varied portions of the land - which was much greater in extent until the final upheaval of Atlantis, or the islands that were later upheaved, when much of the contour of the land in Central America and Mexico was changed to that similar in outline to that which may be seen in the present.

10. The first temples that were erected by Iltar and his followers were destroyed at the period of change physically in the contours of the land. That now being found, and a portion already discovered that has laid in waste for many centuries, was then a combination of those peoples from Mu, Oz and Atlantis.

11. Hence, these places partook of the earlier portions of that peoples called the Incal; though the Incals were themselves the successors of those of Oz, or Og, in the Peruvian land, and Mu in the southern portions of that now called California and Mexico and southern New Mexico in the United States.

12. This again found a change when there were the injections from those peoples that came with the division of those peoples in that called the promise land [Israelites: The Lost Tribes]. Hence we may find in these ruins that which partakes of the Egyptian, Lemurian and Oz civilizations, and the later activities partaking even of the Mosaic activities [i.e. activites of the people of Moses].

13. Hence each would ask, what specific thing is there that we may designate as being a portion of the varied civilizations that formed the earlier civilization of this particular land?

14. The stones that are circular, that were of the magnetized influence upon which the Spirit of the One spoke to those peoples as they gathered in their service, are of the earliest Atlantean activities in religious service, we would be called today.

15. The altars upon which there were the cleansings of the bodies of individuals (not human sacrifice; for this came much later with the injection of the Mosaic, and those activities of that area), these were later the altars upon which individual activities - that would today be termed hate, malice, selfishness, self-indulgence - were cleansed from the body through the ceremony, through the rise of initiates from the sources of light, that came from the stones upon which the angels of light during the periods gave their expression to the peoples.

16. The pyramid, the altars before the doors of the varied temple activities, was an injection from the people of Oz [Peru] and Mu [Pacific Islands]; and will be found to be separate portions, and that referred to in the Scripture as high places of family altars, family gods, that in many portions of the world became again the injection into the activities of groups

in various portions, as gradually there were the turnings of the people to the satisfying and gratifying of self's desires, or as the Baal or Baalilal activities again entered the peoples respecting their associations with those truths of light that came from the gods to the peoples, to mankind, in the earth.

17. With the injection of those of greater power in their activity in the land, during that period as would be called 3,000 years before the Prince of Peace came, those peoples that were of the Lost Tribes [of Israel], a portion came into the land; infusing their activities upon the peoples from Mu in the southernmost portion of that called America or United States, and then moved on to the activities in Mexico, Yucatan, centralizing that now about the spots where the central of Mexico now stands, or Mexico City. Hence there arose through the age a different civilization, a MIX-TURE again.

18. Those in Yucatan, those in the adjoining lands [e.g. Guatemala and Hondurus] as begun by Iltar, gradually lost in their activities; and came to be that people termed, in other portions of America, the Mound Builders.

19. Ready for questions.

20. (Q) How did the Lost Tribe reach this country?

(A) In boats.

21. (Q) Have the most important temples and pyramids been discovered?

(A) Those of the first civilization have been discovered, and have not all been opened; but their associations, their connections, are being re-placed - or attempting to be rebuilt. Many of the second and third civiliza-tion may NEVER be discovered, for these would destroy the present civi-lization in Mexico to uncover same!

22. (Q) By what power or powers were these early pyramids and temples constructed?

(A) By the lifting forces of those gases that are being used gradually in the present civilization, and by the fine work or activities of those versed in that pertaining to the source from which all power comes.

For, as long as there remains those pure in body, in mind, in activity, to the law of the One God, there is the continued resource for meeting the needs, or for commanding the elements and their activities in the supply of that necessary in such relations.

23. (Q) In which pyramid or temple are the records mentioned in the readings given through this channel on Atlantis, in April, 1932? [364 series]

(A) As given, that temple was destroyed at the time there was the last destruction in Atlantis.

Yet, as time draws nigh when changes are to come about, there may be

*Figure 16*
Circular altar stones at the Maya center of Copan. Photo: Corel Gallery.

the opening of those three places where the records are one, to those that are the initiates in the knowledge of the One God:

The temple by Iltar will then rise again. Also there will be the opening of the temple or hall of records in Egypt, and those records that were put into the heart of the Atlantean land may also be found there - that have been kept, for those that are of that group.

The RECORDS are ONE.

24. We are through for the present.

*Figure 17*
Another circular altar at Copan.
Photo: Corel Gallery.

*Figure 18 (left)*
Drawing of circular altar at Copan
shown in figure 17.
From: Spinden (1913).

*Figure 19 (below)*
Tikal also has numerous circular altars.
Most of these are situated
in front of stelae.
Photo: Corel Gallery.

## Summary & Highlights of Cayce's Reading

Let me recap some important parts of the story in this Cayce reading: Around 10,500 B.C. the great continents of Mu (Lemuria) in the Pacific Ocean and Atlantis in the Atlantic Ocean were in their final stages of destruction; remnant islands were all that was left of their original greatness. Poseidia was the last island of the Atlantean continent. Iltar and Atlan were high priests in the worship of the One God, in a world distracted by many gods. In other readings Cayce called these worshipers the "Children of the Law of One." The Yucatan peninsula appeared to be a good land to migrate to and establish a new community. Iltar and his ten followers did just that. They traveled deep into the jungle and built altars and temples. On their altars (see *figs. 16-19*) they did not sacrifice humans, they sacrificed their weaknesses, attempting to make themselves spiritually stronger and purer, their minds more cosmically aware. They did this by altering their consciousness using circular magnetic stones and evoking the spiritual influences from the One Source. But more earth changes occurred, and Iltar's initial temples and altars were destroyed; new temples were built on top of their remnants. In other readings Cayce recounts that Atlan also lost his temples and altars when the island of Poseidia finally sank.

Yucatan, Central Mexico, Southern California, Arizona, and New Mexico were fast becoming lands of mixed peoples from around the world. The Incas of Peru were also on the move, journeying north to join in the great Mayan development. According to Cayce, the remnants of Iltar's initial group also journeyed north to become the Mound Builders in the United States along the Mississippi and Ohio valleys.

Over time the high level of spiritual attunement and worship slipped into self-gratification and glorification, leading to the worship of Baal. Cayce explained that using the same powers and methods, one could create a god or a frankenstein, it all depended upon the ideals and purposes motivating the effort. Apparently, all the best of intentions slipped into darkness and selfishness, and the higher attunement was lost. Human sacrifice crept into once inspired rituals that had so helped the founders reach other dimensions of the universe.

Around 3,000 B.C. remnants of the Lost Tribes of Israel also came to this area of the world. Into Yucatan, Mexico, Southern U.S., and down into western South America they came adding to the mix of ideals, some good and some bad.

The records of the ancient world and its activities remain in Yucatan in one of Iltar's covered temples, in Atlan's cache under the waters off Bimini, and under the ground near the Sphinx in Egypt.

## Findings That Support Cayce's Story

An interesting bit of news that adds to this great story comes from a little-known discovery in China in 1900 by a Taoist monk named Wang Tao-Shih. The monk found a hidden ancient library in a series of caves. The texts in this library speak of an ancient time and place in "Motherland Mu." Mu is the original name for the great Pacific Ocean continent of Lemuria, which actually began before Atlantis. Sir Aurel Stein interpreted and reported on these ancient texts in his two titles, *On Ancient Central Asian Tracks* and *Ruins of Desert Cathay*. In 212 B.C. the crazed Emperor Chin Shih Huang ordered all the books and literature relating to ancient China to be burned. Whole libraries, including the Grand Royal Library, were destroyed. Chinese literature tells of a semi-mythical "Five Monarchs" who ruled China during a golden age of wealth and wisdom. This period is considered to have been paralleled by the early age of the Egyptian Pharaohs, about 2852-2206 B.C.

There have been many attempts to discover the halls of records in Yucatan, Bimini, and Giza. There have also been discoveries that indicate that the dating of the Great Pyramid and the Sphinx may be too young, and that these monuments may well have been constructed closer to the dates that Cayce gave, 10,600 to 10,500 B.C.

In 1992 U.S. Geologist Dr. Robert Schoch and amateur Egyptologist John Anthony West (author of *Serpent in the Sky*, Harper & Row, 1979) announced to the world press that the age of the Sphinx was much older than originally thought. This revelation sent a shockwave through the international community of professional Egyptologists. A summary of of the findings at Giza came in the spring of 1996 in a letter to the Egyptology journal *KMT* (pronounced *k-met*; it is the ancient name for Egypt and means, "The Black Land," owing to the rich, black silt left by the Nile after flooding season). In this letter John Anthony West outlined his and Dr. Schoch's points:

"1. The Sphinx is not wind-weathered as most Egyptologists think, but water weathered, and by rain;

"2. No rain capable of producing such weathering has fallen since dynastic times;

"3. If it had, other undeniably Old Kingdom tombs on the Giza Plateau cut of the same rock would show similar weathering patterns; they do not;

"Ergo, 4. The Sphinx predates the other Old Kingdom tombs at Giza. Simple as that."

Dr. Schoch estimated the Sphinx to have been constructed from between 5,000 to 7,000 B.C. "and that the current head of the figure –

which everyone agrees is a dynastic head – is almost surely the result of recarving." (*KMT*, Summer 1992, p. 53)

Another date-changing piece of evidence comes from the work of Adrian Gilbert and Robert Bauval, published in their best-selling book *The Orion Mystery* (Crown, 1994). Actually, the initial ideas about Giza star alignments came from Edgar Cayce who stated from his trance state in the 1920s that Giza was laid out according to the stars above it. In 1964 Egyptologist Alexander Badawy and astronomer Virginia Trimble published their findings on how the air shafts and passageways in the Great Pyramid aligned with important stars in both the northern and southern heavens. Then, in 1994, Gilbert and Bauval published their findings, identifying many correlations between the stars and structures on the Plateau:

1. The three great pyramids of Giza – Menkaure, Khafre, and Khufu – match the stars Mintaka, Al Nilam, and Al Nitak (*delta, epsilon, and zeta Orionis*) located in the Belt of Orion, noting that the third pyramid (Menkaure) is set off from the other two pyramids just as the third star in the belt (*delta Orionis*) is set off from the other two stars;

2. The alignment is most exact in the year 10,500 B.C., the date Edgar Cayce gave for the construction of the Great Pyramid;

3. The star Saiph is over the pyramid of Djedefre, to the north of Abu Ruwash, and the star Bellatrix is over the "Unfinished Pyramid" at Zawyat Al Aryan to the south. When Orion is on the meridian, the star cluster *lambra Orionis* representing the Head of Orion is over the Dashur pyramids;

4. When Taurus is on the morning horizon, the two pyramids of Dashur, known as the "Red" and the "Bent" pyramids, match the stars Aldebaran and *epsilon Tauri*, the two "eyes" of the bull in the constellation Taurus;

5. The hieroglyphic texts inscribed in the pyramids of Unas (2356-2323 B.C.) and Pepi II (2246-2152 B.C.) refer to the deceased king ascending into the southern skies in the region of the constellation of *Sahu*, which Gilbert and Bauval identify with the constellation Orion. The authors believe that these texts support the idea that there had been some kind of spiritual relationship intended between the Khufu pyramid (the Great Pyramid) and the Orion constellation.

Of all these correlations, the most provocative argument is the curious and inexplicable "misalignment" of the smaller Menkaure pyramid with the bigger Khufu and Khafre pyramids' exactly matching the arrangement of the third star in Orion's Belt (*delta Orionis*). If this isn't evidence that the designers, impeccable in every other dimension of their work, purposefully offset the Menkaure because they were laying out the plateau according to the stars above, then what is the explanation for offsetting the third pyramid? This new star alignment information causes many, including the archeologists who had their dates so well set, to reconsider the age of the Giza monuments. However, nothing that has been carbon dated on the Giza plateau gives a dating older than roughly 3,500 B.C., causing one to be careful about jumping on this 10,500 B.C. bandwagon too soon. The investigation goes on.

A fascinating twist on this alignment discovery is that the three stars are actually in *reverse* order from the pyramids on the ground. In other words, the offset pyramid is the southernmost pyramid of the three, while the northernmost star in the Belt of Orion is offset. The surprise here is that from his trance-state Edgar Cayce identified this too, saying that the poles were opposite during the building of the Giza Plateau. This would mean that the third pyramid would have been the northernmost pyramid, matching the offset star in Orion's Belt. According to Cayce, the Earth's poles were roughly opposite, north was south and south was north, during the ancient times. According to him, the planet has and will change its poles. As recently as 1939, geologists reported that the axis of the inner core of the Earth made a significant shift. Other scientists have found evidence of two major shifts of the planet's axis poles. More on this in the final chapter.

As you might expect, many have gone searching for these record caches, or for *any* records that may shed light upon the great stone builders of the ancient world. The Director of the Giza Plateau has often said that much of ancient Egypt is still uncovered. Excavations are turning up new artifacts all the time. But there is no indication by anything that has been found that there is a record cache of a civilization dating back to 10,500 B.C. There is no specific indication that such exists. Even the texts in the China caves only tell of an ancient motherland Mu; there are no actual records from Mu in the caves. And, unless we are misinterpreting the hieroglyphic records that have already been discovered in Egypt, there is no report of an ancient civilization predating the pharaohic period, of which we have so much evidence. However, the hieroglyphic records do tell that the great Egyptian god Hermes (Thoth) hid his records in the Earth. This is an important message and has driven many to search for the hidden records of Hermes. Since he was a god from the original creation time, his records could well tell of pre-pharaohic ages. His cache may even have artifacts from pre-pharaohic times. In Edgar Cayce's discourses, Hermes is identified as one of the architects of the Great Pyramid and a key influence in the development of the impressive Egyptian civilization. Finding his records would certainly be an important step toward finding the hall of records. His records may even be in the actual hall of records.

Throughout the 1990s and early 2000s, Dr. Joseph Schor of the Schor Foundation and a Life Member of the organization that Cayce founded, the Association for Research and Enlightenment (A.R.E.), in connection with Florida State University, has led research on the Giza Plateau using ground-penetrating radar to locate underground passageways, halls, and chambers. His efforts resulted in some successes and some failures, as this type of investigation often does. One of his most interesting discoveries, yet to be fully investigated, is a supposed chamber some 30' under the Sphinx. The possible chamber or large room is roughly 26' wide, 40' long, with approximately a 30' floor-to-ceiling depth. His team, including Joseph Jahoda, continues to reconfirm and enhance their findings.

Since the 1960s people have been searching for ancient records off the coast of Bimini. In 1998 researchers, funded through the A.R.E. by Don Dickinson, another Life Member and President of the Law of One Foundation, used submarines in an attempt to find submerged ancient structures off the coast of Bimini. Promising formations were found under millennia of sand and a harden, coral-like crust. The search there continues, led by Dr. Joan Hanley of the Gaia Institute, Dr. Douglas Richards of the Meridian Institute, and many others, including Don Dickinson of the Law of One Foundation which has funded many of the expenses.

The A.R.E. also funded a one-man investigation into the archaeological research being conducted in Guatemala at a site Cayce referenced, a site that we will learn much about in this book. Scott Milburn journeyed down the Usumacinta River just over the border of Mexico into Guatemala to the ancient Mayan site of *Y-Okib*, meaning the "entrance" or "cave," now called *Piedras Negras*. He reported on his journey to the A.R.E. Annual Congress in June of 2000.

The records of all of these investigations are stored at the Association for Research and Enlightenment in Virginia Beach, Virginia U.S.A.

Now let's take a deep look into the heart of the Mayan lands for Iltar's legendary records of the prehistoric world of Mu, Atlantis, Oz, and Og, into a time that humanity has all but forgotten.

# Section II

# Archaeological Evidence at Piedras Negras

## CHAPTER 3

# Piedras Negras
## 'The Black Rocks'
## Location of Cayce's
## Hall of Records?

"There where the transverse valley opens towards the river, splendid sand-banks with blackish limestone rocks rising out of them invited us to bathe. The people of that region have named the place Piedras Negras after those rocks. One of these rocks, rising obliquely and pointed at the top, is especially notice-able, because there is carved upon its steeply inclined surface a circular design which resembles that upon the great sacrificial table on the esplanade before the temple of the eight stelae. This fact seems to justify the surmise that on the rock in question were performed the sacrifices intended to appease the water deities; the blood of the victims trickling from the rock and mingling with the waters of the river. I called this rock La Roca de los Sacrificios."

Teobert Maler, Researches in the Usumacintla Valley, 1901.[1]

A nd so writes the first known explorer to view and document the ancient Maya city of Piedras Negras located deep within the jungle lowlands of Guatemala beside the beautiful but treacherous Usumacinta River. Although Maler provides a verbal description of the city which is often colorful, imaginative and decidedly subjective, his excellent photo-graphic documentation of the site was highly praised and is still used as a reference today. His work, done under primitive conditions, served to inspire future scientific interest in Piedras Negras as well as in other ancient Maya lowland cities found in this area of Central America.

The Edgar Cayce readings seem to point to Piedras Negras as the location of the hidden Yucatan Hall of Records. Cayce claimed the records contained information about the origins of civilization from the beginning of time. And Cayce means *really* ancient times since, according to the Cayce chronology, the first Atlantean and Lemurian migrations began sometime after 28,000 B.C. and ended with the demise of Atlantis in 10,500 B.C. These dates seem especially unbelievable given that mainstream scientific data depicts Maya culture as peaking during the middle of the 1st millennium A.D. Evidence for preMaya cultures such as the Olmec provide only a 2000 B.C. start date. Prior to that (2000-6000 B.C.) the area is thought to have consisted of scattered, primitive agricultural settlements which were developed as the hunter gatherer migrants from across the Bering Straits began to settle in Central America. Due to recent emerging evidence the archaeology community is beginning to consider the possibility that the first Americans may have arrived much earlier than 12,000 years ago. This evidence also shows that they came by routes other than the Bering Strait. Combined with modern DNA evidence revealing Eurasian ancestry for some ancient Americans, the possibility of multiple intrusions from other cultures is also now open for consideration. It seems Cayce's version of the history of human civilization is gaining credibility.

*Figure 20*

Shoreline of the Usumacinta river at Piedras Negras during Teobert Maler's expeditions (ca. 1895). *La Roca de los Sacrificios* (Sacrificial Rock) in center pointing up. Many of these photos are of poor quality. Reprinted from: *Memoirs of the Peabody Museum, Harvard University*, Vol. 2, No. 1, 1901.

# The Piedras Negras Scientific Expeditions

What does science tell us about Piedras Negras? Maler made two exploratory visits to Piedras Negras, the first in 1895 and the second in 1899. Herbert Spinden, Sylvanus Morley and other Carnegie Institute researchers visited in 1914, 1921, 1929 and in 1931 during the first of eight seasons of archaeological investigation of the site sponsored by the University of Pennsylvania Museum of Archaeology and Anthropology (Penn).[2] Dr. J. Alden Mason directed the first two seasons of work for Penn (1931-32) and Dr. Linton Satterthwaite, Jr., present during the entire eight seasons of field work, was in charge of the last six years (1933-37 and 1939). Although Penn planned to extend their work further, funding for the Piedras Negras project dried up and they never returned. By 1956, when funding improved, Penn moved on to Tikal, another of the famous Classic Maya cities located in the Guatemala lowlands.

There were no further scientific studies at this ancient and remote site until 1997 when Brigham Young University (BYU) sponsored an archaeological survey in partnership with the Guatemalan *Instituto de Antropologia e Historia*. Stephen Houston and Hector Escobedo are leading the effort which has continued through the 2000 dry season (March - June).[3] The fact that BYU, a Mormon affiliated institution, is studying Piedras Negras is an interesting turn of events in itself given the founding of that particular Christian denomination which is also known as the Church of Jesus Christ of the Latter Day Saints.

The Mormon religion is based on a narrative (now called *The Book of Mormon*) which was carved on a set of gold plates discovered by Joseph Smith under a stone in an earthen mound in rural New York state in 1827.[4] (See *figure 21*.) The plates tell the story of three different transoceanic migrations by Middle Eastern groups — primarily Hebrews. The first migration is said to have occurred after the fall of the biblical tower of Babel around 2300 B.C. The second occurred around 1500 B.C. Some Mormon scholars believe this migration created the Olmec culture at the ancient pre-Mayan site of La Venta. The third migration consisted of 24 Hebrew men and women who left Israel by boat around 600 B.C. and sailed to a promised land which Mormon scholars believe to be Central America. Descendants of this group were said to have later migrated to North America where, around A.D. 421, they buried a record of their history subsequently unearthed by Joseph Smith.

BYU has been very active in Mesoamerican archaeological field work, not only at the Maya sites of Piedras Negras and Palenque, but

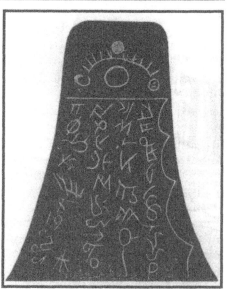

*Figure 21*
The plates translated by Joseph Smith were never photographed. In 1843, six small brass objects with characters similar to those on the plates found by Smith were discovered in a mound at Kinderhook, IL. The historical record is confused, but Smith or one of his close associates translated the Kinderhook plates and believed they were a historical record of Ham. In 1920, the Chicago Historical Society came into possession of one of the Kinderhook plates. Despite the possibility that the Kinderhook Plates are fakes, it should be noted that many thousands of similar artifacts have been recovered from mound sites. Archaeologists usually assume all such artifacts to be hoaxes simply because they don't fit the accepted view of ancient America.

also at the older Olmec and Mixe-Zoquean sites such as La Venta and Izapa.[5] Their archaeological department is fully accredited and research is often conducted in conjunction with other well respected University archaeological programs. Although their motives are certainly based, in part, on the legitimate need for further study of the Piedras Negras site, it is interesting that a Mormon funded University is excavating there. Cayce indicated that remnants of the Lost Tribes of Israel first arrived in North America around 3000 B.C. He then stated that they subsequently migrated down to an area in Central Mexico near present-day Mexico City. Cayce doesn't specify the time frame for their arrival in Central America, but it certainly could have coincided with the 2300 B.C. date given in the *Book of Mormon* or any of the later dates. Could it be that BYU has noted a Hebrew link with Piedras Negras?

## Piedras Negras - An Overview of the Site

From the relatively limited studies conducted at the site, we know that the classic Maya city of Piedras Negras was a large complex extending almost one-half mile from north to south and one-third of a mile from east to west in the central ceremonial area. (See *figure 22.*) It also encompasses several miles of outlying "suburban" type settlements. It was the seat of power for a much larger region and included several smaller Maya sites within its rule. It is thought to have had a population of at least 20,000 at its peak.[6]

The central ceremonial area was divided into five subareas by the Penn expeditions - the South, Southeast, East and West groups with the latter group dominated by the impressively large Acropolis. When considering the size of just the city center, it is obvious that archaeological efforts to date have only 'scratched the surface' at Piedras Negras. Any one of the five subareas contain enough monuments and structures to have kept the Penn expeditions occupied only in that location for the full 8 years. There are 13 major pyramidal structures at the site and 5 of these are in the South group alone. Fortunately, or unfortunately, Penn excavated at least minimally in all 5 subareas.[7]

Penn architect, Fred Parris, surveyed and mapped Piedras Negras during the 1932 and 1933 seasons. His map is divided into 24 squares or sectors which are labeled in alphabetical order beginning with the letter A (in the farthest northwest corner) and ending with V (in the farthest southeast corner). Various pyramids and structures are identified by an alphabetical letter and a number. For example, Pyramid K-5

*Figure 22*
Map showing the major Piedras Negras ceremonial center in relation to surrounding settlements (smaller dots). Adapted from: *Proyecto Arqueologico Piedras Negras: Informe Preliminar No. 1, Primera Temporada 1997.*

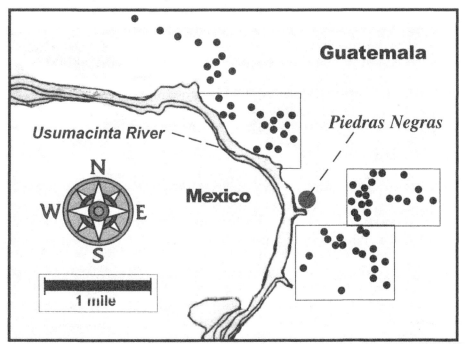

is located in the K block toward the north central area of the map. Since there are so many pyramids and structures referred to in these chapters, it might be useful to refer back to the Parris map. It also might help to keep in mind that the five subareas mentioned above are located mostly in just a few sectors. For example, all of the major pyramids of the South Group are located in sector R. The Acropolis is contained almost entirely in sector J so that any reference to a structure with the letter J in its name would mean an Acropolis feature. The West Group encompasses primarily not only the J sector of the Acropolis, but also the K sector. The East Group is mostly O and P sector structures.

Beginning at Maler's *La Roca De Los Sacrificios* (the Sacrificial Rock), located on the river beach southwest of the site (sector T), primary access into the city is through a small draw which leads northeast into a narrow, crescent shaped plateau/valley. The first group of structures encountered are the pyramid/temples surrounding the South Group Court which are built on a flat plateau that is several feet higher than the river. The northwestern end of the crescent is a valley surrounded on all sides by small hills upon which were built various temples, pyramids, ball courts, steam baths, and palaces arranged in groups which encircle two additional open courtyard areas comprising the East and West Groups. (See *figure 23*.)

## Piedras Negras Is Arranged As A Ceremonial Center

The entire ceremonial center seems to have been built to serve as an orderly structured processional. (See *figure 24*.) Beginning in the South Group (R sector), each subarea is accessed by a prescribed pathway that rises ever higher until it ends at its highest point - the West Group Acropolis (J sector). Surprisingly, the river is not visible from the city and none of the most recent buildings appear to have been built to take advantage of a river view. However, George Andrews has pointed out that the layout of the city seems to parallel the bend in the river.[8]

As during Maler's visit, even today Piedras Negras remains almost totally consumed by jungle. In 1930, Penn archaeologist J. Alden Mason surveyed the site by air and was amazed at his inability to see any of the ruins.[9] It was probably this fact, along with the inaccessibility of the site due to a lack of roads and a nearby series of impassable rapids on the Usumacinta River, that allowed Piedras Negras to be preserved from widespread looting and destruction. BYU, in their 1997 report, also credits the *Comunidades en Resistencia, El Peten*, a faction of Guatemalan guerrilla rebels (and Maya descendants) for protecting the site from looters during the past 20 plus years.[10] However, this protection has been a double-edged sword. As a result of many years of inter-

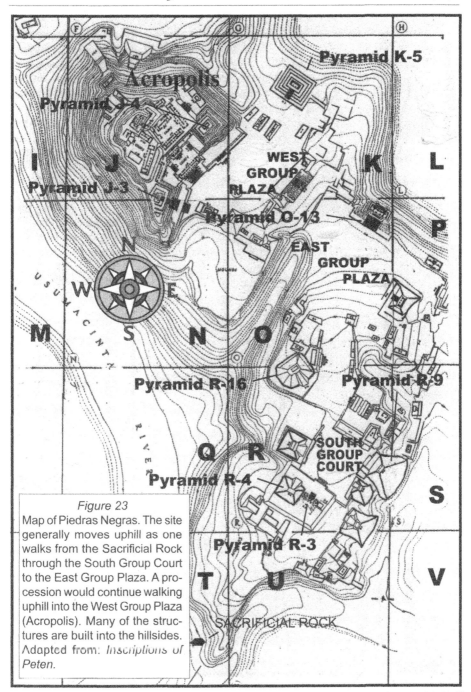

*Figure 23*
Map of Piedras Negras. The site generally moves uphill as one walks from the Sacrificial Rock through the South Group Court to the East Group Plaza. A procession would continue walking uphill into the West Group Plaza (Acropolis). Many of the structures are built into the hillsides. Adapted from: *Inscriptions of Peten.*

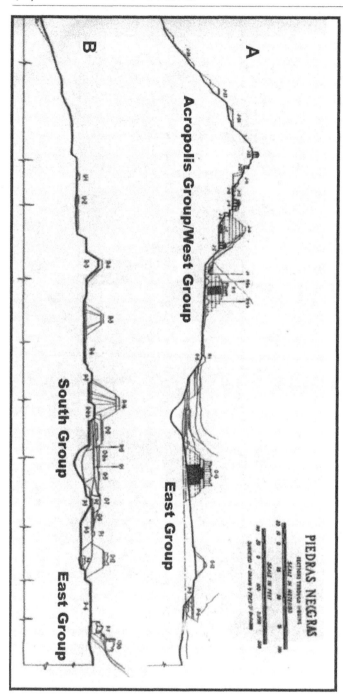

*Figure 24*
Piedras Negras cross section of site showing gradual rise in elevation from one part of the site to another. The map on the prior page does not depict how many of the pyramids and other structures are built into the sides of hills and ravines.

(a). Acropolis/West Group moving down into East Group.

(b). South Group on the left rising up into the East Group.

Reprinted from: *Piedras Negras Archaeology: Architecture*, University Museum, University of Pennsylvania 1944.

nal unrest in the area, Piedras Negras has not been a particularly safe area to visit. In their report on the 1998 season, BYU noted that a side expedition to a nearby site, La Pasadita, had to be cut short due to evidence of military debris and "persistent rumors of land mines in the area."[11]

### The Finest Sculpture Ever Produced In Ancient America

Thanks to Maler, Morley and the Penn expeditions, Piedras Negras became well known among Maya researchers for the many intricately carved stelae and lintels found there. In fact, Lintel 3, discovered by a workman during the 1931 Penn expedition, has been called "the finest sculpture ever produced in ancient America."[12] A lintel is the stone which is placed directly overhead in a doorway. In many cases, the stones Maler and Penn identified as lintels turned out to be wall panels. For this reason, some archaeologists have renamed them panels instead of lintels. In this book they will be called lintels.

Lintel 3 (fig. 25) has 158 hieroglyphs carved on it, six of which date it to around A.D. 757. It portrays an ancient ruler on his jaguar skin-draped throne during a ceremony with seven figures sitting below him and several standing figures on either side. They are portrayed in poses and facial expressions so naturalistic that J. Alden Mason describes them as "reminiscent of Greek art."[13] Also of significance is the attention to detail (fingernails are included) and the high relief resulting in an almost three dimensional look. Drucker, a leading expert in Olmec

---

*Figure 25*
Artistic reconstruction of Piedras Negras, Lintel 3, which is considered to be one of the finest works of Maya artistry was discovered by Penn in 1931. Reprinted from: *Piedras Negras Archaeology: Architecture*, University Museum, University of Pennsylvania 1944.

art, noted that, although Olmec sculpture was created almost 2000 years prior to the Classic Maya era, it was more "dynamic" than most Maya art which he described as "stiff and static." He further stated that Piedras Negras was one of the few exceptions in that it seemed to have achieved a level of realism equal to the Olmec.[14] All of this is thought to have been done using only tools made of jadeite, obsidian and flint since no evidence has been found for the use of metal among the Maya of this period.

Piedras Negras is also famous as the site utilized by the great artist and architect, Tatiana Proskouriakoff, in her discovery of the purpose and meaning of the Maya stelae. Proskouriakoff was present at Piedras Negras during the 1936 and 1937 Penn expeditions. She was asked to produce artistic reconstructions of the various monuments.

*Figure 26*

Artistic reconstruction of the Acropolis at Piedras Negras by Tatiana Proskouriakoff. Reprinted from: *An Album of Maya Architecture*, Carnegie Institution of Washington Publication 558, 1946.

Her drawings were so impressive she was hired by the Carnegie Institution of Washington to do similar work at other Maya sites. (See *figures 26 & 27*.) As a result, she became very familiar with the sculptural artifacts and monuments at many of the ancient Maya cities. The large number of stelae preserved at Piedras Negras and the unusual regularity with which they were produced caused Proskouriakoff to determine that they had been erected to commemorate the birth, death, and ascension to power of the various rulers of the city. Often they contain genealogical information as well.[15] Her discovery provided a critical link which, some 20 years later, lead to the deciphering of noncalendric Maya hieroglyphs. Although not all of the hieroglyphs have been interpreted, a good start has been made.

Piedras Negras is considered unusual in that it contained not only pyramids and temples, but sweat baths. One, in particular, has

*Figure 27*
Artistic reconstruction of the inside of a sweatbath (structure P-7) at Piedras Negras by Tatiana Proskouriakoff. Reprinted from: *An Album of Maya Architecture*, Carnegie Institution of Washington Publication 558, 1946.

been so well preserved that BYU field staff were able to recreate it to full effect.[16] From this and other evidence, it is thought that Piedras Negras was an important religious and ceremonial site that, according to the dated monuments, rose to prominence around A.D. 400 and continued to flourish until A.D. 810.[17] The reason for its demise is unknown, but a growing understanding of the political interactions between neighboring Maya cities indicates its ruling elite may have been overcome by another group.

## How Could Piedras Negras Hold Cayce's Hall Of Records?

If Piedras Negras is an A.D. 1st millennium Maya site, how can it be the location of Cayce's Hall of Records which he said was established during the final Atlantean migration (around 10,500 B.C.)? One possibility is that the Maya built their cities on top of much older (and so far) undiscovered settlements. Linton Satterthwaite, Penn site director in the 1930s, seemed to leave this possibility open in a comment he made regarding his investigation of structures underlying some of the oldest temples. "One is tempted to see a mixture of Maya and non-Maya styles," he stated in a 1939 publication.[18] Although we will discuss this in more detail later, it does seem to hint at outside influences such as Cayce's Atlantean or Hebrew migrations. Cayce indicated in the readings that these outside influences were in some way responsible for the introduction of sacrifice to Maya religious practice. Some scholars have theorized that Mesoamerican cultures developed human sacrifice because they misunderstood that the cosmology of their ancestors was allegorical. They did not realize that the discipline of sacrifice was not meant to be acted out literally, but was to be practiced in the mental and spiritual interior world.[19] Perhaps aspects of sacrificial ritual introduced by the Lost Tribes were subsequently distorted and misused by Maya descendants in later times. If so, then it is also possible that Satterthwaite's "non-Maya" structures are temples built in either an Atlantean or Hebrew style. Some Mormon scholars such as John Sorenson have pointed out many commonalties in temple designs and worship practices during the time of King Solomon and those of the Maya of the Classic period.[20] Perhaps older structures at Piedras Negras will provide even more linkages.

But what do the scientific findings indicate in regard to the many tantalizing clues Cayce provided in the readings regarding an Atlantean Hall of Records and the evidence for prehistoric multi-cultural intrusions? First let's review Cayce's clues.

# A Review of The Edgar Cayce Clues

## Location of the Yucatan Hall of Records

**Clue #1- The records are "in the rock" - written in stone or hidden within a rock building or cave. They may (as in the Egyptian Hall of Records) be inscribed upon 32 tablets or plates.**

• In a February 1932 reading on Atlantis, Cayce stated, "...that record in the rocks still remains - as has that influence OF those peoples...that did escape during the periods of destruction..."[21] A 1941 reading described the Egyptian records as being "tablets" and he stated, "there are thirty-two of these plates."[22] The original Maya reading of 1933 emphasized that the hidden Atlantean records in Egypt, Bimini and Yucatan are identical.[23]

**Clue #2 - There is a temple overshadowing the records.**

• a September 1939 reading spoke of the records being found "in the Aryan or Yucatan land where the temple there is overshadowing same."[24]

**Clue #3 - The records are in a place where stones were uncovered during 1933 by the University of Pennsylvania.**

• In another reading given in December 1933, Cayce stated, "Also the records were carried to what is now Yucatan in America where these stones (that they know so little about) are now - during the last few months being uncovered." This clue caused a follow-up question which mentioned a Pennsylvania museum and led to the identification of the Penn expedition at Piedras Negras.[25]

**Clue #4 - The records are in some sort of chambers which may be entered in 1938 or maybe 2038.**

• In the next sentence of this same reading, Cayce indicated that the records may be discovered if ... "those individuals who will purify themselves...for the gaining of the knowledge and the entering of the chambers where these may be found...In '38 it should come about..." Although this reading was part of a discussion of the 'firestone', it seems to refer to instructions for constructing them which were said to be located in the Hall of Records.

**Clue #5 - The records may be in a second temple or settlement that has been in ruins for many centuries — such as the Maya**

**ruins. There may be evidence of an earlier temple which was destroyed.**

• In the November 1933 reading, Cayce stated that, "the first temples that were erected by Iltar and his followers (who brought over the Atlantean records) were destroyed at the period of change physically in the contours of the land. That now being found, and a portion already discovered that has laid in waste for many centuries was then a combination of those peoples from Mu (Lemuria), Oz (Inca), and Atlantis."[26]

## The Atlantean Firestone Emblem Clues

**Clue #6 - The records contain information about a special Atlantean power source called a firestone and an *emblem* of it may have been found after 1933. Portions of it were carried to museums in Pennsylvania and either Washington or Chicago.**

**Clue #7 - The original Atlantean firestone was a large cylindrical glass cut with facets and had a capstone.**

• In still further readings, Cayce made clear that the records brought to the Yucatan contain information about the making of a special power source used by the Atlanteans which he calls the 'firestone'. In describing the firestone used in Atlantis, Cayce stated that it was a "large cylindrical glass (as would be termed today) cut with facets in such a manner that the capstone on top of same made for the centralizing of the power or force that concentrated between the end of the cylinder and the capstone itself". In fact, he stated that there were stones which were "an emblem of the firestone", or which contained a pattern or instructions for its construction, parts of which were to be carried to museums in Pennsylvania, Washington and Chicago sometime after December 1933 (the time the reading was given).[27]

**Clue #8 - A pattern which will reveal the facets of the firestone crystal will be taken to a museum in Pennsylvania possibly the Pennsylvania State Museum.**

• When asked how many facets the firestone crystal had, Cayce responded, "Would be better were these taken from that pattern of same that will be eventually put in the museum in Pennsylvania" (he later specified the Pennsylvania State Museum).[28]

**Clue #9 - The firestone in Atlantis "was in the form of a six-sided figure" and was "set as a crystal." Also, the form of the crystal was different  earlier in Atlantean history when it was used for**

**spiritual communication than later when it was used as a power source.**

• One reading stated that, in Atlantis, the firestone "was in the form of a six-sided figure, in which the light appeared as the means of communication between infinity and the finite...It was set as a crystal, although in quite a different form as that used there *(meaning it had changed from being a means of communication between man and God in earlier Atlantean times to a source of power for material uses during the later years)*...In the beginning it was the source from which there was the spiritual and mental contact."[29]

**Clue #10 - The firestone pattern or emblem in the Yucatan is in the form of stones (plural) which may have been used as or in conjunction with an altar.**

• The firestone or firestone emblem is further identified not only as consisting of "stones" (note plural is used), but as related in some way to an altar. "The stones that are set in the front of the temple, between the service temple and outer court temple - or the priestly activity, for later there arose (which may give a better idea of what is meant) the activities of the Hebrews from this - in the altar that stood before the door of the tabernacle. This altar or stone, then in Yucatan...is the nearest and closest one to being found."[30]

**Clue #11 - Someone with pure intentions may have discovered the firestone or the information about its use (located in the Hall of Records) by entering chambers in 1938 (or 2038?).**

• One person asked if he might learn to use the firestone and was told those who "gained the knowledge" and were properly purified in body and purpose for "the entering into the chambers where these may be found...In '38 *(1938? or 2038?)* it should come about, should the entity *(the person receiving this reading)* - or others may - be raised."[31] (This clue was not realized at Piedras Negras since Penn was not present at the site in 1938. For some reason, that year was skipped. The final two seasons of investigation by Penn were 1937 and 1939.)

**Clue #12 - The firestone and/or the Hall of Records may be near a sundial that will be uncovered after January 1934 by the University of Pennsylvania where it is found lying between a temple and "the chambers or the opposite temple where sacrifices were made." This will occur "Where temples are being uncovered or reconstructed."**

• Cayce was asked in a January 1934 reading what more might be uncovered in the Yucatan. Unfortunately, it is not clear whether he was referring to the firestone/crystal (it was specifically mentioned by the questioner in his inquiry immediately preceding this one) or to monuments located near the Hall of Records. His response was to describe a "sundial that lies between the temple and the chambers, or opposite temple - where sacrifices were made. For this is the place, is the stone - though erosion has made an effect upon same - in which the body will be particularly interested as related to the other forces or expeditions." When asked for the specific site in the Yucatan where this would be found, the response was, "Where the temples are being uncovered or reconstructed. This has been given *(in an earlier reading and subsequently assumed to be Penn)*, you see."[32]

## Evidence for Atlantean and Other Influences

**Clue #13 - Some of the Maya temples and pyramids that had been discovered up to November 1933 are from the first civilizations - possibly Atlantean.**

• When asked in the November 1933 reading whether the most important Maya temples and pyramids had been discovered, Cayce replied, "Those of the first civilization have been discovered, and have not all been opened; but their associations, their connections, are being replaced - or attempting to be rebuilt."[33]

**Clue #14 - There are Maya sites which contain evidence of Hebrew, Atlantean, Egyptian, Lemurian, and Incan influences.**

• A 1933 reading stated that the ruins "now being found and a portion already discovered that has laid in waste for many centuries, was then a combination of those peoples from Mu *(Lemuria)*, Oz *(Incan)*, and Atlantis...though the Incals were themselves the successors of those of Oz, or Og *(Atlanteans and Lemurians)*, in the Peruvian land, and Mu in the southern portions of that now called California and Mexico and southern New Mexico...Hence we may find in these ruins that which partakes of the Egyptian, Lemurian and Oz *(Incan)* civilizations, and the later activities partaking even of the Mosaic *(Hebrew)* activities."[34]

**Clue #15 - Circular stones "of the magnetized influence" and nonsacrificial altars that have been found in the Maya areas were used by the early Atlantean immigrants to the Yucatan in religious ceremonies. These stones and altars may not be one and the same, but one or the other was used as "sources of light."**

• Cayce stated that artifacts have been found that are Atlantean in origin. First, he mentioned circular stones that are "of the magnetized influence," used during religious ceremonies as the earliest Atlantean remnants.[35] In the next sentence he discussed altars used to cleanse body, mind and soul, but not used for sacrifice until the outside influences intervened sometime after 3000 B.C. He then referred to stones which served as "sources of light" through which "the angels of light" were able to express to the people. It is unclear whether the circular stones and altars are the same thing or whether these are two different artifacts. If they are different then it is also unclear whether the sources of light refers to the altars or the circular stones.[36]

**Clue #16 - The use of family altars in the Maya ceremonial centers will be discovered and are from the Inca and Lemurians.**
• The Cayce readings stated that, "the pyramid and the altars before the doors of the varied activities, was an injection from the people of Oz (Inca) and Mu; and will be found to be separate portions...family altars...family gods..."[37]

**Clue #17 - The remains of the Atlantean immigrants and their settlements in Central America will be hard to find because they performed cremations and possibly burned their settlements. Ashes from these cremations will be found in "one of those temples" that was prepared for this use - possibly a mortuary temple.**
• In September of 1935, Cayce told one individual that he had been an Atlantean immigrant to Central America. "And the entity came into that land known as the Central American land, where the peoples builded many of the temples that are being uncovered today...WHY there are no remains of settlements or the peoples that left the land without showing any burial grounds. For the ENTITY was the one that began the cremations, the ashes of much of which may be found in one of those temples that was prepared for same."[38]

## Other Mysteries in the Search for Cayce's Clues

Although Cayce's clues seem to be pointing to Piedras Negras as the location of the Hall of Records and the firestone emblem, it should be kept in mind that this may not be the correct site. Therefore, it is important to know whether archaeological excavations were going on at any other Maya sites in the area during 1933 or 1938—especially those which might involve museums in Washington and Chicago. There is also a need to clear up confusion regarding the location of the Pennsylvania State Museum which is mentioned specifically in the readings.

## The Penn Museum Confusion

In the A.R.E. Library source file for the 1933 Yucatan readings is a catalog listing and photographs of North and Central American artifacts and dig sites from the 1930s for places other than Piedras Negras. For example, some photos are from *Chichen Itza*. The catalog heading states that it is from the William Penn Memorial Museum, Section of Archaeology. It is stamped with a 1971 Edgar Cayce Foundation copyright. In the book *Mysteries of Atlantis Revisited*, Edgar Evans Cayce and his coauthors state that the William Penn Memorial Museum is in the state capitol at Harrisburg, Pennsylvania.[39] Previous researchers such as Edgar Evans Cayce and archaeologist, Jeffrey Goodman,[40] have tried to locate and differentiate these museums and have ended up assuming that Cayce had meant the Penn expeditions which were actually affiliated with the Penn Museum of Archaeology and Anthropology in Philadelphia.

Carolyn Hatt, in her booklet entitled *The Maya: Based on the Edgar Cayce Readings*, didn't mention the discrepancy between the Pennsylvania State Museum and the Penn Museum and reported that, "the Association (meaning the Edgar Cayce organization - the Association for Research and Enlightenment - A.R.E.) queried the Museum as to what site they were working on in 1933, the following answer came from Dr. Coe: 'The Museum never worked in Yucatan - but in '33 the Museum was excavating at Piedras Negras Guatemala'".[41] This contact would most likely have been made sometime between the December 1933 reading which first mentions the Pennsylvania State Museum and the January 1934 reading in which Cayce answered affirmatively when questioned as to whether an inquiry should be made of the "Pennsylvania State Museum or called University of Pennsylvania". Since Hatt's booklet was published by the A.R.E. Press in 1972, she must have had access to records regarding this inquiry. There was a Dr. William R. Coe who received his doctorate from the University of Pennsylvania. His doctoral dissertation on Piedras Negras artifacts and burials was published by The University of Pennsylvania Press in 1959.[42] Again, the connection is made to Penn, but the reason for the mysterious photographs from other Maya sites in the A.R.E.'s Yucatan reading source file is not explained.

In order to answer some of these questions, I (Lora) visited the State Museum of Pennsylvania, the State Archives, and the State Library in Harrisburg. This was followed by an intensive week at the University of Pennsylvania Museum Library and Archives in Philadelphia in early November of 1999 where I was able to carefully review the Piedras Negras 1930s Penn expedition field notes, both written and photographic. The results of these research efforts were both frustrating and fruitful.

## References

1. Maler, Teobert (1901). Researches in the Central Portion of the Usumacintla Valley. *Memoirs of the Peabody Museum, Harvard University*, Vol. 2, No. 1. Cambridge. (p. 42)

2. Morley, S. V. (1938). *The Inscriptions of Peten, Vol. III*. Carnegie Institution of Washington, Publication 437, Washington.

3. Houston, S., Escobedo, H. and Forsyth, D. (1998). On the River of Ruins: Explorations at Piedras Negras, Guatemala, 1997. *Mexicon*, Vol. XX, pp. 16-22.

4. *The Book of Mormon*, (1963) Salt Lake City, Utah: The Church of Jesus of Latter-day Saints.

5. Sorenson, John (1985). *An Ancient American Setting for the Book of Mormon*. Salt Lake City, Utah: Deseret Book Company.

6. Piedras Negras, Guatemala, July 22, 1999. Brigham Young University, Departments of Anthropology, Geology, Agronomy and Horticulture, internet web site http://ucs/byu.edu/bioag/aghort/PNJacob/PN2.htm

7. *The Inscriptions of Peten, Vol. III*, op.cit.

8. Andrews, George (1975) *Maya Cities*. Norman Oklahoma: University of Oklahoma Press.

9. Mason, J. Alden (1935) Preserving Ancient America's Finest Sculptures. *The National Geographic Magazine*, Vol. LXVIII, No. 5.

10. *Mexicon*, Vol. XX, op.cit.

11. Houston, S., et. al. (1999). Between Mountains and Sea: Investigations at Piedras Negras Guatemala, 1998. *Mexicon*, Vol. XXI, pp. 10-17.

12. Morley, S.V. (1946). *The Ancient Maya*. Stanford University, California: Stanford University Press, p. 63.

13. *The National Geographic Magazine*, Vol. LXVIII, op.cit., p. 548.

14. Drucker, Philip (1952) La Venta, Tabasco A Study of Olmec Ceramics and Art. *BAE Bulletin 153*.

15. Proskouriakoff, Tatiana (1960). Historical Implications of a Pattern of Dates at Piedras Negras, Guatemala. *American Antiquity*, Vol. 25, No. 4, pp. 454-475.

16. *Mexicon*, Vol. XXI, op.cit., pp. 10-17.

17. *The Inscriptions of Peten, Vol. III*, op.cit.

18. Satterthwaite, Linton (1939) Evolution of a Maya Temple - Part 1. *University Museum Bulletin*, Vol. 9, No. 4, p. 6.

19 Sejourne, Laurette (1956) *Burning Water: Thought and Religion in Ancient Mexico*. New York: The Vanguard Press.

20. *An Ancient American Setting for the Book of Mormon.*, op. cit.

21. Reading 354-5

22. Reading 2329-3

23. Reading 5750 1

24. Reading 2012-1

25. Reading 440-5

26. Reading 5750-1

27. Reading 440-5

28. Ibid

29. Reading 2072-10

30. Reading 440-5

31. Ibid

32. Reading 440-12

33. Reading 5750-1

34. Ibid

35. Ibid

36. Ibid

37. Ibid

38. Reading 914-1

39. Cayce, Edgar Evans, et. al., (1997) *Mysteries of Atlantis Revisited.* New York: St. Martin's Press.

40. Goodman, Jeffrey (1977) *Psychic Archaeology: Time Machine to the Past.* New York: G.P. Putnam's Sons.

41. Hatt, Carolyn (1972) *The Maya: Based on the Edgar Cayce Readings.* Virginia Beach, VA: A.R.E. Press, p. 29.

42. Coe, William (1959) *Piedras Negras Archaeology: Artifacts, Caches, and Burials.* Philadelphia: The University Museum.

## CHAPTER 4

# What The University of Pennsylvania Found At Piedras Negras

## On the Trail of the Pennsylvania State Museum

My husband Greg and I arrived in Harrisburg on a late Monday evening. Early the next morning we drove downtown to find the Pennsylvania State Museum. What we found was a modern steel and glass multistory building called "The State Museum of Pennsylvania" located on the corner of Third and North Streets in the heart of downtown not far from the State Capitol Building. Noticing the difference in names, our first order of business was to inquire at the reception desk as to whether this museum was one and the same as the Pennsylvania State Museum. We were assured that it was since the receptionists had never heard of a Pennsylvania State Museum.

We then asked to see any Mayan artifacts especially any from Piedras Negras. A call was made to the curator's office and the message relayed back that there were no such artifacts since the Museum only focused on historical materials from the State of Pennsylvania. We toured the museum anyway and discovered that this statement was not exactly correct. There were displays in the Native American section from many areas of the country other then Pennsylvania. However, we found no artifacts on display from Piedras Negras or any other Central American site. We then returned to the desk to inquire whether such artifacts might have been sent to this museum in the 1930s. Again, a call was made to the curator's office (which we were not allowed to access in person) who suggested we try the State Archives office next door for a listing of items received by the Museum during that time frame.

As we entered the State Archives office at Third and Forster we were quickly greeted by an extremely helpful receptionist, Judy Marcus, who went out of her way to connect us to the right people. This was especially fortunate since a passing archive staff member, upon hearing our inquiry, immediately tried to send us back to the museum. The receptionist suggested we wait and speak with another staff member she believed might be able to help us. Meanwhile we perused the official informational brochure for the archives and noticed that it was "established in 1903 as an administrative unit of the State Library and was combined in 1945 with the State Museum and the Pennsylvania Historical Commission to form the Pennsylvania Historical and Museum Commission."[1]

Another brochure entitled "Research Collections at the Pennsylvania Historical and Museum Commission" contained a listing of museums in the state.[2] The listing for the "State Museum" related that it was "established in Harrisburg in 1905 as the State's official museum" and that its primary purpose is to collect information relative to the history of Pennsylvania. Under archaeology it boasted 1,284 individual archaeology collections including a collection which is "particularly strong in the material culture of Late Woodland and Historic Native Americans dating from A.D. 1000 to the time of European contact." It also stated that the museum includes information regarding the Delaware Indians living in Oklahoma, but made no mention of Central American artifacts. The other museums referenced in the brochure were also solely dedicated to Pennsylvania History. Neither the University of Pennsylvania Museum of Archaeology and Anthropology nor the William Penn Memorial Museum were listed.

Finally, the receptionist returned with her designated staff member who patiently listened as I explained my search (at this point I did not mention Edgar Cayce). He took me to his office and made a call to a Steve Warfel in the curator's office at the Pennsylvania State Museum next door. I reviewed my request again with Mr. Warfel's assistant/secretary since he could not come to the phone. She returned momentarily to inform me that Mr. Warfel had gotten several similar inquiries through the years and surmised that my request had to do with Edgar Cayce. He related that during the 1930s the Pennsylvania State Museum had been called the William Penn Museum, but it did not receive these artifacts. His understanding was that the artifacts were sent to a "Penn or Pennsylvania Museum" in Philadelphia which was disbanded and that no one knows what happened to the artifacts. He suggested that I look for records of that museum in the State Library or in Philadelphia.

The next stop then was the nearby State Library in the Forum Building located at the corner of South Drive and Commonwealth Avenue. There I was assisted by Librarian Bill Nook who, unable to find a reference through his department's sources, sent me to the section on state documents. He also suggested I visit the Free Library of Philadelphia on Vine Street or the one on Locust Street. In the state documents section of the State Library I was able to locate a card in the card catalog under William Penn Museum which mentioned that this was the name of the Pennsylvania State Museum in Harrisburg which, in 1965, had moved into a newly constructed building at its present location at Third and North Streets. There were no references that could be found for either a Penn or a Pennsylvania museum in Harrisburg or Philadelphia. The state librarian assisting me stated that this could mean that it was a privately funded museum since their catalog would only list state funded institutions.

One of the state librarians did find a publication entitled *Commonwealth of Pennsylvania Department of Public Institutions Volume 3, Number 1*, published in September 1935. This source included a listing of new exhibits and artifacts added to the "Pennsylvania State Museum" during the years 1931-1935. All of the artifacts listed were related somehow to Pennsylvania. No Central American artifacts were mentioned and, in fact, the report appeared to provide further verification that the State Museum of Pennsylvania in Harrisburg was once called the Pennsylvania State Museum and that it did not display Central American artifacts even in the 1930s. Interestingly, it was not referred to as the William Penn Museum in the report.

Needless to say, by that point my head was spinning. I now understood the confusion on the museum issue and why other researchers had found it easier to simply assume that Cayce's reference to the Pennsylvania State Museum meant the University of Pennsylvania. Next stop was Philadelphia and the University of Pennsylvania Museum of Archaeology and Anthropology where my efforts were better rewarded. As a result, I never got around to looking for Mr. Warfel's "William Penn or Penn Museum" in Philadelphia.

# The University of Pennsylvania
# Museum of Archaeology and Anthropology

The Penn Museum of Archaeology and Anthropology (*fig. 28*) is located on the Penn campus at 33rd and Spruce Streets. It was founded in 1887 and boasts of having conducted "over 350 research expeditions around the world and collected nearly a million objects, many obtained directly through its own field excavations or anthropological research".[3] It is a Gothic style dark red brick building enclosed by an impressive wall of wrought iron and brick. Behind the massive iron gates and in front of the official public entrance is a classically landscaped garden/patio containing a large shallow cement reflecting pool complete with Greek sculptures. It is a fitting monument to the romance of 19th and early 20th century archaeology. Inside, the museum contains exhibits from ancient cultures all over the world including Canaan/Israeli, Roman, Egyptian, Islamic, Polynesian, African, Asian, Greek, Etruscan and,

of course, the Mesoamerican artifacts from Piedras Negras, Tikal and other sites.

### Piedras Negras Artifacts Displayed at Penn

Although most of the Piedras Negras artifacts originally on display at the Penn Museum were returned to the National Museum in Guatemala in 1947, the center piece of the current exhibit is the massive multi-ton Stela 14 (see *fig. 29*) which was found in front of Pyramid 0-13 by Maler in 1899.

*Figure 28*
The University of Pennsylvania Museum of Archaeology and Anthropology entrance. Photo by Lora Little.

*Figure 29*
Piedras Negras Stela 14 discovered by Maler in 1895, and transported to the Penn Museum in 1932. Reprinted from: *Memoirs of the Peabody Museum, Harvard University*, Vol. 2, No. 1, 1901.

Also on display is an ornately carved, 2 foot high grotesque head thought to depict a Maya rain god. It served as one of four leg supports for Altar 4 (see *fig. 30*) which was also found by Maler on the West Group Plaza floor in front of Pyramid 0-13. Both of these well known artifacts, as well as several others (Stelae 40, 13, 12, Lintels 12, 10, 3, Throne 1, and Miscellaneous Sculptured Stone 1), were taken to Penn by the Eldridge R. Johnson Expedition of 1932 on a temporary loan basis by prior agreement with the Guatemalan authorities.[4] Pictures from the Penn Museum in the 1930s show an impressive display of multiple stelae, lintels and thrones from Piedras Negras.

In a display case in the Mesoamerica Hall were the burial cache items of possibly a royal person (Burial 5) which included a small carved jade pendent that had been inserted into the mouth of the deceased. (See *figure 31*.) Coe remarked that this was a rare practice among the Maya although it has been reported at Palenque (Pacal's burial) and at four burials in Kaminaljuyu, a Preclassic Maya site in Guatemala.[5] Interestingly, an "Opening of the Mouth" ceremony was a common funerary practice among Egyptian burials performed as a means of allowing the soul to "see, hear, smell, breathe, and eat."[6] The display also held a jaguar bone carved with an image of a bird with a cross on its head as well as several small circular and rectangular polished mirrors of both solid and mosaic pyrite. Some of these are believed to have been attached to a headband and worn around the head as depicted by a large sculptured head found in another area of the site by the Penn team. Drucker[7] reported that similar pyrite and hematite pieces were found in the Olmec area near La Venta which Jeffrey Goodman believed to be possible candidates for Cayce's circular magnetized stones (more on this later). At La Venta a statue was uncovered of a woman with hands clasped in a "prayerful"

*Figure 30*
Piedras Negras Altar 4 showing leg supports of carved grotesque head. Reprinted by permission from: University of Pennsylvania Museum Archives.

pose. (See *figure 32*.) Fastened to her chest was a polished hematite disk.[8] In addition, several mosaic pyrite plates were found at Kaminaljuyu, one of which contains on its underside a carving of two persons tending an altar (*fig. 33*). Upon the altar is some sort of offering containing six circular objects while above it rise clouds or possibly "smoke and flames from burning incense."[9] As we will discuss later, discoveries such as these have led researchers to conclude that pyrite and hematite were highly valued minerals used in ancient Maya and Olmec ceremonial activities.

In addition to the exhibits, the Penn Museum houses a 4 story library dedicated solely to archaeology and anthropology, as well as the archives where the original field notes and photography of all Penn field expeditions are preserved. A desire to photograph

*Figure 31*
Carved jade pendant found inserted in the mouth of a deceased and possibly royal person by Penn in 1931 now in the Penn Museum (Burial 5). Reprinted from: *Piedras Negras Archaeology*, 1959, courtesy of the University of Pennsylvania Museum.

*Figure 32*
Right: Statue from Mesoamerican Olmec site (La Venta ca. 1500 B.C.) of woman with a polished hematite pendant fastened to her chest. Reprinted from: *BAE Bulletin* 153, 1952.

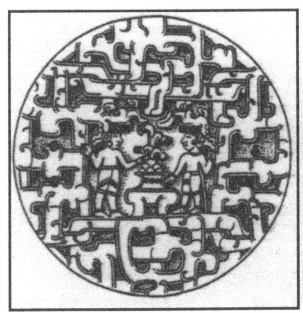

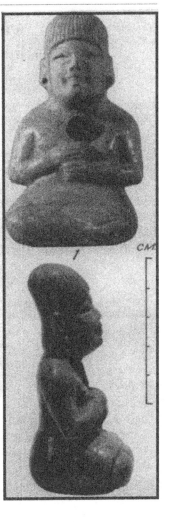

*Figure 33 (above)*
Carved backside of mosaic pyrite plaque from Preclassic Maya site at Kaminaljuyu, Guatemala. Reprinted from: *Excavations at Kaminaljuyu, Guatemala*. Carnegie Institution of Washington Publication 561, 1946.

Stela 14 and the other Piedras Negras artifacts lead me eventually to Mr. Allessandro Pezzati, reference archivist, through whom I applied and gained access to the Penn archives. Due to copyright restrictions the Museum does not allow general photography of exhibits for publication. The good news was that the archives had hundreds of high quality photographs of Piedras Negras artifacts. The bad news was, as might be expected, they were available at a price. For this reason, every attempt has been made to select only those photos related to our Hall of Records search.

## Evidence for Excavations
## by Washington and Chicago Museums

I was first advised by the archive staff to visit the museum library in order to be certain the information I was requesting was not already available in published form. There I found many of the references I had seen in my primary sources. All of these were very helpful. However, as my sources had warned, publication of a final comprehensive report on Piedras Negras was never accomplished, although a detailed review and dating of the site monuments throughout the 1937 season, coauthored by Dr. Linton Satterthwaite, was included in Sylvanus Morley's 1938 *The Inscriptions of Peten*.[10] Dr. Satterthwaite also published a few preliminary reports for the University as well as various specialized journal articles most of which were reviewed for this book.

*Figure 34*
Map of the Peten area showing location of various ancient Maya sites.

**PETEN**

The Peten region is also known as the southern lowlands. It extends through much of Guatemala, as well as parts of Mexico and Belize.

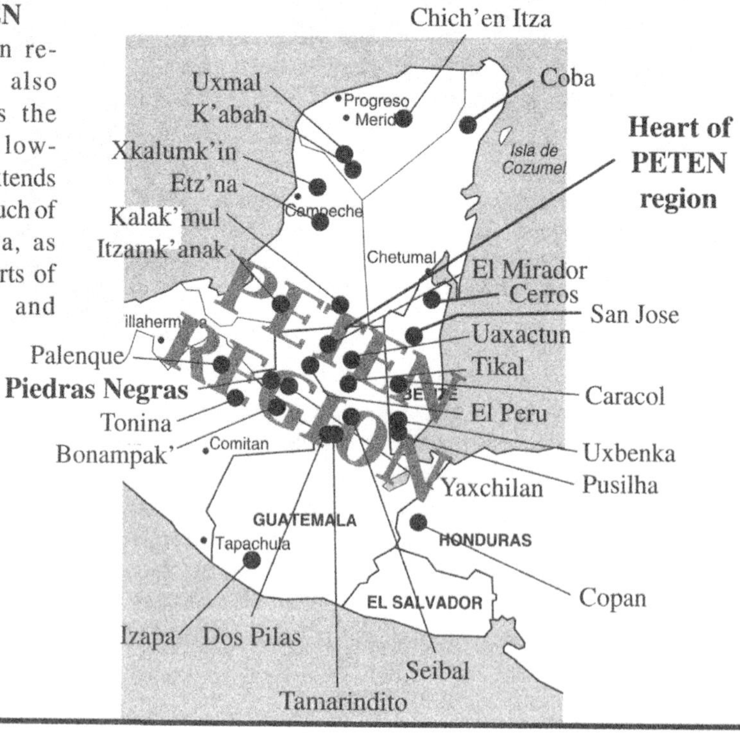

Chich'en Itza

Uxmal
K'abah
Progreso
Merid
Coba

Xkalumk'in
Etz'na
Kalak'mul
Itzamk'anak

Isla de Cozumel

**Heart of PETEN region**

Campeche

Chetumal

El Mirador
Cerros
San Jose
Uaxactun
Tikal
Caracol
El Peru
Uxbenka
Pusilha

illahermosa
Palenque
**Piedras Negras**
Tonina
Bonampak'
Comitan

Yaxchilan

GUATEMALA
Tapachula

HONDURAS

EL SALVADOR
Copan

Izapa
Dos Pilas

Seibal
Tamarindito

Also of interest in Morley's *The Inscriptions of Peten*, was a listing of all scientific explorations in the Peten area year by year up to and including 1937. The listing also briefly summarized each area of focus.[11] Since Cayce indicated that some artifacts would possibly be found both during and after 1933, and that some would be taken to museums in Chicago, Pennsylvania, and Washington, it is important to be aware of any other sites excavated during this time period especially by representatives from institutions located in these cities.

The Peten area includes the departments of Peten and Izabal in Guatemala, parts of the states of Chiapas & Campeche in Southern Mexico, and eastern areas of Belize. (See map, *figure 34*.) Ongoing expeditions in 1933, in addition to Penn's work at Piedras Negras, included the Sixteenth Central American Expedition sponsored by the Carnegie Institution of Washington. That expedition focused mostly on surveying sites for potential study. However, they were doing excavations at Uaxactun in Guatemala in 1933 — the 8th year of intensive exploration there. It was further reported that in 1931 the Fourteenth Expedition of the Carnegie Institution uncovered "12 previously unreported stelae, 13 altars, 8 lintels, and 5 steps" at Yaxchilan, a site located on the Mexico side of the Usumacinta river 30 miles south (upstream) of Piedras Negras.[12] This site, along with Palenque, was visited by Dr. Satterthwaite during the 1934 and 1935 Piedras Negras seasons.[13] Given the close proximity of all of these sites, it was important to the early archaeologists in the area to compare them for similarities. For example, Andrews noted that, although Piedras Negras and Yaxchilan "were built and occupied around the same time, their design and layout are significantly different."[14] Later he pointed out that "the clarity of the internal circulation scheme which is apparent at Piedras Negras is not found at most other sites."[15]

A listing of field work in the entire Maya area during the fall of 1933 and the spring of 1934 was also reported in an issue of the journal *Maya Research*. It showed that the Carnegie Institution of Washington was investigating the Nunnery Group at Chichen Itza, as well as in Campeche and Uaxactun. Could this expedition be somehow related to the mysterious William Penn Museum listing of artifacts from Chichen Itza in the A.R.E. library files? Even more interesting is the reference to a 1934 joint expedition of the Carnegie Institution and the Field Museum in Chicago to San Jose in Belize. It was noted that during the 1931 season the leader of this expedition, the renowned Mayanist, J. Éric Thompson, then Assistant Curator of Central and South American Archaeology at the Field Museum, "hoped to solve certain problems of history raised by the discovery of pottery of a non-Maya type in burials at this typical Maya center."[16]

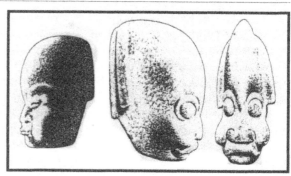

*Figure 35*
Example of elongated heads from Maya stone carving on display at the National Museum in Mexico City. Reprinted from: Carnegie Institution of Washington Publication 606, 1954.

Thompson reported in his book, *Maya Archaeologist*, his 1931 discovery of a strange bundle style burial (knees to the chin) containing a human skull with an unusually elongated head accompanied by five pottery vessels "not of local manufacture." (See *fig. 35*.) One of these vessels, approximately one foot in length, was shaped like an hourglass. Near the skull was a flint stone carved in the shape of a dog. Although Thompson was not ready to conclude that these were signs that this person was a "foreigner," he did admit that the skull and artifacts were unlike any other found at the site or in the area.[17]

Upon his return to the San Jose site in 1934, while excavating in a newly discovered set of mounds, Thompson reported finding a cache containing a highly polished pyrite disk perforated with two holes assumed for suspension around the neck, two pieces of ore with a high percentage of lead, and "remains of the only copper until then reported from a Classic site". Thompson viewed the copper as a sign that San Jose was occupied longer than some of the larger cities and concluded that, since lead was not known to have been used by the Maya, those pieces must have been included "as curiosities because of their unusual weight."[18] Of course, as mentioned earlier, pyrite and hematite pieces are significant since, according to Goodman, they may be the magnetized stones Cayce mentioned as remnants of early Atlantean civilization.[19]

### The Penn Museum Archives and the Piedras Negras Field Notes

As expected, however, none of the reports available in the library proved to be as productive as a thorough analysis of the original Penn Piedras Negras field notes. And I was not disappointed as I slowly leafed through the well-organized boxes of notes, diaries, photographs, drawings and letters. Mr. Pezzati runs a professional and efficient operation and was very cooperative during my days there. After explaining the general purpose of my search, including a brief review of the Edgar Cayce/ Hall of Records story, he remarked that in his 12 years in the archives he was not aware of anyone else on the Cayce trail requesting this information. I mentioned that Jeffrey Goodman, who has degrees in archaeology and geology, had indicated reviewing the site reports (which may not have included the actual field notes) in his 1977 book.[20] He did not recall the name, but admitted that date would have been prior to his tenure with the museum. He wished me luck with the project and expressed his hope that a "Mayan Hall of Records" would someday be found.

So how do Cayce's clues compare to the scientific data? Quite well, actually. I was able to corroborate Goodman's findings from his review of the published Penn reports and much more.

## What Was Found In 1933

One of the reasons for searching the field notes was to determine exactly what was found at Piedras Negras during the 1933 season and what may have been taken to the Penn Museum. As mentioned earlier, Cayce stated specifically that the Atlantean records were taken to the Yucatan "...where these stones (that they know so little about) are now - *during the last few months* - being uncovered." This reading was given in

*Figure 36*
Piedras Negras Throne 1 found in Acropolis Court 1 transported to Penn Museum in 1932. Reprinted by permission from: University of Pennsylvania Museum Archives.

December of 1933. The Penn expedition worked at Piedras Negras from March through July of 1933.

In the same reading Cayce stated that an emblem of the firestone "*will* be brought to this America... A portion to be carried, as we find, to the Pennsylvania State Museum."[21] Note that the uncovering of the area near the records seems to have occurred a few months before December 1933, while the transporting of the firestone related artifacts to the various museums was predicted to occur after that date. This could mean that the artifacts were found in 1933 (or earlier), but just not received at the museum until 1934. Given the transportation difficulties reported at Piedras Negras, this seems possible.

Although it does not quite fit Cayce's time frame, published reports tell us that some of the monuments packed for transport to Pennsylvania in 1932 did not arrive until sometime between January and April of 1933.[22, 23] This shipment of artifacts contained four large stelae (40, 13, 12, & 14), a sculptured throne (#1; see *fig. 36*), Lintels 3, 10, & 12 (the latter contains one of the oldest dates found at the site - A.D. 514), one of the Altar 4 supports, artifacts from Burial 5 including a pyrite mosaic disk, and Miscellaneous Sculptured Stone 1 (a round portable stone altar 10 inches in diameter with partly eroded inscriptions discovered in 1931).[24,25] It is tempting to view the Piedras Negras stelae (with their then undeciphered inscriptions) as Cayce's "stones that they know so little about."[26] Large stone monuments such as the stelae *were* an important discovery at Piedras Negras for the 1931 and 1932 seasons. *However, these items do not meet the criteria of having been uncovered within the past few months of 1933*. In addition, judging from recent advances made in hieroglyphic decipherment, these monuments appear to have been created long after the time of Cayce's Atlantean migration.

Since many of the large monuments (stelae, lintels, altars and thrones) had already been transported to museums in Pennsylvania and Guatemala during the 1931 and 1932 seasons, the main goal of the 1933 season at Piedras Negras, according to Mason, was "to obtain as completely as may be a dated history of the evolution of buildings and ceramics".[27] Morley reported that the 1933 Penn expedition, led by Dr. Linton Satterthwaite excavated South Group pyramids R-3, R-5, structures S-2 and S-4 and cut trenches into the remaining mounds in that subarea. Excavations were also undertaken in West Group structures K-6 (ball court), J-2, K-5 (pyramid/temple), and J-6 (Acropolis palace court where Throne #1 was found) with "trenches cut through all the remaining mounds" on the Acropolis.[28] Preliminary clearing of South Group Pyramid R-9 was also accomplished. In the field notes,

Satterthwaite reported that during 1933 he excavated 11 temples, 17 palaces, 2 ball courts, and a number of sweathouses.[29] Unfortunately, that covers a large portion of the site. Still, it does allow us to narrow our attention to the South and West Groups since a great deal of excavation seems to have taken place there. So, were the stones Cayce referred to found? A review of the field notes yielded *few candidates that met all of Cayce's criteria* although there were ten discoveries during the 1933 season that seemed to be worth noting. Significantly, five of these were located in the West Group and four were in the South Group. The remaining one was in a cave just north of the East Group.

## Ten Significant Discoveries at Piedras Negras During 1933

### The West Group/Acropolis

First of all, in ball court K-6 in the West Group, a carved stone lintel or wall panel (Miscellaneous Sculptured Stone 9; see *fig. 37*) was found which contained one of the latest dates inscribed at the site. It was also carved with an unusual "glyph-style hand ending sign and bird head." (See *fig. 38*.) A picture of it was sent to Morley for dating. It was speculated that it could be part of a throne.[30] The second discovery, also found in the K-6 ballcourt (Misc. Sculptured Stone 10; see *fig. 39*), is a carving of two ball players seemingly in action. It is unique in that, unlike most Maya carvings, the two figures are etched on a totally blank background. However, their type of dress is typical of the Maya ball player as found at other sites. Since it contained no glyphs, it was not dated.[31] A third discovery was the remains of house structures surrounding the ceremonial areas—a new development. They were thought to be the dwellings of priests and nobility.[32] In a fourth discovery, five underlying structures were found while excavating in the Acropolis palace area (J-6) near the site where Throne #1 was found.[34]

The fifth, and most compelling, discovery in the West Group was a giant stucco mask uncovered on the corner of Pyramid K-5. (See *fig. 40* and cover photo.) It was so startling to the researchers that they stayed an extra 10 days in July (enduring the beginning of the rainy season) just to complete its excavation. It is somewhat similar to decorative masks discovered on monuments at other Maya sites in the lowlands such as Uaxactun as well as in the Northern Yucatan and the Mexican highlands. It is 9 feet high and depicts a mythological, possibly jaguar, face. Satterthwaite believed it represented the Sun god.[45] There is evidence that similar stucco masks decorated the corners of Pyramid

*Figure 37*
Miscellaneous Sculptured Stone #9 found in the K-6 ball court of the West Group. Reprinted by permission from: University of Pennsylvania Museum Archives.

*Figure 38*
Drawing of hand ending sign glyph from Misc. Sculptured Stone 9 (West Group Ball Court). Reprinted from: *The Inscriptions of Peten Vol. III*, Carnegie Institution of Washington, 1938.

*Figure 39*
Misc. Sculptured Stone 10 depicting Maya ball players (West Group Ball Court). Reprinted by permission from: University of Pennsylvania Museum Archives.

*Figure 40*

Close up of giant (9 ft.) stucco mask uncovered on corner of Pyramid K-5. Picture taken shortly after excavation in July 1933. Reprinted by permission from: University of Pennsylvania Museum Archives. (Cover contains a more recent photo - note results of weathering over the years.)

---

K-5 (see *fig. 40*) on each of its multiple terraces. In 1933 only this one and part of another were found. Upon their return in 1934, Penn researchers discovered that the second partial mask had been destroyed, most likely by weathering.[46]

The mask is also similar to one found on a late Preclassic temple (ca 50 B.C.) discovered at Cerros, a Maya site in Northern Belize (formerly called British Honduras).[47] Cayce identified that area as one of the places where "evidences of this lost civilization" of Atlanteans would be found.[48] According to Schele and Freidel, the Cerros temple was dedicated to the Jaguar Sun god and was used by the king to commune with the supernatural world of the ancestors on behalf of all the people.[49] The mask on Pyramid K-5 at Piedras Negras meets Cayce's clue of something being uncovered and certainly "care" had to be taken in its uncovering. Also, it was uncovered "within the past few months" of 1933.

*Figure 41*
Tatiana Proskouriakoff's drawing of Pyramid K-5 as it might have looked during the Maya occupation of Piedras Negras. Note giant stucco masks on each terrace. Reprinted from: Carnegie Institution of Washington Publication 558, 1946.

However, although it may represent a Sun god, it is not a stone (it is made of stucco) and it does not seem appropriate to call it a "sundial that lies between the temple and the chambers, - or opposite temple - where sacrifices were made."[50] Also, it was not taken to a museum.

### South Group

A sixth discovery made in 1933 resulted from trenching excavations of Pyramid R-3 in the South Group which showed that there were at least 4 underlying substructures. In a 1933 Museum Bulletin article Satterthwaite noted, "It may even turn out that there was an extensive city of buildings on low platforms before the first real pyramid was erected here."[33] A seventh discovery was a short stone column buried under Stela 24 in front of Pyramid R-9. (See *fig. 42.*) It was listed in the field notes photo catalog and described as being flat on one side and containing "questionable signs of carving." It could not be dated.[35] It may be a

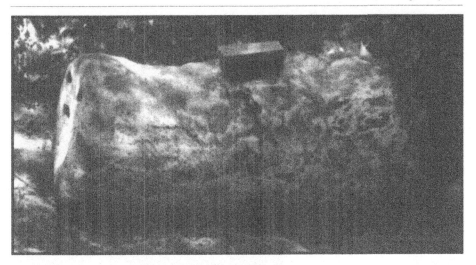

*Figure 42*
Short stone column found under Stela 24 at Piedras Negras 1933. Reprinted by permission from: University of Pennsylvania Museum Archives.

candidate for Cayce's firestone emblem since it is eroded and slightly cylindrical and even had to be uncovered. However, it does not contain any decipherable carvings and does not appear to be an emblem of anything. An eighth discovery was a large stucco head buried under the floor in Pyramid R-5. (See *fig. 43.*) The face was painted red and in the field notes Satterthwaite commented that the forehead did not show the typical Maya flattening considered attractive at that time.[36] In other words, it could be a portrait of a nonMaya person or perhaps an ancestor.

A ninth discovery was Burial #10 located below the plaza floor in front of Structure U-3 in the South Group. It was described by Satterthwaite as the "most elaborate chamber of all".[37] It was apparently a royal burial interred in a concrete vault with a wooden roof. The tomb design included 2 niches and stepped ends. (See *fig. 44.*) In one of the niches was a tripod dish (dated by style as Late Classic) containing the mutilated remains of an 8 year old child possibly included as a sacrificial offering. Many objects of carved jadeite (a precious stone to the Maya) beads, pendants and ornaments as well as shell beads, bird claws and flint chips were found in the burial chamber. It also appeared that the primary occupant's remains had been removed and there was evidence of a fire.[38] In 1997 BYU uncovered a similarly burned elaborate burial (#13) chamber near Pyramid 0-13 in the East Group. Current understanding of Maya funerary rituals and information gleaned from hieroglyphic decipherment have led BYU to conclude that burials 10

*Figure 43*
Life size stucco head discovered under floor in Pyramid R-5 (South Group). Forehead does not show typical Maya flattening. Picture taken in the field during 1933. Reprinted by permission from: University of Pennsylvania Museum Archives.

*Figure 44*
Unusual burial chamber for Burial 10 in South Group. Note niches on sides and steps on either end. Reprinted from: *Piedras Negras Archaeology*, 1959, University of Pennsylvania Museum.

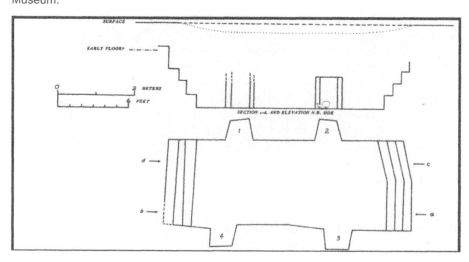

and 13 are probably examples of later rulers performing burning/ reinterment rituals to honor earlier rulers or nobility. This ritual was known to have been common among Maya sites in the Usumacinta drainage area. BYU's conclusions were further reinforced by references made to this type of ritual on a panel discovered near Pyramid O-13.[39] In addition, Satterthwaite found evidence of a burned wooden building at one of the lowest and oldest levels of the Acropolis during his excavations in 1933.[40] This burning ritual may be tantalizing evidence of an Atlantean presence. Cayce indicated that the ancient Atlantean immigrants did not leave many remains of their settlements or burials because they practiced cremation. In fact, he predicted that "the ashes of much of which *(cremations)* may be found in one of those temples that was prepared for same."[41] Both of the burned burials were found near temple sites. Although the burials themselves are probably not Atlantean, the cremation ritual could be a remnant of Atlantean tradition reserved centuries later for royalty only. Or perhaps ancient Atlantean ancestral ashes were preserved and spread over the royal burials as a means of honoring the dead.

## Cave Burial Near The East Group

A tenth significant discovery made in 1933 was Burial #6 found in a cave located in the hills just north of (behind) the East Group. Satterthwaite described it in his field notes as containing "unusual bone tubes (which) permits suggestions that these are the insignia of a holy man of some sort, perhaps a hermit who was buried where he lived." He further wrote in his notes that "a religious association for the place is borne out by the final disposition of the cave, resembling a shrine, using the fissure in front walled up to give the desired gloom."[42] The bone tubes were carved with the serpent motive of the Maya style. Dr. Mary Butler who excavated them described them as: "Two bone tubes about 13 cm. (5 inches) long, abut 2.3 cm. (almost 1 inch) in diameter, decorated in each case on the front with a wide band formed by two parallel lines enclosing a conventionalized snake head, shown in profile with simplicity and restraint. The backs were plain except for bands of rosettes encircling each end. The designs were carved in low relief. The serpent band in one case slanted from left to right, in the other from right to left, so that the two formed a complementary pair, probably worn on the breast. Three holes were bored in one tube in front of the snake head, arranged as at the points of a triangle; on the other tube, two of the corresponding holes were present, the third being begun but not carried through the bone. On these tubes were traces of red paint.

They were found beside the skull, about 20 cm. (7.8 inches) away from it, and about on a line with the nose." They are listed as "Destroyed in camp fire" by Coe.[43] It is known that a campfire destroyed one of the buildings in 1932, but, mysteriously, the field notes in Satterthwaite's handwriting, with drawings of the burial, are dated as May of 1933.[44] This burial is especially important since it was located in a cave. The significance of caves to our search for the Hall of Records will be discussed in the next chapter.

## What Was Sent to the Penn Museum?

Of course, to remain on the trail of Cayce's clues, we need to know which items were sent back to the Penn museum. The field notes contained an Object Catalog dated 1933. It listed items collected during the 1933 expedition and notes that they were "lent by Guatemala Government 1933." It appeared to be the packing list of items sent to the Penn Museum from the 1933 expedition. Of the ten discoveries previously mentioned, those sent to the Penn Museum were Misc. Sculp-

---

### 1933 Expedition Object Catalog of Items Sent to the Penn Museum

The 1933 object catalog listed 256 items some of which are groups of pottery sherds numbered as one item. The largest number of items (56) came from the Acropolis Court 1 area (J-6 & J-7) and includes a carved obsidian knife. Other areas mentioned on the list and their corresponding number of artifacts are:

**West Group (Total=168):**

# of artifacts    area recovered

(56) J-6/J-7 Acropolis
(53) West Group surface collected by architect (included mostly pottery figurines and fragments)
(32) J-2 Acropolis
(13) K-6 West Ball Courts
(10) J-22 Above Court 2 Acropolis
(45) Burial #5 near J-5 Acropolis
  (4 groups of pottery sherds and a fragment of cranium)

**South Group (Total=80):**

(28) Burial #10 near Structure U-3
(22) R- 3 Pyramid (including figurine heads, mano stones and a fragment of Misc. Sculptured Stone #11)

**South Group (continued):**

# of artifacts    area recovered

(14) House mounds area - surface collections of architect
(5) R-5 Pyramid
(4) R-1 Pyramid
(4) R-11 South Ball Courts
(2) Surface collections of architect Fred Parris
(1) R- 4 Pyramid

**Northeast Area (Total=25):**
(25) Burial #6 Cave

**East Group (Total=8):**
(8) Surface collected by Fred Parris

**Miscellaneous/Various Positions (Total=5):**

**Southeast Group (Total=1):**
(1) Structure S-2

tured Stone 10 of the ballplayers, as well as objects from Burial 10, and cave Burial 6. The other seven discoveries were either sent to the Guatemala Museum (for example, the stucco head from Pyramid R-5) or left at the site (the two giant stucco masks from Pyramid K-5).[51] A listing of all the items sent to the Penn museum by location appears in the table on the prior page. As can be seen, the largest number were found in the West Group/Acropolis area (168). Out of these 168, 56 were discovered in the Acropolis. The second largest number was found in the South Group (80). Among these items were some very compelling descriptions. Some of them may even be emblems or patterns of the firestone. Of particular interest, and worthy of discussion, are pieces of calcite, pyrite, and hematite.

### Calcite, Pyrite and Hematite Discovered in 1933

One of the most intriguing objects transported to the Penn Museum in 1933 was a "fragment of a stone vessel, possibly alabaster, White - translucent" found in the Acropolis area (J-2).[52] Coe described the vessel as "globular."[53] One of Cayce's clues about the hall of records refers to an **emblem of the firestone crystal** which Cayce described as a "large cylindrical glass" object. Thus, the translucent and circular characteristics of this item seem significant. Satterthwaite later wrote that he believed this object was a sign of "late trade relations with the Gulf Coast

*Figure 45 (right)*
Sample piece of calcite. Photo reprinted from Corel Gallery.

*Figure 46 (below)*
Sample piece of pyrite. Photo reprinted from Corel Gallery.

region or farther afield."[54] This would date it to the Postclassic period. However, Coe had the sample analyzed and determined it to be made of calcite, not marble or onyx, which means it could be much older. He further noted that it was smooth on both sides and speculated that it was part of a "globular" shaped vessel about 10 inches in diameter.[55]

Calcite (*fig. 45*) is abundant in Mexico and, interestingly, when heated, calcite has the unusual characteristic of becoming fluorescent. Fluorescence is a quality that exists when a mineral contains particles called *activators* that react to ultraviolet light (such as from the sun) and gives off a glow that can be seen.[56] This particular quality sounds a lot like the Atlantean firestone since Cayce stated that it was kept under a dome that was removed "so that the activity of the stone was received from the sun's rays, or from the stars; the concentrating of the energies that emanate from the bodies that are on fire themselves..."[57] Also, calcite's crystallization at the molecular level is hexagonal which brings to mind Cayce's description of the firestone crystal as being six-sided. Could this artifact be one of the stones that served as Cayce's "sources of light"? There is a reference in the *Book of Mormon* to a Hebrew named Jared who was among the first immigrants to Central America (2300 B.C.) who "did molten out of rock sixteen small stones; and they were white and clear, even as transparent glass..." to provide lighting for his ship during the long oceanic voyage. He prayed to God for help until "the Lord stretched forth his hand and touched the stones one by one with his finger" illuminating them.[58]

---

*Figure 47 (below, left)*
Drawing of a slightly beveled pyrite disk (front, back, and profile) from a buried cache in Piedras Negras Acropolis (J-6). Photo reprinted from: *Piedras Negras Archaeology*, 1959, University of Pennsylvania Museum.

*Figure 48 (below, right)*
Drawing of oval pyrite ornament with scroll design found in Piedras Negras Acropolis (J-2). Photo reprinted from: *Piedras Negras Archaeology*, 1959, University of Pennsylvania Museum.

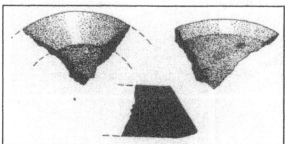

Other artifacts of note listed in the 1933 catalog included 2 solid pyrite (*fig. 46*) pieces. These polished pyrite stones (*fig. 47*) are possible candidates for Cayce's Atlantean magnetized stones as well as the "sources of light" used in religious ceremonies. One was found within the fifth substructure level under the Acropolis (J-6) near where Throne 1 had been discovered. It was found with several objects placed in a ceramic jar as a cache offering. This highly polished fragment was slightly beveled and assumed to have been used as a mirror.[59] An even more interesting piece was an "iron pyrite or hematite ornament probably from inlay-oval, polished on front with incised scroll" found buried in an area near the front steps leading into Court 1 of the Acropolis (J-2).[60] Coe lists this artifact (*fig. 48*) in his report as being pyrite.[61] What is especially significant is that it may be related to the enigmatic and ancient scroll/spiral design rock carvings (petroglyphs) found near the river at Piedras Negras. (More on the scroll petroglyphs in the next chapter). If these pieces are the magnetized stones mentioned by Cayce as artifacts from the Atlantean immigrants, this would provide additional support for the idea that the scroll is an Atlantean symbol.

At this point it seemed important to determine whether pyrite was really the key ingredient for Cayce's magnetized stones. Also, why did so many of the Penn references label these stones as "pyrite or hema-

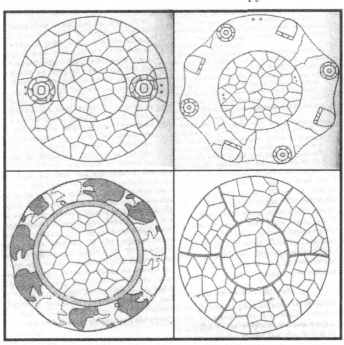

*Figure 49*
Examples of pyrite mosaic designs from Kaminaljuyu, Guatemala, a Preclassic Maya site. Drawing reprinted from: Carnegie Institution of Washington Publication 561, 1946

tite?" Is there a difference? Actually, there are several very important differences.

Pyrite is composed of iron sulfide and sometimes contains small amounts of cobalt, nickel, silver and gold. It's more recognizable name is *fool's gold*. It is not magnetic. It can occur in crystal form usually in single or multiple cube shapes. Cubes, of course, are one type of six-sided figure, however, pyrite does not crystallize hexagonally at the molecular level, but instead crystallizes isometrically.[62] Solid pieces of pyrite are known to have been polished and used by Native Americans (including the Maya) possibly as mirrors and as dental inlays. It was also, with great difficulty, cut into polygonal (often six-sided) shaped flakes and carefully constructed into circular mosaic plaques, not for use as mirrors, but for ornamentation. (See *fig. 49*.) Pyrite has been found in burials in many sites in Central and North America. The mosaic plaques were most prevalent in the Guatemala highlands and in Arizona. Kidder, Shook and Jennings studied pyrite plaques from multiple sites and came to believe that, due to their consistency and quality of craftsmanship, they were probably produced by unusually skilled specialists from one location.[63] Pyrite is found in raw form throughout the world, but is especially plentiful in Bolivia, Spain, Italy, Utah, Colorado, Pennsylvania, Illinois and New York.

Coe noted that, like hematite, discoveries of *solid* pyrite disks are rare in Mesoamerica although large numbers have been found in caches buried in Caracol (Belize) and further north at Teotihuacan, Mexico which is known to have been a widely used ceremonial site. Most Mesoamerican pyrite is found in the form of mosaic plaques such as the one discovered at Piedras Negras in Burial 5 in 1932 (*fig. 50*) which is still on display at the Penn Museum. Coe found this plaque of particular interest since few have been uncovered in the Maya lowland areas. Strangely, pyrite disks did not, for example, show up in the nearby Maya city of Uaxactun (except for a few very small pieces assumed to have

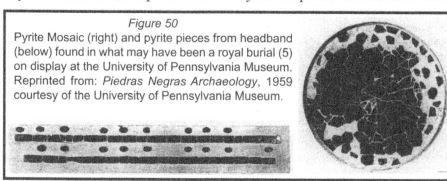

*Figure 50*
Pyrite Mosaic (right) and pyrite pieces from headband (below) found in what may have been a royal burial (5) on display at the University of Pennsylvania Museum. Reprinted from: *Piedras Negras Archaeology*, 1959 courtesy of the University of Pennsylvania Museum.

been broken off of a mosaic plaque) although "many richly stocked burials" were found there. Hematite, however, was found at Uaxactun - a significant point which will be discussed later. Also, of interest is that several of the pyrite pieces on the mosaic plaque from Burial 5 were cut into six-sided shapes. In fact, the center of the design is made up of pieces that form a hexagon. Coe also reported that a hexagon shaped piece of pyrite probably from a mosaic was found among debris unearthed at Piedras Negras near the South Group (Pyramid R-10). This artifact was not on the 1933 object list and Coe did not give the date of its discovery. He did state that it was located in the museum at Guatemala and he only included a drawing of it in his book. This would suggest that it was sent directly to Guatemala from the field.[64]

During the 1998 season at Piedras Negras, while digging into the axis of Pyramid 0-13 in the East Group, BYU uncovered what they called "one of the largest known caches in the Maya Lowlands" which had in it not only a large number of eccentric shaped stones, but also "9 pyrites (interspersed with jade, Spondylus, and hematite flecks)" which they believed to be part of a still undiscovered royal burial.[65] BYU also reported finding an unusual carved solid pyrite disk within Burial 13 during the 1997 season. They considered it a likely royal burial since within it were found over 100 pieces of worked jade collar ornaments, a mosaic jade plaque and many other clay and pottery artifacts. The polished and ground pyrite disk was 2 inches in diameter and carved on one side with hieroglyphs dating it to the Maya Classic Period around the time of Piedras Negras Ruler 4. A name glyph indicated the owner was a person who went by the name of Turtle and was an *ajaw* meaning "lord of the underneath" of a site called *Hix Wits* (Feline Hill).

*Hix Wits* is a mysterious city referred to on monuments at both Piedras Negras and its southern neighbor, Yaxchilan. BYU describes it as a "lost city" since it has never been located. It appears to have been a subject city to Piedras Negras since a representative from there is shown giving tribute on one sculpture. However, some rift may have occurred in that relationship since on the pyrite disk is carved the head of the *ajaw* with, as BYU described it, "drops of blood coursing from his severed neck." At Yaxchilan *Hix Wits* is referred to earlier as an enemy and later as supplying a bride to its sister city. BYU speculates that this lost city may be located in Guatemala at an undiscovered site near Piedras Negras.[66] Is this another possible reference to Cayce's Hall of Records? A city located at least partly underground and perhaps populated during the Maya period by caretakers of the secret records who called themselves "lords of the underneath." We will investigate evidence for underground chambers in the next chapter.

It appears that more pyrite than hematite has been found at Piedras Negras and other Maya sites. Schele and Freidel reported that hematite is found in volcanic areas and is rare. It was considered by the Maya as "superior even to the iron pyrite that the lowland Maya also imported." The Maya ground some of the hematite into a purple-red powder. When the powder was applied to the body it created a glitter effect.[67] Coe reported that red paint probably made from hematite was found on two of the skeletons in Burial 5 (1932 season), and on the bone tubes in Burial 6 (1933 season) at Piedras Negras, as well as in traces on some of the stelae at the site and on the Inscribed Cliff petroglyph. He also noted that the powdery red hematite coloring was found at many other Maya and Olmec sites mostly related to burials. For example, the remains of the famous Maya ruler Pacal, found in a tomb at Palenque, was wrapped in a red painted shroud. Interestingly, red paint burials have been reported in Peru and in North America, as well, especially in New England and Wisconsin among Archaic period burials (ca. 3000 B.C.).[68] Of most significance is Coe's statement in regards to the red paint tradition that, "The possibility of an Old World origin ought not to be neglected." Although he doesn't elaborate, this is an amazing statement from a mainstream archaeologist during the 1950s! [69]

## Hematite: Cayce's Magnetized Stones from the Atlantean Era?

Although hematite and pyrite are similar minerals, they are not the same. Both contain iron, however, hematite is iron oxide and sometimes contains trace amounts of titanium. Most significantly, like calcite, hematite crystallizes hexagonally. Hematite (*fig. 51*) is also paramagnetic. The term paramagnetic means it has a weak magnetic attraction. Of particular interest is the fact that hematite becomes strongly magnetic when heated.[70] Hematite crystals and polished mirrors have been found in Maya excavations mostly during the Late Preclassic period and diminishes thereafter.[71] A 1955 National Geographic expedition to the Olmec site of La Venta found two complete concave mirrors of similar size in two different locations. Both finds were laid out as part of a deliberate and unusual design consisting of 9 celts (ax heads) made of jade and serpentine. In the first two rows, 4 celts were laid side by side, the third row contained one celt and below, in a fourth row, was a mirror. But what was even more significant was that the mirrors were found to consist of a naturally occurring aggregate of magnetite ($Fe_3O_4$), hematite ($Fe_2O_3$), and ilmenite ($FeTiO_3$), an iron oxide containing titanium.

*Figure 51*
Samples of polished (left) and unpolished hematite (right) from New Jersey gem shop.

Other similar mirrors were found later some of which "*did not match any known geological source.*"[72]

Magnetite is a highly magnetic mineral and both hematite and ilmenite are paramagnetic. In addition, during expeditions at the Olmec site of San Lorenzo in the 1970s, archaeologists reported finding a grooved hematite bar which they believed may have been used as a lodestone compass.[73] Although their actual use is a mystery, researchers believe that the hematite mirrors were used as pendants and to reflect the sun in order to create smoke (by burning) during ceremonial rituals. Many of them contain holes and may have been worn by ruler priests who "flashed the sun's light in the eyes of the audience."[74] Because the drilled holes seem to have been carelessly placed on some of the specimens, archaeologists believe that they may have been obtained elsewhere through trade and the holes added later. They also speculated that "the pieces date from an earlier period of Olmec cultural development and exist at the La Venta site as treasured heirlooms or antiques." The fact that most were found in important ritual offerings, even when broken or fragmented, was also cited as a sign that they may have "an association with ancient times."[75] In addition, Carlson noted that no *pyrite* mirrors were found at La Venta even though that material would have been just as easily obtained. Pyrite, being a non-oxidized metal, decomposes in an oxidizing environment such as a burial. Minerals composed of the iron

*Figure 52*
Olmec jaguar mask pavement from La Venta. It is a symbolic form of the jaguar. Photo by: Lora Little.

oxides, such as hematite, do not decompose over time. It certainly sounds as if the hematite/magnetite/ilmenite pieces could very well be Cayce's "stones of the magnetized influence" brought over by the Atlantean immigrants.[76] If so, then perhaps the pyrite pieces were attempts by later groups to imitate the prized ancient Atlantean stones.

Cayce also indicated that the magnetized stones were used as sources of light and for spiritual communication. The archaeological data seems to support this characteristic as well. At Cerros in Northern Belize, hematite was found as part of a headband in a King's burial obviously as highly prized as jade, the Maya's most valued mineral. Schele and Freidel, who are considered experts in Maya cosmology, surmise that hematite was used to represent spiritual power and sacred energy and that it would "aid him (the deceased king) in his communication with the sacred world of the supernatural."[77] On sculptures at La Venta, hematite pendants were depicted around the neck of *God I* - the fire god or fire serpent. The mirror image has also been found associated with

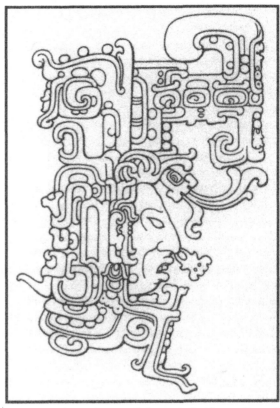

*Figure 53*
Maya drawings of the serpent footed God K with smoking axe/mirror on his forehead.

jaguar images indicating it was a symbol of power. One of the La Venta mirrors was found buried just above an Olmec jaguar mask pavement.[78] (See *fig. 52*.) Archaeologist Michael Coe stated that the mirrors may also be associated with the Maya *God K* who, like his Aztec counterpart, *Tezcatlipoca*, is often depicted as serpent footed with a smoking mirror protruding from his forehead.[79] (See *fig. 53*.) He is associated with the four creations of ancient times and the four directions. (This is an interesting 'coincidence' given the hematite compass discovery mentioned above.) In addition, Carlson found language links between the Maya word for mirror and words meaning "rulership, succession in office, brilliance, lightning, contemplation, meditation, and imagination."[80] In the Tzotzil language the word for mirror is the same as the word for window and is used in the context of the gods looking at man through the mirror/window. As Carlson puts it, "Tezcatlipoca could look into the hearts of men with his smoking divinatory mirror". He further pointed out that mirrors are still used by Maya shaman today for divination and in healing ceremonies.[81]

## What the 1933 Piedras Negras Discoveries Tell Us About the Hall of Records

The primary purpose of detailing the many artifacts uncovered at Piedras Negras in 1933 is to determine whether what was actually uncovered and catalogued by the archaeologists fits Cayce's clues and descriptions about the location of the Hall of Records. Some readers may have found the detail somewhat tedious. However, given the controversial nature of Cayce's Hall of Records — and his archaeologically unacceptable view of the influence of Atlantis and Mu — it is a virtual necessity to be meticulous and thorough. If what Cayce stated is true, then the 1933 archaeological record from Piedras Negras — or perhaps a nearby site — should fit his descriptions. From our review of the artifacts uncovered at Piedras Negras during 1933, it does seem that several of Cayce's descriptions are consistent with what was actually found.

To summarize, we have a few artifacts from 1933 that partially line up with Cayce's clues for the emblem of the Atlantean firestone crystal and magnetized stones. These are the calcite vessel and the fragments of pyrite/hematite. In addition, cave Burial #6 (with its holy man occupant) seems to be an interesting lead since cave habitation is a more ancient type of settlement. Of course, the most important Cayce clue related to the 1933 expedition is that the Hall of Records is located near **"where these stones (that they know so little about) are now during the last few months - BEING uncovered."**[84] The calcite, pyrite, and hematite stones on the 1933 object catalog were uncovered in the Acropolis. However, these may not be the stones referred to in that clue. Therefore, it would seem to be important to note the specific areas which were most actively scrutinized during the 1933 season.

As shown in the table on page 65, a lot of time was spent excavating both in the South Group (which is thought to be the oldest area) and at the Acropolis (especially around Court 1) during 1933. Also, the last two weeks of the season were spent at Pyramid K-5 near the Acropolis uncovering the giant stucco masks. Although it is not clear whether Cayce was referring to these subareas within the site, or to the Piedras Negras site as a whole, it does seem logical to keep in mind that anomalies associated with these subareas may be particularly significant. Cayce stated that the Hall of Records was near the place where stones were being uncovered. Perhaps the entrance to the Hall of Records is located in one of the subareas.

What else from Piedras Negras could fit Cayce's "uncovering of the stones" clue? Interestingly, one feature noted in the excavations of all three subareas were large numbers of cylindrical stone column altars both in front of and within the temples. These are unusual features in that they often had dedicatory caches of objects under them and they were not believed to have been used for sacrifice. None of these altars were transported back to Penn during 1933 according to the object catalog. However, many of them were located in structures excavated in 1933 as were the so-called drum-shaped portable altars.[85] In addition,

---

### Other Objects Transported to the Museum During 1933

Other notable objects mentioned in the 1933 field catalog for transport to Penn were:

- A bone awl 4 inches in length and the cut section of a conch shell both from cave burial #6.
- A pottery ball with crudely incised cross 1 inch in diameter (This item appears to also have been listed by Coe who describes it as being made of red limestone[82]).
- A "flattened spheroidal worked stone. Harder than limestone. Possibly a hammer stone" 8 cm (3 inches) in diameter and a thickness of 6 cm (2.3 inches) found Pyramid R-1, South Group.
- A "broken slab with partly finished incised glyphs and sketches" found in the Acropolis J-6 area.
- Miscellaneous sculptured stone #11 (fragment from Pyramid R-3).
- A small hemispherical stone object from Pyramid R-3

- A leaf shaped flint knife from Burial #10
- A fragment of a cylindrical clay object open at both ends and carved with a kneeling human figure found at J-2 (Coe identifies this as an earspool although it is much larger than other earspools).[83]
- A small pottery disk 1 inch in diameter found in the K-6 ball court
- A "Flake from quartzite river pebble, apparently struck off intentionally. Ovoid in shape. Max. Dms. 3.5 cm (1.37 inches). Again we have a possibility for the firestone emblem. Unfortunately its archaeological provenance (location from which it originated) is questionable since it is listed as a surface collection of the site architect somewhere in the West group.
- Several metates and mano stones assumed to have been used to grind corn or other grains.
- Dozens of partial and whole figurines most of which were "surface collected by the site architect (Fred Parris)."

---

the object catalog for 1933 lists several rectangular, ovoid and cylindrical *mano stones* and *metates*. These are the preferred grinding stone still in use today in Central America.[86] Two limestone objects, one rectangular and one square and of "unusual form...ground flat on one side, roughly convex on other" are listed as "possible" mano stones.[87]

## Expanding The Search at Piedras Negras

Overall, the focus of the Piedras Negras excavations during 1933 produced some possibilities related to the Cayce clues—especially the hematite and pyrite objects and the calcite vessel fragment. Since Cayce also indicated that discoveries would be made **both before and after 1933**, the next logical step was to broaden the search to include any relevant anomalies uncovered at Piedras Negras by Penn or BYU. For example, what have the archaeological explorations uncovered that differentiate Piedras Negras from other Maya sites?

It must be kept in mind that the Classic Maya period during which most of the known Piedras Negras monuments were erected was many thousands of years after the arrival of the Atlantean records. However, it is possible that the site still contains some clues that point to its Atlantean heritage. Also, there may be monuments or artifacts discovered before or after 1933 that match Cayce's clues. In the next two chapters we'll examine those. You may be surprised at what we found!

## Chapter References

1. The Pennsylvania State Archives: Pennsylvania Historical and Museum Commission, brochure #3/99/10M.

2. Research Collections at the Pennsylvania Historical and Museum Commission, 1999.

3. University of Pennsylvania Museum of Archaeology and Anthropology Brochure and building map.

4. Morley, S. V. (1938) *The Inscriptions of Peten, Vol. III.* Carnegie Institution of Washington, p. 3.

5. Coe, William (1959). *Piedras Negras Archaeology: Artifacts, Caches, and Burials.* Philadelphia: The University Museum, pp. 133-134.

6. Pinch, Geraldine (1994) *Magic in Ancient Egypt.* London: British Museum Press, p. 152.

7. Drucker, P. (1952) La Venta, Tabasco: A Study of Olmec Ceramic and Art. *BAE Bulletin 153.*

8. Goodman, Jeffrey (1977) *Psychic Archaeology: Time Machine to the Past.* New York: G.P. Putnam's Sons.

9. Kidder, Alfred, Jennings, Jesse, and Shook, Edwin (1946) *Excavations at Kaminaljuyu, Guatemala.* Carnegie Institution of Washington Publication 561, p. 130.

10. *The Inscriptions of Peten Vol. III,* op. cit.

11. Morley, S. V. (1938). The Inscriptions of Peten, Vol. I. *Carnegie Institution of Washington, Publication 437,* Washington.

12. Ibid, p. 103

13. Ibid, p. 100

14. Andrews, George (1975) *Maya Cities.* Norman Oklahoma: University of Oklahoma Press, p. 133.

15. Ibid, p. 136.

16. Blom, Franz (Ed.) (1934). Ma*ya Research* Vol. 1, No. 1 pp. 17-18.

17. Thompson, J. Eric (1963). *Maya Archaeologist.* Norman: U. of Okla. Press, p. 241

18. Ibid, pp. 244-245.

19. *Psychic Archaeology,* op. cit., pp. 80-81.

20. Ibid

21. Reading 440-5

22. Mason, J. Alden (1935) Preserving Ancient America's Finest Sculptures. *The National Geographic Magazine,* Vol. LXVIII, No. 5.

23. Satterthwaite, Linton Piedras Negras Field Notes, 1933 Report, University of Pennsylvania Museum Archives.

24. *The Inscriptions of Peten Vol III,* op.cit., p. 4.

25. Satterthwaite, Linton. Piedras Negras Field Notes, 1932 Packing List, University of Pennsylvania Museum Archives.

26. Reading 440-5

27. Mason, J. Alden (1933) The Piedras Negras Expedition. *The University Museum Bulletin*, Vol. 4, No. 5, p. 93.

28. *The Inscriptions of Peten, Vol. I*, op.cit., p. 99.

29. Satterthwaite, Linton. Piedras Negras Field Notes, 1933 Report, University of Pennsylvania Museum Archives.

30. Piedras Negras Field Notes, Photo Catalogs and Photographs, Box 19, Photo Catalogs, 1931-33 University of Pennsylvania Museum Archives.

31. Satterthwaite, Linton (1933) The Piedras Negras Expedition. *The University Museum Bulletin*, Vol. 1, No. 5, pp. 121-126.

32. Ibid

33. Ibid, p. 126

34. Ibid

35. Piedras Negras Field Notes, Photo Catalogs and Photographs, Box 19, Photo Catalogs, 1931-33, University of Pennsylvania Museum Archives.

36. Satterthwaite, Linton. Piedras Negras Field Notes, Box 6, Notebook 6, R-1 to R-10 University of Pennsylvania Museum Archives.

37. Satterthwaite, Linton. Piedras Negras Field Notes, Preliminary Notes on Piedras Negras Burials, 1933. University of Pennsylvania Museum Archives.

38. *Piedras Negras Archaeology* op. cit., pp. 126-127.

39. Houston, S., Escobedo, H. and Forsyth, D. (1998). On the River of Ruins: Explorations at Piedras Negras, Guatemala, 1997. *Mexicon*, Vol. XX, pp. 16-22.

40. Satterthwaite, Linton (1935) *Piedras Negras Preliminary Report No. 3: Palace Structures J-2 and J-6*. Philadelphia: University of Pennsylvania Museum, p. 42.

41. Reading 941-142.

42. Satterthwaite, Linton (1943) P*iedras Negras Architecture* (Draft) in Field Notes, Reports and Publications, University of Pennsylvania Museum Archives.

43. *Piedras Negras Archaeology* op. cit. pp. 61-62.

44. Linton Satterthwaite, Piedras Negras Field Notes, Miscellaneous Observations, Box 7, Notebook 8, University of Pennsylvania Museum Archives.

45. Satterthwaite, Linton (1933) The Piedras Negras Expedition. *The University Bulletin*, Vol. 4, No. 5, pp. 120-126.

46. Satterthwaite, Linton (1940) Evolution of a Maya Temple - Part II. *The University Bulletin*, Vol. 8, No. 2-3, pp. 18-27.

47. Schele, Linda and Freidel, David (1990) *A Forest of Kings*. New York: William Morrow, p. 103.

48. Reading 364-4.

49. *A Forest of Kings*, op. cit. p. 111.

50. Reading 440-12

51. Satterthwaite, Linton. Piedras Negras Field Notes, Object Catalog 1933, Box 13, University of Pennsylvania Museum Archives.

52. Piedras Negras Object Catalog 1933, op.cit.

53. *Piedras Negras Archaeology* op. cit., p. 38.

54. Satterthwaite, Linton (1943) Animal head feet and a bark beater in the Middle Usumacinta region. *Carnegie Institution of Washington, Division of Historical Research Notes on Middle American Archaeology and Ethnology,* No. 27, Cambridge, p. 180.

55. *Piedras Negras Archaeology* op.cit., p. 38.

56. Online Mineral Gallery (http://www.minerals.net/mineral) copyright Hershel Friedman, 1997-1999.

57. Reading 440-5

58. *The Book of Mormon*, (1963) Salt Lake City, Utah: The Church of Jesus of Latterday Saints., p. 483.

59. Piedras Negras Object Catalog 1933, op.cit.

60. Ibid

61. *Piedras Negras Archaeology* op.cit., p. 43.

62. Online Mineral Gallery (http://www.minerals.net/mineral) copyright Hershel Friedman, 1997-1999.

63. *Excavations at Kaminaljuyu, Guatemala* op. cit., p. 126-133.

64. *Piedras Negras Archaeology* op.cit., p. 42.

65. Houston, S. et al. (1999) Between Mountains and Sea: Investigations at Piedras Negras, Guatemala 1998. *Mexicon*, XXI p. 13.

66. *Mexicon*, XX op. cit., p. 19.

67. *A Forest of Kings* op. cit. p. 463.

68. Snow, Dean (1976) *The Archaeology of North America*. London: Thames and Hudson, Ltd., p. 6.

69. *Piedras Negras Archaeology* op.cit, pp. 134-136.

70. Online Mineral Gallery. op. cit.

71. *A Forest of Kings* op. cit., p. 463.

72. Heizer, Robert and Gullberg, Jonas (1981) Concave Mirrors from the Site of La Venta, Tabasco: Their Occurrence, Mineralogy, Optical Description, and Function. In Elizabeth Benson (Ed.) *The Olmec and Their Neighbors: Essays in Memory of Matthew W. Stirling*. Washington, D.C.: Dumbarton Oaks Research Library and Collections, p. 116.

73. Carlson, John (1981) Olmec Concave Iron-Ore Mirrors: The Aesthetics of a Lithic Technology and the Lord of the Mirror. In Elizabeth Benson (Ed.) *The Olmec and Their Neighbors: Essays in Memory of Matthew W. Stirling*. Washington, D.C.: Dumbarton Oaks Research Library and Collections, p. 117-147.

74. Carlson, John. The *Olmec and Their Neighbors*, op. cit., p. 113.

75. Ibid, p. 115.

76. Reading 5750-1.

77. *A Forest of Kings* op. cit., p. 121.

78. Carlson, John.*The Olmec and Their Neighbors*, op. cit.

79. Coe, Michael (1973) *The Maya Scribe and His World*. New York: Grolier Club, p. 16.

80. Carlson, John.*The Olmec and Their Neighbors*, op. cit., p. 127.

81. Ibid, p. 126.

82. *Piedras Negras Archaeology* op. cit. p. 39.

83. Ibid, figure 59q.

84. Reading 440-5.

85. *Piedras Negras Archaeology* op. cit.

86. Sharer, Robert (1994) *The Ancient Maya: Fifth Edition*, Stanford: Stanford U. Press.

87. Piedras Negras Field Notes, Object Catalog, op. cit.

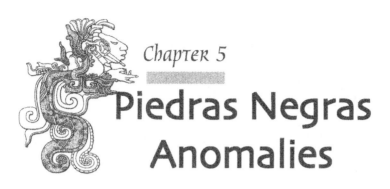

Chapter 5

# Piedras Negras Anomalies

Piedras Negras is a fascinating Maya site. It contains many unusual features such as primitive rock carvings, strange abstract inscriptions, nonMaya architecture in substructures under existing pyramids, large underground caverns, and shows many connections to the ancient Maya creation story. Even the archaeologists admit that it does not fit the usual pattern of the Classic Maya city. Penn researchers, Coe and Satterthwaite, concluded that Piedras Negras was a conservative community in that certain architectural features such as the distinctly Classic Maya vaulted roof were adopted much later there than at neighboring Maya sites.[1, 2] Several sources described Piedras Negras as seeming reluctant to change early established ceremonial patterns and being resistant to diffusion. In other words, it didn't seem to try to keep up with its sister cities nor did these cities seem to keep up with it.

Piedras Negras was also unique, according to Coe, "in the widespread presence of sweathouses, column altars in temples, the prominence of caches, and the apparent rarity of burials in temple structures."[3] The Penn expeditions located only 10 burials, although BYU discovered an additional 39 during their first three seasons. Most of these burials were not found within temples.[4] In addition, Piedras Negras had unusually large quantities and varied styles of so called "eccentric forms" (fig. 54) which are small sculpted, seemingly abstract, shapes made primarily from obsidian (volcanic glass), but also flint, and other materials. Their actual use is unknown, although they were often found buried in groups (called caches) at various levels of the temples. It is thought that they were a type of religious offering and may also have been used for bloodletting ceremonies.[5] Recent evidence has revealed that some of them were probably shaped to represent lightning. Lightning was considered to be a powerful force that embodied the spiritual substance of the universe and was therefore connected to the special Maya rituals designed to enhance communication with the supernatural world.[6] Apparently, these rituals were very much a part of life in Piedras Negras. In this chapter we will explore the many unusual features at Piedras Negras and how they relate to our search for the lost Hall of Records and to Cayce's story of Atlantis.

# Rock Carvings

### The Sacrificial Rock

Among the most unique discoveries at Piedras Negras were three rock carvings that are not a part of the city monuments. First is the

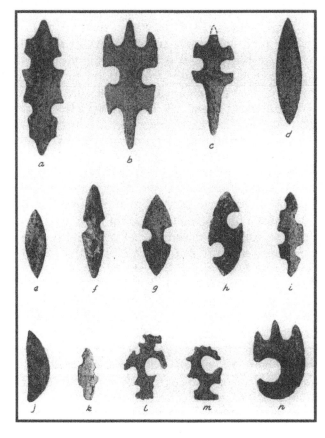

*Figure 54*
Examples of sculpted stones in abstract shapes which archaeologists call "eccentrics" found at Piedras Negras. Reprinted from: *Piedras Negras Archaeology*, 1959, courtesy of the University of Pennsylvania Museum.

Sacrificial Rock, so named by Maler because it contains a design that is similar to another altar (Altar 1) in the city that he was certain was used for human sacrifice.[7] The carved design (*fig. 55*) depicts a side view of two persons sitting opposite each other. The figure on the left sits a little lower and holds a square book or box-like object in outstretched hands. The higher figure seems to lean forward either to observe or to accept the object. The scene is framed in a double line of concentric circles segmented as if to include hieroglyphic symbols although none are clearly visible. Maler described the carving as eroded, while Morley, who stud-

*Figure 55*
Sacrificial Rock located in the rive bed at Piedras Negras. Chalk outlines were added for emphasis by Penn expedition 1935. [White line down middle is also on negative.] Photo reprinted by permision from the University of Pennsylvania Museum Archives.

ied it in 1929, claimed it was simply unfinished.[8] In his field notes from 1935, Satterthwaite noted the possibility of "one or two very lightly incised small glyphs" in the lower inner circle area, but did not attempt to decipher them.[9] Morley dated the carving to near the end of the Classic period (A.D. 830) although he based this solely on its resemblance to Altar 1 which does contain that date as well as several other very ancient dates (more on the mysterious dating periods of Altar 1 later).[10]

The Sacrificial Rock is located in the river bed at the beach entrance to the city. It is below the water level during the rainy season and therefore is protected from overgrowth by the jungle. The rock is a natural tear shaped, table top outcropping of black limestone. It is rounded on the beach side and its pointed end faces southwest toward the Mexico side of the river.[11] Of all of the artifacts at Piedras Negras, the Sacrificial Rock looks most like a sundial which Cayce indicated would be one of the features "uncovered" in the future (after 1933) by Penn near the Hall of Records. The sundial may also be the stone that contains the emblem of the Atlantean firestone. It fits the time line Cayce gave (in that it was studied most closely by Penn during the 1935 season), however, it did not have to be "uncovered," per se, and was not taken to any of the museums. It also does not appear to be located "between the temple and the chambers," as Cayce further described, unless the chambers refers to some other feature of the site such as a temple or cave located on the other side of the river.[12] While in the field, Satterthwaite received reports of mounds located across the river in a valley well north of the Sacrificial Rock. He did not follow-up since he concluded that they would have been practically inaccessible to the ancient Maya at Piedras Negras. As a result, they were not explored.[13] But what is especially odd about the Sacrificial Rock is that it almost appears to have been designed to be a signpost. It is the first feature a visitor traveling by river would notice. However, it doesn't have any of the usual city emblem glyphs on it. Instead, it has two figures which appear to be exchanging or viewing something that looks a great deal like a book or tablet. Since we are searching for a Hall of Records, it is certainly more than just a bit interesting. But there is more.

## The Spiral Petroglyphs - Atlantean Symbol?

A second set of nonmonumental carvings was found by J. Alden Mason in 1931 on flat rocks in the river bed opposite the West Group about 440 yards downstream from the Sacrificial Rock. They were not studied or recorded until the 1935 season. The rocks slope 10 degrees and are below the high water mark, but, fortunately, are 50 yards above the river in low water. Found at this location were primitive petroglyphs pecked into the rock in the shape of double and single circular spirals or scrolls. Satterthwaite wrote in his field notes that there were 40 of them irregularly arranged. They range in size from 6 to 16 inches in diameter. Some were drawn clockwise while others are counterclockwise. He further noted that they were "very much eroded and seeming of great age."[14]

In a 1935 publication, Satterthwaite stated that the spiral petroglyphs (*fig. 56*) "do not differ from rock carvings in Colorado and Pennsylvania, Transjordania and South Africa which have been referred to primitive cultures." He also believed that they could not have been made by the Postclassic Maya since a fragment (*fig. 57*) chipped from the cliff was discovered reused as a vault slab in Court 1 of the Acropolis during the 1932 excavations.[15, 16] This, along with other evidence, led Penn to conclude that the rocks along the river were used as a quarry for construction materials. Thus, it appears that these spiral petroglyphs were not particularly valued during the Classic Maya period which provides more weight to their being of a more ancient origin. In the field notes, Satterthwaite wrote that all of the petroglyph carvings (including the Inscribed Cliff) could "be the work of a relatively primitive Maya

*Figure 56*
Spiral or scroll petroglyphs (rock carvings) at Piedras Negras throught to possibly be preMaya. Chalk outlines were added for emphasis by Penn expedition 1935. Photo reprinted by permission from the University of Pennsylvania Museum Archives.

*Figure 57*
Fragment of rock from spiral carvings found re-used as a vault stone in Court 1 of the Acropolis in 1932. Photo reprinted by permission from the University of Pennsylvania Museum Archives.

*Figure 58*
La Venta Altar 3 showing two figures facing each other as is also on the Piedras Negras Sacrificial Rock. Partly eroded spirals can be seen framing the carving. From *Stone Monuments of Southern Mexico*, Stirling (1943).

*Figure 59*
Drawing of the coiled serpent used in Egypt and India to symbolize the kundalini life force. Source: *Egyptian Motifs*, Dover Publ.

*Figure 60*
Primitive spiral rock carvings from Arizona. Reprinted from Corel Gallery.

*Figure 61 (above left)*
Tres Zapote Monument C containing spiral design which appears to depict men under water or underground? From *Stone Monuments of Southern Mexico*, Stirling (1943).

group who were receiving stimuli from the center of the area to the east."[17] Spirals were a common decorative feature at Tres Zapote, an Olmec site located to the east of Piedras Negras on the Gulf Coast dating to 1500 B.C. They were not so common at the Olmec site of La Venta, although a carving of two seated (and bearded) figures very similar to those depicted on the Piedras Negras Sacrificial Rock (and Altar 1) was found on La Venta Altar 3 (*fig. 58*). Instead of being framed by concentric circles the figures are surrounded by a series of spiral and scroll designs.[18]

Spirals have been found at ancient sites throughout the world. They are often associated with themes of death and rebirth and are frequently seen with megalithic prehistoric burials. It is thought that the symbol may have originated from observations made of the movement of water or the sinking of an object into the depths. It could also reflect the movement of the stars and was used at some ancient sites as markers for star sightings as well as for the solstice.[19] A pecked petroglyph depicting a cross surrounded by two concentric circles was found in several locations around Teotihuacan. One, located on a nearby mountain slope, lines up with the heliacal rising of the Pleiades constellation which occurs on one of only two days each year when the sun is at its zenith. The spiral is related to the Maya glyph of the univalve shell and represents the underworld. It is also thought to be related to the spiral shaped Los Casorios (Wedding Party) constellation that makes up the head of the bull of Taurus and includes the star Aldebaran.[20]

Spirals are maternal symbols since they occur so frequently in nature and were considered in some cultures to be living things. The spiral staircase in medieval churches was said to symbolize the secret path to heaven... "revealed only to those who have ascended into heaven."[21] The single spiral was used in ancient Egypt (*fig. 59*) to represent the coiled serpent.[22] Ancient (3000 years old) texts in India used the word kundalini (meaning coiled serpent) to describe the potential life force energy that when awakened through certain spiritual practices unites our physical, mental and spiritual bodies and creates a connection "between infinity and the finite" to use Cayce's words.[23, 24]

Could the spiral petroglyphs at Piedras Negras be related to the firestone which Cayce said was initially used as a means of creating communication with God or to the power of the magnetic stones used by the Atlanteans who immigrated to the Yucatan? The exact composition of the rocks onto which the spirals are carved is not clear, but it appears that they are not composed of magnetic minerals. Satterthwaite described them as "black rocks" in a 1935 article, while Morley stated that they were carved on "native limestone."[25, 26] The black rock in the riverside cliffs nearest to the Acropolis was analyzed by BYU and determined to be black chert stained with manganese dioxide. Chert is an impure form of flint and is composed of microcrystalline quartz. It also usually includes the remains of micro-organisms. It is not magnetic. The remaining rock was identified by BYU as limestone which is composed of at least 50% calcite. The black color of some of the limestone at Piedras

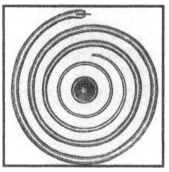

Negras is caused by the presence of dolomite. Interestingly, calcite, quartz (chert), and dolomite (like hematite) all form hexagonal crystals at the molecular level which provides another correlation to the six-sided form of Cayce's firestone.[27, 28] Although the rock cliffs are not known to be magnetic, could

*Figure 62*
Serpent spiral mound in Iowa. From *The Serpent Symbol*, E. G. Squier (1851).

the site have been chosen by the Atlanteans for the Hall of Records because its geologic makeup at the molecular level symbolizes a hexagon?

There is some evidence that the spiral designs could be a symbol for ancient spiritual practices. As mentioned in the last chapter, a pyrite ornament with an incised scroll design was found in the Acropolis area at Piedras Negras during the 1933 season.[29] In addition, Schele and Freidel believe that spirals may have both a sacred and an astronomical connection for the Maya. Early Maya temples dedicated to the Sun god, such as at Cerros, were arranged so that the king entered walking in a clockwise spiral and left by walking around in a counter clockwise spiral "thus emulating the movement of the sun from east to west." In this holy of holies area the king performed fasting and bloodletting rituals in order to obtain a trance-like state in which contact was made with the supernatural world.[30]

Another possibility is that the spiral and/or the concentric circle design is a symbol for Atlantis (*fig. 63*). In *Criteas*, Plato described the great city on the island of Atlantis as having a circular layout. In fact, it resembled a spiral in that it was laid out in the form of three concentric circles created by moats of water surrounded at some further distance by a fourth circle. A canal was built which dissected the circles. On the island in the center of the innermost circle was the palace and the main temple. All of the circles were built on "a smooth plain...being itself encircled by mountains" not unlike the terrain surrounding Piedras Negras.[31] Interestingly, Cerros, in Belize, is built overlooking a bay on the Caribbean coast and its inner ceremonial center was completely surrounded by a shallow semicircular canal connected to the bay. Since Cerros is a very early Maya site, this design could be another Atlantean remnant.

Or perhaps the spirals are an ancient symbol for the Atlantean records buried nearby. Double spirals or scrolls symbolize both evo-

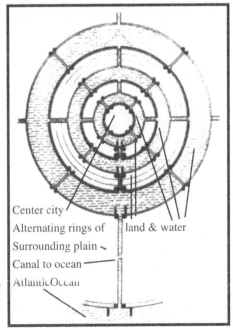

Center city

Alternating rings of   land & water

Surrounding plain

Canal to ocean

Atlantic Ocean

*Figure 63*
Drawing of the layout of the ancient city of Atlantis as described by Plato in *Criteas*. Adapted from Zhirov (*Atlantis*, 1970).

*Figure 64*
Hebrew scroll. Reprinted from: *The Jewish Encyclopedia*, 1905.

lution (unwinding) and involution (winding in) and can represent the cycles of life or of the cosmos.[32] This would be a fitting emblem to mark the location of the records since, from Cayce's readings, we are given to understand that they contain a history of civilization possibly going back to the time of creation. In addition, the double spirals at Piedras Negras are reminiscent of the scroll form and could have been carved to represent written documents. Since Cayce indicated a Hebrew connection to the Maya, it should be noted that the Hebrew *Torah* originated in written scroll form around 900-600 B.C. The most primitive versions were written on animal hide and rolled onto scrolls which were turned counter clockwise on one side and clockwise on the other.[33] (See *fig. 64.*) Although a few badly decomposed Maya animal hide and bark books called codex have been unearthed, most are recopied versions of older manuscripts created around the time of Spanish colonization and none were found in scroll form. Also, in one reading Cayce seemed to indicate that the Atlantean records were preserved in stone.[34] Despite this, it seems possible that, if Piedras Negras is the site of the Hall of Records, there might be some ancient markings, however cryptic, directing a knowledgeable person to the location of the Hall of Records.

## The Inscribed Cliff: An Iltar Connection?

The third nonmonumental carving was a cliff inscription 16 feet above ground level discovered by Maler in 1895 southeast of the South Group. (See *fig. 65.*) The Piedras Negras area contains many overhanging cliffs. This particular one is located outside the ceremonial center approximately 220 yards southeast of Structure V-1. After studying it during the 1935 season, Satterthwaite described it as being similar to the spiral petroglyph carvings on the river banks in that it was "pecked" into the "living rock." He also noted that it was well preserved and still

*Figure 65*

Photograph from 1935 of the Inscribed Cliff at Piedras Negras depicting the cosmic turtle/ Maize god emergence symbols. Chalk outlines were added for emphasis by Penn expedition. Photo reprinted by permission from the University of Pennsylvania Museum Archives.

*Figure 66*

Example of two headed cosmic monster or dragon used frequently in Maya art that resembles carving on Inscribed Cliff at Piedras Negras. Reprinted from Dover.

*Figure 67*
Linton Satterthwaite's drawing of the Inscribed
Cliff. Reprinted from: *The Inscriptions of Peten*,
Carnegie Institution of Washington, 1938.

had traces of red paint in the carved lines. As mentioned in the last chapter, hematite based red paint was widely used by the Maya especially in ceremonial activities.[35]

Interestingly, the description of what the carving depicts varies from observer to observer. Maler sketched it as two portrait type heads in profile facing in opposite directions, although he noted that the head to the left was eroded.[36] Satterthwaite saw it as similar to the "two-headed dragon well known to Maya art though only a few lines of the head on the left survive." (See *fig. 66*.) Today, Maya researchers call this type of drawing the "cosmic monster." The noneroded head Satterthwaite identified as the famous Long Nose god (Itzamna) of Maya mythology (*fig. 67*). He also noted that in the middle of the carving was the hieroglyphic cartouche for the day sign *Ahau* (*fig. 68*) which is also the Maya word for "lord." *Ahau* is the last and most important of the twenty Maya day signs. It is also the day of which Itzamna, the Maya Creator, is patron. On the cliff inscription, beside the day sign, is a bar (which represents the number 5) and one smaller than normal and irregularly located dot (which may represent the number 1) which would indicate the day sign 6 *Ahau*.[37] This would be equivalent in our calendar to a month and day number (such as November 3). It does not, however, give any information about the year. In 1935 Satterthwaite wrote to Morley that he and his field associate could find no evidence for additional dots which may have been removed or eroded. But, for some reason, Morley dismissed the dot altogether and interpreted the inscription as 5 *Ahau*. Even though there were no additional glyphs to indicate the year, Morley proceeded to outline a very speculative theory as to why it would have been carved during the Early Classic Maya period.[38]

In the 1997 BYU report, the inscription was referred to as "the carved Pauahtun/God K/8 *Ahau* (9.13.0.0.0) turtle petroglyph discov-

*Figure 68*
Closeup of the Maya Ahau day sign glyph from
Inscribed Cliff. Note bar and small dot to the
left of the day sign possibly depicting the num-
ber 6. Reprinted from: *The Inscriptions of Peten*,
Carnegie Institution of Washington, 1938.

ered by Maler."[39] Where they got the 8 (as opposed to 5 or 6) *Ahau* date is not clear. However, it is assumed that BYU was referring to this same cliff inscription since it was the only petroglyph Maler reported finding at Piedras Negras. Also, Satterthwaite did concede that the carving could be a side view of the body of a turtle which was an important Maya symbol.[40] In excavations nearby, BYU discovered broken pottery pieces (called pot sherds), as deep as 6 feet below ground level at the base of the cliff. They also identified five niches (one containing pot sherds) on the cliff below the turtle and a ledge above the cliff which could have held a human body. They concluded that the inscription was "highly suggestive of maize-god emergence scenes connected to such turtles."[41] This means that the site was most likely used for ceremonial activities that included a reenactment of the sacred creation story related to the turtle shell. In one of the Maya creation myths (*fig. 69*), the First Father, Itzamna, (also called the Maize-god) paddles with two companions in a canoe to the place of the three stones of creation which become a turtle's shell through which "he can be reborn and create the new universe." The Maya date this creation event as occurring on August 13, 3114 B.C., a date that brings us closer to the chronology of Cayce's story. In addition, there is evidence that, for the Maya, the three stones of the turtle's shell may have been represented by the movement of the three stars in the belt of Orion.[42] (More on this in the chapter on astronomical alignments.)

Piedras Negras seems to have been very closely connected to the turtle symbol. For example, the Emblem Glyph used by the Maya to identify Piedras Negras contains a turtleshell symbol.[43] Fitzsimmons noted in his review of Piedras Negras mortuary anniversaries that there was a "proliferation of 'turtle' titles at Piedras Negras" among the persons mentioned on the various monuments.[44] In fact, the inscriptions found at Piedras Negras indicate that it was ruled by only two families, the most prominent of which was the Turtleshells. This pattern of a two family dynasty is unique to Piedras Negras and was based on intermarriage between maternal first cousins.[45] Is it possible that the Turtleshell family name was derived from the ruling families' descent from the great "First Father" god, Itzamna?

Researchers have so far uncovered at least four Maya Classic era ruling dynasties that claimed mythological ancestry and the Turtleshells of Piedras Negras are one of those.[46] Could Itzamna be Cayce's Atlantean — Iltar — paddling over the Atlantic and up the Usumacinta to begin a new life or a new creation? If the Atlanteans were as advanced both spiritually and technologically as Cayce asserted, it seems plausible that they could have been perceived as gods. Over thousands of years the real story of their existence may have been com-memorated through what we view as mythology. For example, the Maya credit Itzamna with the invention of books and writing and say he named the various places in the Yucatan. This would certainly fit the profile of Cayce's Iltar. In the Yucatec Maya language, Itzamna is called the *Hunab* meaning "one god" in that he is creator of the universe and encom-passes everything. Cayce identified Iltar as being a member of the "Sons of the Law of One" who practiced monotheism.

Although he is the ultimate god for the Maya, Itzamna is also thought to be an aspect of another well known Mesoamerican god, Quetzalcoatl (also believed to be known as Kukulcan). This god is de-picted as having both good and evil characteristics. Some myths credit Quetzalcoatl/Kukulcan with bringing enlightenment and peace, while other stories portray him as introducing human sacrifice and bloodlet-ting rituals. In some versions the negative side of Quetzalcoatl is actu-ally a competitor and associate named Tezcatlipoca (*fig. 70*). He was said to have entered the land of Quetzalcoatl and served as a bad influ-ence to the people. In the same way, Itzamna represented for the Maya both life and death, day and night, and good and evil.[47] This duality is depicted by the two headed cosmic monster, similar to the cliff inscrip-

*Figure 69*
Itzamna (Iltar?) paddling his boat over the Atlantic. From one of the codex.

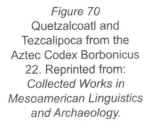

Figure 70
Quetzalcoatl and
Tezcalipoca from the
Aztec Codex Borbonicus
22. Reprinted from:
*Collected Works in
Mesoamerican Linguistics
and Archaeology.*

tion carving, which is frequently portrayed in Maya art. Given that Cayce's story of the Atlantean migration included immigrants with both high and low moral character (Sons of the Law of One and the Sons of Balial) this duality could also be a reflection of both of these powerful groups. Some of the Atlanteans would have been looked upon as creators and life givers while others might have been excellent representations of the lower tendencies of man. Perhaps the double headed cosmic monster and the Ahau day sign on the Inscribed Cliff carving at Piedras Negras represent the dual nature of Itzamna as personified by the god-like Atlantean immigrants.

Another interesting connection involves God K (*fig. 71*), which BYU identified with this cliff inscription. God K is known as the serpent footed god, K'awil, who was the embodiment of the conduit from the supernatural world into the middle world (earth). In Maya cosmology, newborn souls must pass through the gullet of the serpent to assume their new bodies. God K was one of the three gods who, with Itzamna, paddled to the new creation. He is also associated with the hematite mirrors which may be Cayce's Atlantean magnetized stones. As noted in the last chapter, he and Quetzalcoatl's negative alter ego, Tezcatlipoca, are often depicted with a smoking mirror/axe in their foreheads representing the flowing out of the spiritual substance of the supernatural world through the hematite mirror. God K was known to the Maya as the Vision Serpent since he was a means of communication or transformation from one world to another. The Vision Serpent is sometimes rep-

Figure 71
God K in his role as the Vision Serpent is shown emerging from the mouth of a snake. From *American Indian Design*, Dover Publ.

resented as coiled into a spiral form which makes God K surprisingly similar to another serpent symbolized concept mentioned earlier in relation to the spiral petroglyphs - the coiled kundalini energy that, when unleashed, links man with the spiritual world. In some Maya art, rulers are depicted holding the Double-headed Serpent Bar to convey that they are "grasping the path to the underworld."[48] (See *figure 72*.) Amazingly, these concepts are known to go back in Mesoamerican history at least as far as the Olmec culture and possibly farther.[49] Could they be based on early Atlantean beliefs and, if so, why did they change over time to become associated with Maya bloodletting ceremonies?

Perhaps it was because of the negative influence of the Tezcatlipoca character who sounds a lot like one of Cayce's Atlantean Sons of Balial. As a result of the power-hunger and self-gratifying tendencies of this negative influence, the Maya ancestors may have gradually lost their ability to use the Atlantean hematite mirrors to commune with the One God. Over time they had to resort to self-mutilation, bloodletting, and possibly hallucinogenic drugs in order to put themselves into an altered state of

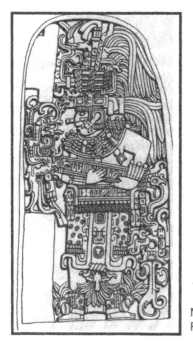

Figure 72
Maya ruler grasping the double headed serpent bar. From *American Indian Design*, Dover Publ.

consciousness. In doing this they could have been communing more with images from their own subconscious than with the spiritual world. Eventually the God K/Vision Serpent experience would have become so closely associated with bloodletting rituals, that this would explain the Maya belief that they were, in effect, feeding blood to the gods in order to elicit communication with the otherworld. It is known that, for the Maya, God K was often symbolized as the idol or cave god and was "the process by which spirit is manifested within material objects." By smearing them with blood, the Maya came to believe that places and objects could be imbued with supernatural power.[50] The large number of eccentric shaped knife-like stones and stingray spine artifacts found throughout the site indicates that bloodletting rituals were in full swing at Piedras Negras. At some point these rituals moved from personal bloodletting to include human sacrifice. Schele reported that modern Maya shaman are wary of bloodletting rituals and often use a substitute offering such as incense or candles to communicate with the spiritual world. They believe that the old rituals were dangerous because they led to direct contact with the underworld (the subconscious?) which can "result in the loss of soul and body and accusations of witchcraft."[51] Certainly, it could have led to an unbalanced mental state over time.

Since the Inscribed Cliff is a primitive type of monument and not part of the manmade temple complexes at Piedras Negras, it is possible that it was carved prior to the construction of the great city center. Perhaps it was a sacred spot in some way associated with Iltar/Itzamna and his group. For example, it could have been the place where the ancient Atlantean spiritual ceremonies were performed. These ceremonies would have predated the Maya bloodletting rituals and would instead have been based on the original Iltar/Sons of the Law of One inspired Atlantean rituals. Perhaps it was the site of spiritual ceremonies where Iltar/Itzamna — using the hematite mirrors — activated the kundalini energy and communed with the One God.

## The Strange Design on Lintel 6

Another anomaly at Piedras Negras involves the discovery of an unusually carved stone depicting a mysterious, abstract design. (See *figure 73*.) It is unlike any other design at the site although Maler reported and copied somewhat similar carvings in 1897 and 1900 at three other sites nearby. Two of those designs, as at Piedras Negras, he believed to have been carved on the underside of door lintels so that it could only be seen from the inside of the building.[52] What makes the Piedras Negras design especially noteworthy in our search is that it is a wheel or circle 1 foot in diameter with six spokes that gives the impression of a six-sided star and it appears to have been drawn with one continuous line. It seems quite possible that it may relate to Cayce's firestone which he said was "in the form of a six-sided figure." Also, since it resembles a six-sided star similar to the modern Hebrew symbol, it might even be evidence for the presence of the Lost Tribes. In addition, it could also be related to a Maya game board that was used as a sundial in ancient times. Of course, one of Cayce's clues about the lost Hall of Records related to the uncovering of a sundial.

Maler discovered the design during his 1895 expedition to Piedras Negras. It was etched into a 4.4 feet long, 4 feet wide and 3.5 inches thick stone slab that had been recently carried from the ruins by local woodcutters. They had taken it to their camp (located 93 yards northeast of the Sacrificial Rock) and used it as a table top. Maler assumed that it was the lintel stone from the top of a doorway so he named it Lintel 6 (*fig. 74*). When the workers abandoned their camp the stone became overgrown by the jungle.[53] Penn relocated the lintel in 1931, but did not remove it. They tentatively dated it to the "Early Middle Period (???)."[54] Note the question marks in the dating indicating that they really had no idea when it was carved. Penn also seemed to reinforce the unusual quality of the inscription since they were unable to

*Figure 73*
Photograph of Piedras Negras Lintel 6 as it currently appears.
Photo by John Montgomery.

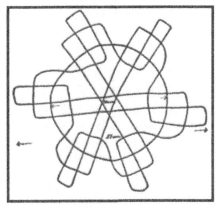

*Figure 74*
Maler's 1895 drawing of the mysterious six spoked design on Piedras Negras Lintel 6. Reprinted from: *Memoirs of the Peabody Museum, Harvard University*, Vol. 2, No. 1, 1901.

categorize it or to determine its purpose. In another report, Satterthwaite reviewed and described several of the lintels discovered at Piedras Negras, but noted, "Lintel 6 we eliminate since it has neither carved inscription nor design, but merely an incised abstract figure."[55] Although it was not mentioned in the BYU reports, a recent picture of it on site at Piedras Negras was available through the internet as of July 1999 indicating that it is still where Penn left it.[56]

## Was Lintel 6 used as an Ancient Sundial?

One of the designs similar to Lintel 6 was found by Maler at El Cayo, a small set of ruins located on the Mexico side of the Usumacinta river. El Cayo is approximately 15 miles south of Piedras Negras which puts it almost halfway between Piedras Negras and another large Maya site, Yaxchilan. Maler discovered the design on the inside of a lintel that was part of the temple doorway. The temple was one of 5 separate temple buildings constructed on top of one large platform. Maler described the El Cayo design as shaped like a "St. Andrew's Cross," (*fig. 75*) but, again, drawn with one continuous overlapping line. He found no other carvings within any of the other temple structures. In his discussion he speculated that the design "must have had some special significance, perhaps astronomical." He further noted that "they may intimate that these rooms were devoted to the astronomer-priests, to whom the calculation of the chronology was intrusted."[57] It needs to be noted that although Maler identified the stone as a lintel, the building from which it came had already collapsed. In several in-

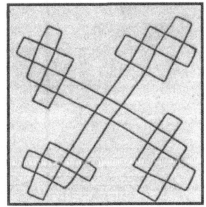

*Figure 75*
Maler's drawing of the St. Andrew's Cross at El Cayo. Reprinted from: *Memoirs of the Peabody Museum, Harvard University*, Vol. 2, No. 2, 1901.

stances at Piedras Negras, Maler's lintels turned out to be something else.[58]

Because of the uniformity of the carved squares, it is possible that the El Cayo design is the remains of a Maya *patolli* or other game board. Patolli is an ancient game of chance played by the Maya as well as the later Aztec. In modern times the game has become associated with gambling and drinking. Boards pecked into monuments have been found at several sites although most are in the form of a square rather than a cross.[59] (See *figure 76*.) Archaeologist Adrian Digby has theorized that the patolli board may have been used in conjunction with a sundial in ancient times. He has identified sun symbol hieroglyphic inscriptions depicting a shape he calls crossed trapezes (*fig. 77*) that were most likely used to record the movement of the sun. Interestingly, one of the working models of the crossed trapeze design he proposed resembles two equilateral triangles — one with the apex pointing up and the other down. Although the bottom point does not show on his model, these two triangles would form a six-sided star not unlike the Star of David which will be discussed in more detail shortly. Pebbles were utilized on the Patolli board and Digby stated that they could have been used to mark the sun's progress through the day and/or the solar year. When the

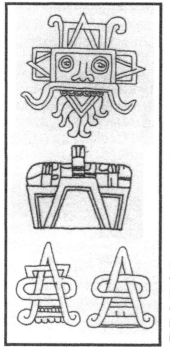

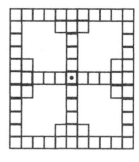

Figure 76
Schematic of a typical Patolli board - after Wanyerka.

Figure 77
Examples of hieroglyphic crossed trapezes/sun symbols which may have been used in conjunction with the Patolli board as a sundial. a. Piedras Negras Stela 90, b. Uxmal, Casa del Adivino c. Codex Nuttell d. Cuilapan, Mixtec inscription Reprinted from: Carnegie Institution of Washington Publication 546, 1943.

Spanish arrived, the Patolli game was banned as it was thought to be related to the pagan Maya religion. If it were indeed a sundial, it would certainly have been viewed as a part of the old superstitions. Digby believed that the Maya turned Patolli into a gambling game to fool the Spanish into believing it was harmless.[60]

Could Digby's theory mean that Lintel 6 is, indeed, a sundial? Cayce indicated that care should be taken in uncovering it and that it would be associated with the firestone emblem. However, although uncovered, Lintel 6 was not moved during the 1930s and was relocated by Penn in 1931 rather than at some date after 1933 as the Cayce clues indicate. Still, it is a compelling and mysterious design.

## Similar Designs at other Mesoamerican sites

The other two designs, which were discovered by Maler at La Mar and San Lorenzo, (*figs. 78-79*) are more similar to Lintel 6 from Piedras Negras. Like Lintel 6, these designs are circles with spokes, although instead of six spoke projections, they both have only four. Both also appear to have been drawn with a continuous line. The first of these was located by Maler at another small set of Maya ruins located 21 miles northeast of El Cayo near a tributary of the Usumacinta. At

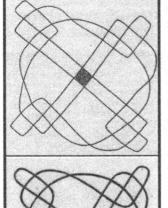

this site, called La Mar, Maler found the design on the underside of a lintel in a structure facing north around the main plaza.[61]

The third example of the matching designs was found by Maler in April of 1900 at another small Maya city, called San Lorenzo, located on the Lacanton river in the Mexican State of Chiapas. At this site the design was one of several carved on "an enormous bed of stratified limestone which the natives call *El Planchon de las Figuras* located a quarter of a

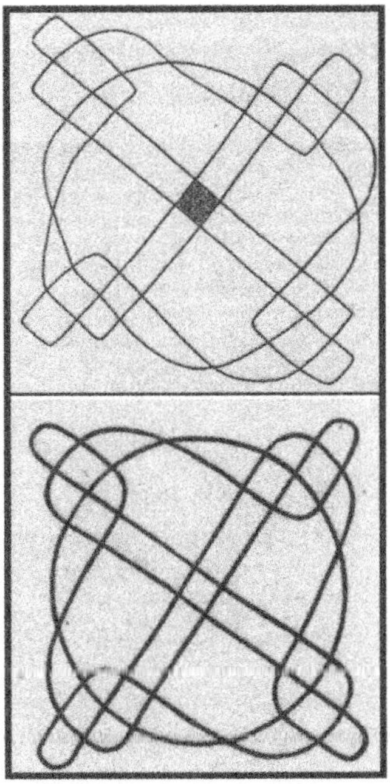

*Figure 78 (top)*
Abstract design similar to Lintel 6 discovered by Maler at La Mar. Reprinted from: *Memoirs of the Peabody Museum, Harvard University*, Vol. 2, No. 2, 1901.

*Figure 79 (bottom)*
Closeup of design that resembles Lintel 6 from the San Lorenzo rock carvings. Reprinted from: *Memoirs of the Peabody Museum, Harvard University*, Vol. 2, No. 2, 1901.

mile from the ruins of the main temple." The "almost horizontal" rock bed is only visible during the dry season and, according to Maler, was "one hundred and fifty meters long [492 feet], and from thirty to forty meters wide [98-131 feet]." In order to sketch the most prominent carvings he had to wait until late afternoon (5:00 P.M.) when the sun was at a particular angle to the carvings because they could not be seen clearly at any other time.[62] This seems to support the possibility of an astronomical connection.

Not only does the limestone rock bed at San Lorenzo contain the Lintel 6 design, but if Maler's drawings are accurate, it also displays some other rather fantastic pictures. (See *figure 80*.) In light of the previous discussion of the Piedras Negras spiral petroglyphs, the concentric circles are most significant. Maler stated that the figures surrounding the circle seemed to have been deliberately grouped. He noted that the largest figure (in the upper right hand corner) is a 13 by 3 foot "plaza surrounded by temples." To our modern eyes this portion of the petroglyphs looks like some von Daniken inspired rocket ship. An animal figure to the left of the circles was described by Maler as being 5.6 feet long and to "resemble a long-extinct saurian, but is probably a mythical beast." Also notable is the six pointed star in the upper left quadrant which was not mentioned by Maler in his text. Maler concluded that the concentric circles were used as an altar to honor the ancestors and to appease the "much feared water god."[63]

El Cayo, La Mar, and San Lorenzo are considered to be minor Maya sites and were not mentioned in either the 1946 nor the 1994

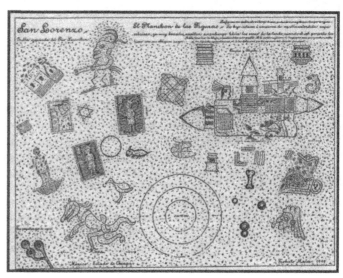

*Figure 80*
El Planchon de las Figuras discovered by Maler at San Lorenzo in the Mexican State of Chiapas. Reprinted from: *Memoirs of the Peabody Museum, Harvard University*, Vol. 2, No. 2, 1901.

edition of *The Ancient Maya*, a key source book on Maya studies.[64, 65] El Cayo and La Mar are believed to have been subject cities ruled by Piedras Negras. In fact, there is evidence in the inscriptions that relatives of the Piedras Negras ruling dynasties resided there and at El Cayo held ruling positions.[66] Maler's 1897 photographs of the stelae (he did not photograph the Lintel 6 look alike designs) at El Cayo and La Mar were mentioned briefly in Proskouriakoff's *Maya History*. In her analysis of Maler's pictures, Proskouriakoff described the artistry of the El Cayo stelae as similar to those found at Yaxchilan during the Postclassic Maya period. She also noted that the figures on the La Mar Stela 2 seem to be in a dancing pose and "carry in one hand small rectangular objects with two projecting strings at one end, possible *scrolls of paper...*" Unfortunately, Proskouriakoff does not mention the lintel wheel designs at these sites or at Piedras Negras.[67]

El Cayo is currently under investigation by the University of Calgary. It was also studied in the 1950s and 60s and determined to have evidence of Preclassic settlement. Unfortunately, it was heavily looted during the 60s and 70s.[68] In 1997 it was also the focus of a very dangerous altercation between archaeologists and local residents from the criminal element which made the international news services. This has added to the danger factor for BYU given El Cayo's proximity to Piedras Negras.

Have any other six-sided figures been discovered? In 1992 a tri-axial pecked cross petroglyph was discovered at the Lagarto Ruins in Southern Belize (British Honduras). It is a six-pointed design enclosed by 25 pecked dots forming a circle. Each of the six spokes consists of three dots each and extends outward from a center dot. Although, as mentioned earlier, pecked crosses have been found at other Maya sites and especially at Teotihuacan, they normally have only four axis. One of these four axis pecked crosses was found at Uaxactun, a Guatemalan site near Piedras Negras. The only other six-pointed cross that has been reported was a painted version discovered at Roberto's Cave in Laguna during the late 1980s. The purpose of the pecked crosses has not been confirmed but it is thought to mark alignments related to the movement of the sun or of significant star groupings.[69]

## Lintel 6: Firestone Emblem or Ancient Hebrew Symbol?

Lintel 6 at Piedras Negras is significant in relation to Cayce's clues for the firestone and the Hall of Records. It is a six-sided figure like the firestone, is an eroded carving on stone, and seems to be a good candidate for an "emblem" of something. Also, it did have to be uncovered. But it wasn't found in 1933 ("within the past few months" as Cayce stated) and was not taken to the Penn museum nor to any others from what can be ascertained from the scientific literature. Regardless, it does seem to relate to another aspect of the Cayce Maya story. The six-sided characteristic of the Piedras Negras design, the Lagarto pecked cross, and the six-pointed star at San Lorenzo immediately bring to mind the Hebrew Star of David. Could this be evidence for Cayce's story of the migration of the Lost Tribes of Israel to Central America sometime after 3000 B.C. or for the Mormon stories of migrations from 2300 to 600 B.C.? According to the *Jewish Encyclopedia*, the modern Star of David was not officially adopted as a symbol of Judaism until 1873 because Hebrew rabbinical tradition opposed the use of symbols or images to represent God. However, the Magen Dawid or Shield of David, a six-pointed star design made from two equilateral triangles, was used among Hebrew people for thousands of years. An example has been found on a third century tombstone.[70] The Seal of Solomon was also sometimes depicted as a six-pointed star although in other instances it only had five points. According to Arabic tradition it was imprinted on a ring which was used by Solomon to command demons.[71]

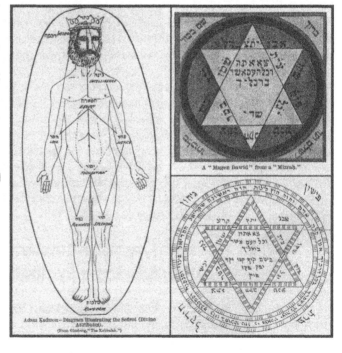

*Figure 81 (right top)* The traditional *Magen Dawid* or Shield of David. Reprinted from: *The Jewish Encyclopedia*, 1905.

*Figure 82 (left side)* Depiction of Adam Kadmon with six pointed star. Reprinted from: *The Jewish Encyclopedia*, 1905.

*Figure 83 (right bottom)* Shield of David used as an amulet. Reprinted from: *The Jewish Encyclopedia*, 1905.

The Shield of David can also be traced to the Hebrew mystical teachings of the Cabala which claims to have origins to the time of Adam Kadmon (the first Adam according to the Gnostic teachings from which the Cabala originated). The Cabala is made up of teachings that have been preserved from antiquity and is found within the mystical traditions of many ancient cultures including those in the Orient. It was known by Plato and was evident in the ancient religion Zoroasterianism which flourished in Persia in the 6th century B.C. It has also been traced to ancient Chaldea. The Cabala teachings are believed to have entered Hebrew tradition during the time of the Essenes before the birth of Christ, but may have been present among the Hebrew people even earlier since it is said to contain secret teachings given to Moses by God at Mt. Sinai.[72] The six-pointed star within a circle is known to have been used on cabalistic amulets to ward off evil in the middle ages.[73] The Hindu religion also used a similar hexagonal figure as a symbol of protection.[74] Although this does not prove a Hebrew link with the Maya, it does suggest the possibility of an ancient Old World connection either through Asian origins or Hebrew ones. As we will discuss in a next chapter, the significance of the six-sided figure may have originated with the Atlanteans. Regardless, Lintel 6 is an interesting anomaly at Piedras Negras and remains an enigma among Maya inscriptions.

## Underground Location for Hall of Records?

Probably the most intriguing discovery of the 1998 BYU expedition was the location of a huge cenote near the site. Cenotes are large caverns or holes created by underground rivers and are believed to have provided a water source for many ancient Maya population centers especially to the southeast of Piedras Negras in the Yucatan area. This particular cenote, currently dry, is the largest recorded in Guatemala. It measures 328 feet in diameter and 217 to 394 feet deep. The 1998 report indicated that researchers tried to explore it although they stated "*initial* attempts at exploration were stymied by the steep drop." The 1999 report confirmed their inability to access the bottom and recommended doing deeper excavations along the floor of the pit. No further information has been given regarding artifacts or other discoveries made near the cenote. The BYU researchers do, however, speculate that this cenote could explain the more ancient name for the Piedras Negras site which was *y-okib*, a Maya word meaning "entrance."[75] In Maya hieroglyphics, letters and words are often depicted by a symbol or logograph. This word's logograph contains the element for cave. Could this be a reference to the existence of an ancient underground Hall of Records?

*Figure 84*
Chicomoztoc or seven caves in which the ancestors of the early Toltecs resided from the *Historia Tolteca Chichimeca.* Reprinted from: *Collected Works in Mesoamerican Linguistics and Archaeology.*

In one reading Cayce indicated that the stones related to the Atlantean firestone or the records of them could be discovered by "entering into the chambers where these may be found."[76] It is possible that Cayce's chambers are underground caverns.

The Piedras Negras area is not only the location of a large cenote, it is also loaded with caves that, so far, have been mostly unexplored. Maler mentions the presence of caves in the area several times in his 1901 report. In fact, during his 1899 explorations he reported using a cave south of the city as a campsite.[77] The 1998 BYU report indicated that a portion of their group explored caves near an ancient Maya site called La Pasadita, located south of Piedras Negras. They did not report any specific findings, but stated that their goal was to "document the caves with cultural material that are abundant in the area."[78] As mentioned earlier, the Penn expedition found a cave burial (#6) in 1933 near the Eest Group subarea which they concluded contained the remains of a holy man.[79] This is not surprising since caves were rich in religious symbolism for the Maya who considered them to be entrances to the underworld.

During the 1999 season BYU performed a detailed geological analysis of the Piedras Negras vicinity reporting the presence of dolomitic limestone underlain by carbonate chalk (which does not create caves easily). Due to the presence of underground streams, however, it does facilitate the creation of cenotes and they reported finding many others near the largest one. They further noted that, "Caves are few, small, limited to dolomitic rocks, and mostly deriving from collapse rather than dissolution." In 1999 BYU excavated in three caves, two of which were located south of the ceremonial center and one, quite notably, "overlooking the Northwest Group Court" - not far from the Acropolis. All of the caves were found to contain human burials which included ritual animal offerings of primarily birds (representing the upper world) and aquatic species (the underworld) and food supplies such as was the custom in ancient Egyptian burials.[80] Even if BYU is correct regarding the low quantity of caves, there could still be some that are so far undiscovered.

As Schele and Freidel pointed out, to the Maya, "the world was alive and imbued with a sacredness that was especially concentrated at special points, like caves and mountains."[81] Through these sacred points it was possible to access the underworld which contained the spirits of the ancestors and of the various gods. This is believed to have been accomplished during sacred ceremonies involving the reigning king. In fact, his power may have been directly related to his ability to connect with the supernatural world.[82] This would explain why some Mesoamerican structures were built over caves. For example, the Pyramid of the Sun at Teotihuacan seems to have been deliberately constructed so that it is directly above a multi-chambered cave which is believed to be manmade.[83] In a 1996 report, Manzanilla and associates described in detail the remains of several long underground caverns under Teotihuacan in Central Mexico which were used for ceremonies and burials. They believe that the caverns were originally quarry pits for volcanic rock used in the construction of all but one of the structures at the site. Only the Pyramid of the Sun was constructed of nonvolcanic materials. In fact, they believe it was built using materials which could be gathered from the top soil in the area. This could mean that it was built earlier than the rest of the site as some have claimed. It could even have been built during the time of the Atlanteans or of the Lost Tribes.[84] This report also provides support for the idea that the early Mesoamericans had the technological capability to build large underground caverns for ceremonial or other uses.

But how do caves relate to the early Atlantean immigrants? Graham Hancock in his book, *Heaven's Mirror*, pointed out that the Aztecs believed their ancestors came from a island they called Aztlan. They also understood that their ancestors at first lived in caves located in the heart of a mountain.[85] Richard MacNeish, in his research into the caves of the Tehuacan Valley near present day Mexico City, found evidence of human occupation dating back to 10,000 B.C.[86] Since there is, so far, no evidence for ancient temples or house structures during that time frame, it could be that Iltar and his followers utilized caves just as the other native groups were doing. Piedras Negras could have been selected for settlement not only for its remoteness, but also because of the large number of cenotes and caves in the area. Perhaps the Hall of Records can be found in one of these caverns. Cayce's story might also explain the Maya's belief in caves as access points to the ancestors and to the spiritual world. As mentioned before, Cayce included the Atlanteans as one of the ancestral groups of the Maya. He also said that the Atlanteans were spiritually advanced in that they were able to communicate directly with God.[87] Perhaps the ancestors were simply actual, historical cave-dwelling people honored for their special abilities.

## Presence of Older Possibly Non-Maya Substructures at Piedras Negras

As Jeffrey Goodman[88] noted in his comparison of the Cayce readings with the findings of the Penn archaeologists, Satterthwaite did report evidence of "older possibly non-Maya substructures"[89] under Pyramid K-5. This structure is located in the West Group near the Acropolis in what is believed to be the most recently constructed area of the site. The oldest level found within Pyramid K-5 was much larger, shorter, and plainer and there was evidence that it had been destroyed prior to erection of the new levels. Given the non-Maya style and the fact that it may have been destroyed, Goodman proposed that this could be the first temple erected by the Atlantean Iltar.[90] Cayce had stated that these temples were destroyed, but, according to a 1933 reading, were "now being found and a portion already discovered that has laid in waste for many centuries, was then a combination of those peoples from Mu (Lemuria), Oz (Inca), and Atlantis." In the same reading he also indicated that they had been destroyed "at the period of change physically in the contours of the land."[91]

With regards to the possibility of a natural destruction, the 1997 BYU expedition found depressed areas with "extraordinarily deep deposits of earth and clay." They concluded from this evidence that the area had suffered multiple episodes of erosion due to water.[92] Given their geological analysis of the site it could also indicate the collapse of underground caverns. Could this feature reflect Cayce's changes "in the contours of the land?" These eroded areas were found in the eastern sector of the oldest portion of the site, the South Group. Perhaps Iltar first put the records in a cavern that collapsed. He might then have moved them further inland to a second underground location at the site. Another interesting finding is that there is more than one type of destruction present at Piedras Negras. Curiously, Satterthwaite also reported evidence that the entire site seemed to have been deliberately vandalized probably at the time the city was abandoned. Almost every face was mutilated and Throne 1 appeared to have been deliberately broken as if an attempt had been made to remove all symbols of power.[93] Proskouriakoff noted that this seems only to have been true at Piedras Negras.[94] Was there something special about the power or the history of Piedras Negras that it had to be so carefully erased?

The older, possibly non-Maya, substructures of Pyramid K-5 were first identified in 1932 by J. Alden Mason who performed a limited excavation. (See *figure 85*.) A second partial excavation was done in 1933 by Satterthwaite resulting in the discovery of the large stucco Sun-Jaguar masks on the corners of the building. Satterthwaite finally got around to performing a complete excavation of the structure during the 1939 season.[95] He dated the earliest levels to around A.D. 430 which made it equal in age to Pyramid R-3 in the South Group and Pyramid 0-13 in the East Group. Coe's analysis of pottery remains at the various levels

*Figure 85*
One of the substructures (not the oldest) found under Pyramid K-5 depicted as it may have looked when in use. Artistic reconstruction by Tatiana Proskouriakoff. *An Album of Maya Architecture*, Carnegie Institution of Washington Publication 558, 1946.

of these three structures determined that the earliest level of Pyramid K-5 was constructed around 80 years later. He did concede that perhaps there were lower levels that had not so far been located.[96] Iltar's temple would have been built around 10,000 B.C. by Cayce's chronology and that date is certainly not within the dating boundaries of the Penn expedition. However, it is interesting that the 1933 reading stated that "the portions now being discovered" had "laid in waste for *centuries*" as opposed to millennia which would be correct chronology by scientific standards.

Also of significance is the fact that Satterthwaite noted that the temple area of the oldest substructure of K-5 was larger, more open to viewing by the general populace, and allowed room for more participants than in later versions. This led him to surmise that priestly exclusivity was a more modern development.[97] Is it possible that the change to a more elaborate pyramid design with smaller temples reflects Cayce's story of the more egalitarian Atlantean "Sons of the Law of One" style of temple worship being replaced by descendants of the "Sons of Balial" who preferred hierarchies and focused on "satisfying and gratifying of self's desires?"[98] Or could the change in temple design possibly have been influenced by the intrusion of Hebrew styles of worship wherein the ceremonies in the tabernacle of the Holy of Holies were limited to those descended from the priestly line? Since Cayce gave an early B.C. date to the arrival of the Lost Tribes of Israel, it seems important to know the dates of these older substructures, something which Coe and Satterthwaite have attempted to do.

Coe reported that similar older substructures were excavated beneath pyramids R-3 in the South Group and O-13 in the East Group.[99] One of Satterthwaite's hypothetical assumptions was that city occupation and building of ceremonial structures occurred simultaneously throughout the site. Using a highly questionable architectural dating system based on a limited number of hieroglyphic dates from stelae and lintels and some additional speculative hypotheses, Satterthwaite proposed that Piedras Negras had been occupied initially around the beginning of the 9th baktun (around A.D. 400). That is considered the Early Classic period of Maya history. Coe called this dating method "worse than nothing if taken literally" as he attempted to utilize analysis of ceramic caches to date the various excavated substructures.[100] Although the assumed dates - also questionable per Coe - for various ceramic styles (developed using data from multiple Maya sites) fit Satterthwaite's dating of the then known substructures of pyramids R-3 (*fig. 86*) and 0-13, it did not coincide with the location of caches from Pyramid K-5. Ceramic styles that had been thought to be more recent were found in

*Figure 86*
Megalithic stairway leading from South Group Plaza to first platform that supports Pyramids R-3 and R-4. Photo reprinted by permission from the University of Pennsylvania Museum Archives.

layers that Satterthwaite had dated as older causing Coe to propose later dates for these substructures. He further speculated that, if Satterthwaite's theory regarding occupation was true, then it could be assumed that construction began in the South Group and gradually spread to the East and West Groups. Also, Coe believed this meant that at least 2 more substructures should be present in K-5.[101] All of this would indicate that the Penn expeditions created a lot more questions than they answered regarding the true age of the site. Evidence from the more recent BYU excavations seems to bear this out.

During the 1997 season, BYU performed test pitting in 200 locations near the Acropolis, in the East Group (behind Pyramid K-5), and in the South group.[102] Penn had concluded from their excavations that Court 1 in the Acropolis contained a 10-part substructure history that began with buildings constructed of more temporary materials. Postholes with remains of mud and stucco walls were discovered at the lowest levels reached by Penn.[103] BYU reported being skeptical of Penn's conclusions in that their excavation revealed that the Acropolis appeared to be built over a "buried and stuccoed building on a different orientation from the standing building above" which they dated to the Early Classic (A.D. 250-600) period. They noted, however, that under the Early Classic deposits was a concrete layer (not bedrock) through which they could not probe. Were these signs of even earlier deposits and/or Iltar's structures? At the same location they also discovered an unusual worked outcropping of bedrock which, for some mysterious reason, had been left uncovered in the building plan.[104] In the 1998 season they explored further and reported an "abyss accessed by steps" near the outcropping which they stated was characteristic of Early Classic ceremonial ritual. This led to the discovery that the West Group Plaza located directly in front of the Acropolis covered a buried substructure that was most likely the home of the Early Classic rulers and which was a "smaller palace of more open, accessible form." They noted that it appeared that the Maya had chosen at the end of the Early Classic period to do a major and deliberate renovation which emphasized "dramatic enclosure and spatial exclusivity."[105] This could be more evidence for the injection of outside influences as proposed by Cayce.

Dates on stelae erected throughout the site had indicated to Morley and Satterthwaite that the South Group contained the oldest structures. It is also situated closest to the river access making it the most likely location for the first settlements. The 5 major pyramids in this group are unusual in that they are built of larger stone blocks than those in the other subareas and have megalithic stone stairways leading from the plaza to a first very large terrace platform. All levels after these have stairs constructed of much smaller stones located on different sides of the pyramid than the megalithic stairways. Again, there appears to be evidence of later construction that may have changed the orientation of the entire ceremonial center. Also unusual is Pyramid R-16 which appears in the transition corridor leading north from the South Group into the East Group Plaza. Like the other South Group pyramids this structure is built on a large terrace, however, it is the only one which is not parallel to its terrace platform. Its platform faces east while the pyramid on top faces more southeasterly. Satterthwaite, in trying to understand this odd orientation, noted that its medial axis lines up with a pyramid on the Acropolis to the north (more about alignments and their relation to celestial objects later).[106] BYU 1997 test pits near R-16 showed "4 m. [13 feet] deep rubble and as-yet-unplumbed sterile deposits."[107]

In his investigations of Pyramid R-3 in the South Group (which occurred during the 1933 season), Satterthwaite wrote in a 1934 preliminary report that, "There is nothing primitive about the pyramid, either in structure (within Maya limits) or its design, and it presupposes a considerable prior period of experience in substructure building. If this is one of the earliest pyramids still in use when the city was abandoned, either the evidence of such a prior period lies buried under other pyramids of the city, or pyramids were first built here after being developed elsewhere."[108] He believed it was the latter option. However, BYU data indicates otherwise. Probes near Pyramid R-5 (which is located adjacent to R-3) pointed to remains of an Early Classic structure under 13 feet of debris.[109]

Also of interest, in an area largely unexplored by Penn in the eastern sector of the South Group, BYU found a Late Classic period structure under which was buried a circular building which they dated to the Early Classic period (A.D. 250 - 600).[110] This is of particular note since circular buildings assumed to be astronomical observatories have been found in Chichen Itza and Caracol. Also, the firestone in the Cayce readings was housed under a dome in a circular building in Atlantis.[111] Although the dating is too late for this to be an Atlantean remnant, perhaps it is a copy of an even earlier building yet to be found. This is not so far-fetched given recent intriguing evidence uncovered by BYU

*Figure 87*
A line of portable drum shaped altars at Piedras Negras uncovered during the Penn expeditions. Reprinted by permission from: University of Pennsylvania Museum Archives.

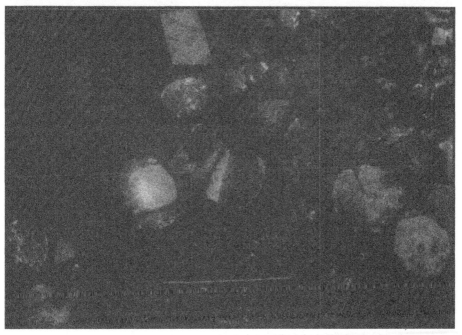

*Figure 88*

Example of a table top altar (Altar 2) at Piedras Negras which was found in front of Court 1 of the Acropolis. Reprinted by permission from: University of Pennsylvania Museum Archives.

that indicates Piedras Negras may be much older than originally proposed. In the South Group and in the U sector located near the river and the Sacrificial Rock, deposits from the Late Preclassic (400 B.C. - A.D. 100) and the Protoclassic eras (A.D. 100-250) were found. Even more significant was the discovery of Middle Preclassic era (1000 - 400 B.C.) deposits "with suggestions of even earlier material" which caused them to conclude that "occupation is far longer than previously thought and buried remains undisturbed by Pennsylvania promise a rich trove of earlier architecture."[112]

# Altars as Remnants of Atlantean and Other Early Civilizations

Altars are specifically mentioned in the Cayce readings and are included in several Hall of Records and firestone clues. First is the reference to artifacts still in existence in the Yucatan that are remnants from the Atlantean and other preMayan civilizations. In describing the Atlantean artifacts, Cayce identified magnetized circular stones used for religious ceremonies in one sentence and then, in the next sentence, he began to discuss altars used to cleanse body, mind and soul.[113] It is not clear whether the altars are the same as the magnetized circular stones, but the wording may indicate that the people gathered around the altars and utilized the circular stones as a separate tool. As mentioned previously, there is evidence that the magnetized circular stones are the relatively small hematite disks or mirrors discovered at Piedras Negras and elsewhere.[114] If that is true, then these Atlantean influenced altars may or may not actually be rounded. If the magnetized stones and the altars are one and the same, then the altars would necessarily be not only circular but "of the magnetized influence." It does not appear that the altars at Piedras Negras were magnetized. The 1999 BYU report stated that the carved monuments at Piedras Negras were made from "thick bedded limestone" which they found near the river bed. Buildings were also faced with this same limestone. The darker dolomitic limestone, found above, at the level of the site, and on higher hills, was used for wall construction since it was more easily broken into blocks.[115]

However, regardless of the shape or magnetic quality of the altars, Cayce clearly stated that they were definitely not used for human sacrifice by the Atlanteans. In fact, altars for human sacrifice were introduced several thousand years later, according to Cayce. In this same reading he went on to identify "The pyramid and the altars before the doors..." as remnants of the Lemurian and Oz (Incan) influence which he said "...will be found to be separate portions."[116] Satterthwaite has confirmed Cayce's description as Goodman reported in his book.[117] Satterthwaite noted that the temples which contain the altars and the pyramids upon which they were built "may have originated and at first developed apart from each other."[118] Cayce went on to explain that there were also altars to be found that were family altars of a type mentioned in the Scriptures and were the beginning of the people turning back to the self-gratifying tendencies of the "Balial activities."[119] Again, Cayce is unclear as to whether the altars that are found in front of the temples are the family altars or if this is a another type of ancient altar. The latter possibility appears likely since there are three different types of altars reported at Piedras Negras. First are the table top altars (*fig. 88*) found in the West and East Group Plazas which certainly could have been used for human sacrifice. The second type, found within and in front of the temples, are cylindrical or column-shaped. The third type are small, drum-shaped stones (*fig. 87*) that could be easily moved. The archaeologists called these "portable altars" and they could be Cayce's family altars since they were often found outside of the temple areas.

*Figure 89*
Depiction of human sacrifice from Piedras Negras Stela 11. Reprinted from: Spinden, *A Study of Maya Art,* 1913.

In his review of the Piedras Negras material, Goodman pointed out the significance of the discovery of the 2 cylindrical (column) altars at Pyramid K-5 (West Group). They are unusual in that they were found to be positioned with one inside and one outside the temple chamber similar to those Cayce described.[120] Satterthwaite noted that this positioning was carried through from the earliest to the latest levels of the structure and that these altars were most likely not used for human sacrifice. He based that on the discovery of a more flat topped designed altar carved on a stela (#11) at the site which depicts human sacrifice. (See *figure 89.*) Also, the cylindrical altars were coated with soot which he believed associated them with ceremonies in which copal (an ancient Maya incense still used today) was burned.[121] Goodman cited this as support for Cayce's assertion that human sacrifice was a later aspect of Maya ceremonies influenced by the sacrificial traditions of the "Mosaic" influence and the loss of the Atlantean spiritual practices.[122] Of course, this assumes that the cylindrical altars are much older than this structure has so far been dated.

Cayce placed the arrival of the Lost Tribes sometime after 3,000 B.C., although the mutation of Hebrew sacrificial rites into human sacrifice may have occurred over a long period of time.[123] In a 1946 article Satterthwaite stated very clearly that the cylindrical column altars are indeed quite old. "These burned column altars are present in and before the earliest Piedras Negras temples, so far as we can judge, and they seem to carry the ritual of the incense-burner back to a time long preceding that of the spiked example actually recovered (a pottery incense-burner dated A.D. 736)."[124] Interestingly, this pattern may also be present in Hebrew temple design (*fig. 90*). These ancient temples typically were set up with a room just outside the Holy of Holies (where the Ark of the Covenant was placed) which contained an incense altar. Just outside the incense room was another space which contained a pool of

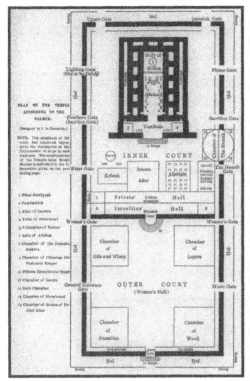

*Figure 90*
Example of Hebrew temple design. Reprinted from: *The Jewish Encyclopedia*, 1905.

water and a sacrificial altar.[125]

But what else did Cayce tell us about the Atlantean altars? In one reading Cayce gave a description of temples on the Atlantean island of Poseidia and said that they contained "sacred fires where these were offered, the sacrifices that were gradually builded by the people in their attempt to appease those forces in nature..." In that same reading, Cayce stated that in the temple were "large or semi-circular columns of onyx, topaz, and inlaid with beryl, amethyst, and stones that made the variations in catching the rays of the sun..." These activities were carried by the migrating Atlanteans to other parts of the world (according to Cayce) and show up as sun worship.[126]

Amazingly, there is evidence at Piedras Negras that seems to correlate well with Cayce's Atlantean temple description. A 1934 article by Satterthwaite discussed the discovery of the rounded ("more or less cylindrical") column altars in 10 out of 12 pyramid temples he excavated at Piedras Negras. He went on to note that these temples contained unusual niches with ventilating flues which he believed were related to the "fires around such stones, set within almost all of the temples, were an essential part of the rites of Piedras Negras temple ritual from fairly early to late times." Interestingly these niches and flues were unique in that they were not found in other Maya sites in the middle Usumacinta region.[127] In regards to the various types of stones and gems Cayce claimed were used on the Atlantean columns, one common characteristic of onyx (calcite variety), amethyst and beryl is that their molecular crystallization is hexagonal (a six-sided configuration which brings to mind the six sided firestone).[128] None of these minerals or gemstones (except calcite) were reported to have been found at Piedras Negras. However, another hexagonal crystal mineral has - hematite.[129] In the next chapter the significance of altars to our search for the firestone and the Hall of Records will be shown as we explore the uncovering of the sundial!

# References

1. Coe, William (1959). *Piedras Negras Archaeology: Artifacts, Caches, and Burials.* Philadelphia: The University Museum, pp. 143-144.

2. Satterthwaite, Linton (1938) Evidence for a logical sequence of roof types on a Maya building at Piedras Negras. *Science*, Vol. 88, p. 504.

3. *Piedras Negras Archaeology*, op. cit., p. 144.

4. Houston Stephen, et al (1998) Between Mountains and Sea: Investigations at Piedras Negras, Guatemala, 1998 *Mexicon*, XXI, op. cit. p. 15.

5. *Piedras Negras Archaeology*, op. cit., p. 144.

6. Freidel, D, Schele, L. and Parker, J. (1993) *Maya Cosmos*. New York: William Morrow. p. 200.

7. Maler, Teobert (1901). Researches in the Central Portion of the Usumacintla Valley. *Memoirs of the Peabody Museum, Harvard University*, Vol. 2, No. 1. Cambridge.

8. Morley, S. V. (1938). The Inscriptions of Peten, Vol. III. *Carnegie Institution of Washington, Publication 437*, Washington.

9. Satterthwaite, Linton (1934) Piedras Negras Field Notes, Box 7, Notebook 8, University of Pennsylvania Museum Archives.

10. *The Inscriptions of Peten Vol. III*, op. cit. p. 302.

11. Satterthwaite, Linton (1935) The Black Rocks. *University Museum Bulletin*, Vol. 6, No. 1.

12. Reading 440-12.

13. Satterthwaite, Linton (1943) Piedras Negras Archaeology: Architecture, Part 1, No. 1, Introduction. Philadelphia: University of Pennsylvania Museum, p. 28.

14. Satterthwaite, Linton (1935) Piedras Negras Field Notes, Box 7, Notebook 8, University of Pennsylvania Museum Archives.

15. *University Museum Bulletin* Vol. 6, No. 1, op. cit., p. 8.

16. Satterthwaite, Linton (1936) Notes on the Work of the Fourth and Fifth University Museum Expeditions to Piedras Negras, Peten, Guatemala. *Maya Research*, Vol. III, No. 1, p.86.

17. Satterthwaite, Linton Piedras Negras Field Notes, Box 17, University of Pennsylvania Museum Archives.

18. Drucker, Philip (1952) La Venta, Tabasco A Study of Olmec Ceramics and Art. *BAE Bulletin* 153,

19. Biederman, Hans. (1994) *Dictionary of Symbolism: Cultural Icons and the Meanings Behind Them*. New York: Meridian.

20. Aveni, Anthony (1977) Concepts of Positional Astronomy Employed in Ancient Mesoamerican Architecture. In Anthony Aveni (Ed.) *Native American Astronomy*. (pp. 3-19) Austin Texas: University of Texas Press.

21. Julien, Nadia (1996) *The Mammoth Dictionary of Symbols*. New York: Carroll & Graf Publishers, Inc.

22. *Dictionary of Symbolism: Cultural Icons and the Meanings Behind Them*. op. cit.

23. Reading 2071-10.

24. Ancient Vedic Texts

25. University *Museum Bulletin*, Vol. 6, No. 1, op. cit., p. 8.

26. *The Inscriptions of Peten Vol. III*, op. cit., p. 302.

27. Houston, Stephen et al (2000) Among the River Kings: Archaeological Research at Piedras Negras, Guatemala, 1999. *Mexicon*, XXII, pp. 8-17.

28. Online Mineral Gallery (http://www.minerals.net/mineral) copyright Hershel Friedman, 1997-1999.

29. Piedras Negras Field Notes, 1933 Object Catalog, University of Pennsylvania Museum Archives.

30. Schele, Linda and Freidel, David (1990) *A Forest of Kings*. New York: William Morrow, p. 111.

31. Zangger, Eberhard (1992). *The Flood From Heaven: Deciphering the Atlantis Legend*. New York: William Morrow and Company, Inc.

32. Dictionary *of Symbolism: Cultural Icons and the Meanings Behind Them*. op. cit.

33. Singer, Isidore (Ed.) (1905) *The Jewish Encyclopedia, Vol. XI*. New York: Funk and Wagnalls Company, pp. 126-134.

34. Reading 364-3.

35. *University Museum Bulletin*, Vol. 6, No. 1, op. cit.

36. *Memoirs of the Peabody Museum, Harvard University*, Vol. 2, No. 1, op. cit.

37. University *Museum Bulletin*, Vol. 6, No. 1, op. cit., p. 8.

38. *The Inscriptions of Peten Vol. III*, op. cit., p. 298-301.

39. Houston, Stephen (1997) On the River of Ruins: Explorations at Piedras Negras, Guatemala, 1997. *Mexicon XX*, p. 18.

40. *The Inscriptions of Peten Vol. III*, op. cit. p.299.

41. *Mexicon XX*, op. cit., p. 18.

42. *Maya Cosmos* op. cit., p. 92.

43. Proskouriakoff, Tatiana (1993) *Maya History*. Austin: University of Texas Press, p. 102.

44. Fitzsimmons, James (1998) Classic Maya Mortuary Anniversaries at Piedras Negras, Guatemala. *Ancient Mesoamerica*, 9, p. 273.

45. Fox, James and Justeson, John (1986) Classic Maya Dynastic Alliance and Succession. In Victoria Brickler (Ed.) *Supplement to the Handbook of Middle American Indians Vol. 4*. (pp. 7-34). Austin Texas: University of Austin.

46. Kubler, George (1973) Mythological Ancestries in Classic Maya Inscriptions. In Merle Robertson (Ed.) *Primera Mesa Redonda De Palenque Part II*. (pp. 23-43). Pebble Beach California: Pre-Columbian Art Research

47. Sharer, Robert (1994) *The Ancient Maya*. Stanford, California: Stanford University Press, p. 526-531.

48. Maya *Cosmos, op. cit.*, p. 201.

49. Ibid p. 196.

50. Ibid pp. 199.

51. Ibid p. 204.

52. Maler, Teobert (1901). Researches in the Central Portion of the Usumacintla Valley. *Memoirs of the Peabody Museum, Harvard University*, Vol. 2, No. 2. Cambridge.

53. *Memoirs of the Peabody Museum, Harvard University*, Vol. 2, No. 1, op. cit., p. 75.

54. *The Inscriptions of Peten Vol. III*, op. cit., pp. 110-111.

55. Satterthwaite, Linton (1936) *Piedras Negras Preliminary Papers: A Pyramid without Temple Ruins (Structure J-3)*. Philadelphia: University of Pennsylvania Museum, p. 12.

56. Piedras Negras Guatemala, at internet address: http://member.aol.com/lakamha/png.html.

57. Ibid, p. 85.

58. *The Inscriptions of Peten Vol. III*, op. cit. p., 35

59. Wanyerka, Phil (1999) Pecked Cross and Patolli Petroglyphs of the Lagarto Ruins, Stann Creek District, Belize. *Mexicon*, XXI, pp. 108-112.

60. Digby, Adrian (1974) Crossed Trapezes: A Pre-Columbian Astronomical Instrument. In Norman Hammond (Ed.) *Mesoamerican Archaeology: New Approaches.* (pp. 270-283) Austin Texas: University of Texas Press.

61. *Memoirs of the Peabody Museum, Harvard University*, Vol. 2, op. cit., p. 93-94.

62. Ibid, p. 204-205.

63. Ibid, p. 206.

64. Morley, S. G. (1946) *The Ancient Maya.* Stanford, California: Stanford University Press.

65. The *Ancient Maya*, op. cit..

66. *Supplement to the Handbook of Middle American Indians Vol. 4*, op. cit.

67. *Maya History*, op. cit., p. 169.

68. Mathews, Peter and Aliphat, Mario (1999) The El Cayo Archaeological Project. *University of Calgary Web Site*, http://www.ucalgary.ca/Uof C/faculties/SS/ARKY/cayo/elcayo.html.

69. Wanyerka, *Mexicon*, XXI, op. cit.

70. *The Jewish Encyclopedia, Vol. VIII*, op cit., p. 252.

71. *The Jewish Encyclopedia, Vol. XI*, op cit., p. 448.

72. *The Jewish Encyclopedia, Vol. III*, op. cit., p. 458.

73. The *Jewish Encyclopedia, Vol. I*, op. cit., p. 549.

74. *The Jewish Encyclopedia, Vol. VIII*, op. cit., p. 252.

75. Houston, et al., *Mexicon XXI*, op. cit. p., 16.

76. Reading 440-5.

77. *The Inscriptions of Peten Vol. III*, op. cit., p. 4.

78. Houston, et al *Mexicon XXI*, op. cit., p. 10.

79. Satterthwaite, Linton Piedras Negras Field Notes, University of Pennsylvania Museum Archives.

80. *Mexicon XXII*, op. cit., p. 7.

81. *A Forest of Kings* op. cit., p. 67.

82. Ibid, pp. 101-103.

83. *Native American Astronomy* op. cit., p. 5.

84. Manzanilla, Linda, Lopez, Claudea and Freter, AnnCorrine (1996) Dating Results From Excavations In Quarry Tunnels Behind the Pyramid of the Sun at Teotihuacan. *Ancient Mesoamerica*, 7, 245-266.

85. Hancock, Graham (1998) *Heaven's Mirror: Quest for the Lost Civilization.* New York: Crown Publishers, Inc., p. 12.

86. McNeish, Richard (1969) Speculation about How and Why Food Production and Village Life Developed in the Tehuacan Valley, Mexico. *Archaeology*, 24(4): 307-315.

87. Reading 364-7.

88. Goodman, Jeffrey (1977) *Psychic Archaeology: Time Machine to the Past.* New York: G.P. Putnam's Sons.

89. Satterthwaite, Linton (1939) Evolution of a Maya Temple - Part I. *The University Bulletin,* Vol. 7, No. 4, pp. 3-14.

90. *Psychic Archaeology,* op. cit.

91. Reading 5750-1.

92. *Mexicon XX,* op. cit., p. 18.

93. Satterthwaite, Linton (1937) Thrones at Piedras Negras. *University Museum Bulletin* Vol. 7, No. 1, pp. 18-23.

94. *Maya History,* op. cit., p. 168.

95. *Piedras Negras Archaeology,* op. cit., pp. 151-156.

96. *The University Bulletin,* Vol. 7, No. 4, op. cit., p. 3.

97. Ibid, p. 7.

98. Reading 5750-1

99. *Piedras Negras Archaeology* op. cit., pp. 149-156.

100. Ibid, p. 151.

101. Ibid, pp. 152-154.

102. *Mexicon,* XX, op. cit.

103. *Maya Research,* Vol. III, No. 1, op. cit., p. 84.

104. *Mexicon XX,* op. cit., p. 20.

105. Ibid, p. 13-14.

106. The *Inscriptions of Peten, Vol. III,* op. cit., p. 10-15.

107. *Mexicon XX,* op. cit., p. 18.

108. Satterthwaite, Linton. Piedras Negras Field Notes, Preliminary Paper Draft. Box 18, University of Pennsylvania Museum Archives, p. 75.

109. *Mexicon XX,* op. cit., p. 18.

110. Ibid, p. 20.

111. Reading 440-5

112. *Mexicon XX,* op. cit., p. 21.

113. Reading 5750-1

114. *Psychic Archaeology,* op. cit.

115. *Among the River Kings,* op. cit., p. 3.

116. Reading 5750-1.

117. *Psychic Archaeology,* op. cit.

118. *The University Bulletin,* Vol. 7, No. 4, op. cit., p. 6.

119. Reading 5750-1.

120. *Psychic Archaeology,* op. cit.

121. *The University Bulletin,* Vol. 7, No. 4, pp. 3-14.

122. *Psychic Archaeology,* op. cit.

123. Reading 5750-1

124. Satterthwaite, Linton (1946) Incense Burning at Piedras Negras. *University Museum Bulletin,* Vol. 11, No. 4, p. 21.

125. *Jewish Encyclopedia* Vol. XII, op. cit., p. 95.

126. Reading 364-12.

127. *Maya Research,* Vol. III, No. 1, op. cit., pp. 76-78.

128. Online Mineral Gallery, op. cit.

129. *Piedras Negras Archaeology* , op. cit.

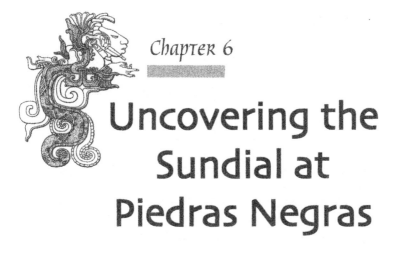

## Chapter 6

# Uncovering the Sundial at Piedras Negras

In a January 1934 reading discussing the potential discovery of the Atlantean firestone emblem, Cayce was asked what "more may be uncovered, that we can tell him?" The "him" referred to the leader of the Penn expedition. Cayce's response was to warn the leader to use "precaution in the uncovering of the stone, or what may appear in the *uncovering of what might be termed the sundial* that lies between the temple and the chambers or opposite temple - where sacrifices were made. For this is the place, this is the stone - though erosion has made an effect upon same - in which the body will be particularly interested..."[1] In other words, the firestone emblem and possibly the Hall of Records is very near something that could be called a sundial.

As mentioned previously, the Sacrificial Rock is the artifact at Piedras Negras that most looks like a sundial, but it did not have to be uncovered and it does not (at this time) appear to be located between a "temple and the chambers..." However, the carving etched on its surface very nearly matches that on Altar 1 which was discovered on the West Court Plaza in 1895 by Maler. Altar 1 is located in front of the Acropolis and is near several pyramid/temples. It is one of only two table top rounded altars and, at first glance, is reminiscent of the famous Aztec calendar stone which is also often referred to as a sundial.[2] In addition, it meets Cayce's clue that it would be found "where the temples are being uncovered or reconstructed" since Penn was excavating in the Acropolis and nearby at Pyramid K-5 in 1933.[3]

# The Strange Dates of Altar 1

As with the Sacrificial Rock (*fig. 92*), the upper surface of Altar 1 (*fig. 91 & 93*) contains a carving that shows two persons sitting facing each other with outstretched arms holding a square object (a book or tablet?) between them. Unlike the Sacrificial Rock, Altar 1 has, not one, but two concentric rows of glyphs forming a circle around the two figures. The circular altar top has a diameter of 7 feet and is supported underneath by three rectangular blocks 5 feet in height. Unfortunately, in 1895 Maler reported that the top of the altar had been broken into two parts, probably by a falling tree. He had it cleaned and photographed. By 1914 when Morley arrived, the table top was broken into four parts. The 1931 Penn expedition uncovered the fourth piece "under humus where it had fallen."[4] Both Maler and Morley reported that the carvings on the top were very badly eroded so that the remaining traces of hieroglyphic writing could not be read. However, the sides of the table top

---

*Figure 91*
Photograph by Maler in 1895 of Altar 1. Reprinted from: *Memoirs of the Peabody Museum, Harvard University*, Vol. 2, No. 1, 1901.

and the three block supports were covered with very readable glyphs which Morley recorded and interpreted.

## Altar 1 Dates: 5000 B.C., 4000 B.C., & August 13, 3114 B.C.

And this is where things get very interesting. Morley devoted nine pages in his *Inscriptions of the Peten* to explaining the rationale for his interpretation of the calendric glyphs on Altar 1. This was because he determined that five of the dozen or so dates recorded on the altar were *prior to* 3114 B.C. — the ancient beginning date for the Maya Long Count (and also the Maya date for the creation of the world). In fact, the oldest date on the altar was some 16 centuries earlier, around 5000 B.C., and the second oldest was around 4000 B.C.! Altar 1 also contains the August 13, 3114 B.C. creation date. Only four of the glyph dates on Altar 1 are within the Maya Classic period, although three of them are much earlier than Morley believed this altar could have been carved.

The earliest Maya era date found on Altar 1 (A.D. 430) is prior to any other date found within the entire Piedras Negras site. The next

---

*Figure 92 (below left)*
Drawing by Maler in 1895 of the carving on the Piedras Negras Sacrificial Rock. Reprinted from: *Memoirs of the Peabody Museum, Harvard University*, Vol. 2, No. 1, 1901.

---

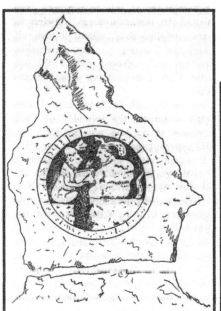

*Figure 93*
Drawing by Maler in 1895 of the carving on top of Piedras Negras Altar 1. Reprinted from: *Memoirs of the Peabody Museum, Harvard University*, Vol. 2, No. 1, 1901.

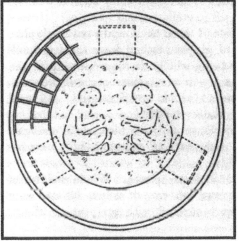

oldest Maya era date is the same as the date found by Penn at Piedras Negras (on Lintel 12) equating to A.D. 514 (which places it in the Early Classic Period).

But another date peculiarity was found on Altar 1. It also depicts the most recent date found on any monument at the site: A.D. 830. Based on this date, and the altar's design, Morley concluded that Altar 1 was the final monument erected at Piedras Negras. Morley admitted that immediately prior to A.D. 830, the few monuments erected were much plainer as if the civilization was beginning to fail. Regardless, he proposed that there was a sudden upsurge in elaborate monument construction to commemorate the end of the baktun (400 year period) which occurred on that date.[5]

### 3114 B.C. to A.D. 2012

Apparently Morley's dating didn't make sense to the esteemed Mayanist J. Eric Thompson, so he revised it. He decided that Altar 1 was erected in A.D. 692 because this date corresponded to a significant katun (20 year period) ending date. Interestingly, Thompson considered the A.D. 830 date to be a projection into the future. Given what we know about the history of the Maya cities, this date may have prophesied the decline of Piedras Negras and many other sites in the Peten. In fact, the same date was included as a future date on inscriptions at Palenque as well. Thompson's analysis of the dates on Altar 1 also disagreed with Morley's two earliest dates, although he confirmed one of the ancient dates which he noted may signify either the 3114 B.C. creation date or a future date i.e. A.D. 2012.[6] He further conceded that it could represent both past and future dates at the same time. If so, then obviously, Maya cosmology was very highly developed which would provide more support for Atlantean ancestry.

But why would the residents go to so much trouble to record future and highly ancient dates. What do these dates signify? Proskouriakoff did not totally support Thompson's rejection of Morley's two oldest dates and stated that they probably "deal with astrological computations."[7] Could they perhaps be evidence of a more ancient settlement history for Piedras Negras that links it to Iltar and the Atlantean records? This seems highly possible since recent hieroglyphic decipherment has revealed that Altar 1 depicts the Maya story of the first creation as do texts on Copan Stela 23, Coba Stela 1, and the Palenque Tablet of the Cross. (See fig. 94.)

On August 13, 3114 B.C. the texts say that "it was seen, the first image of the turtle, great holy lord" was manifested at a place called "Lying-down-sky, First-Three-Stone-Place." The image of the turtle is believed to be the three stars in the "belt" of the constellation of Orion, a

## Other Maya Dates Recorded on Monuments:
## 400 Million Years B.C. to A.D. 4772

Piedras Negras is not the only Maya site with monuments that contain both ancient and future dates. One stela at Quirigua records a date 90 millions years ago while another at the same site contains a date 400 million years ago.[10] An ancient date discovered in 1999 at the nearby site of Palenque describes a king, *Jinich Ahkal Mo'Nab*, who ruled in the early 8th century (after the famous ruler, Pacal) and claimed to be the reincarnation of a primordial god known to Mayanists as GI (pronounced G one). The inscription records the ancient reign of GI' (pronounced G-one-prime - the First Father) as beginning March 10, 3309 B.C.[11] The First Father's birthday is given as June 16, 3122 B.C. In addition, a text in the Temple of the Cross records the date December 7, 3121 B.C. as the birthday of an ancestral goddess (named "Lady Beastie" by the scientists because she was depicted with a strange birdlike head) who, at the age of 761, gave birth to the three gods (GI, GII, & GIII) who ruled over Palenque.[12] On one of the panels in the Temple of Inscriptions at Palenque, Pacal appeared to give his reign greater historical significance by linking it to a remote ancestral god who, according to the panel, existed over 1 million years in the past! As at Piedras Negras, the future dates included the year A.D. 830 which is the end of the katun. But Pacal went further to note that the calendar round date of his accession would occur for the 80th time 8 days after the end of the first piktun (an 8000 year cycle). Since the Maya creation date is August 13, 3114 B.C., it places Pacal's accession on a date equivalent to October 23, A.D. 4772. This has caused some scholars to conclude that the Maya did not really believe that the world would be destroyed at the end of the current era (A.D. 2012) as some have claimed.[13]

Who were these ancient gods that they had actual — quite specific —birth dates? Could they be remnants of earlier lost civilizations? Interestingly, the Palenque inscriptions are much more involved in outlining the important dates of Lady Beastie, called the First Mother, than they are for GI, the First Father.[14] It is as if it was more important to record the maternal line — a tradition reminiscent of Hebrew custom. Cayce indicated that the early civilizations were matriarchal. In many of the past life readings he gave for people living in the Yucatan after the Atlantean destruction, females were in positions of power. He also noted that the Atlanteans had lifespans that were much longer of those of today.

*Figure 94*
Temple of the Cross at Palenque containing creation tablets. Photo by: Lora Little.

grouping also known to be correlated to the three great pyramids of Giza in Egypt.[8, 9] These and other remarkable astronomical connections will be explored in more detail in the next chapter .

## Firestone Emblem Uncovered?

But there is more to the story of Altar 1. As you will recall, Cayce cautions Penn to take care in uncovering the sundial "or what may appear at the uncovering" because this was the place where they would find what they were looking for (i.e. the firestone emblem and possibly the Hall of Records).[15] (See *fig. 95 & 96.*) Coe reported that the Penn expedition in May 1931 uncovered a pottery bowl containing cache offerings beneath Altar 1. The contents of the bowl included, among the usual items, "2 small pieces of crystalline hematite and a hematite disc." These were taken to the Penn Museum where Coe was able to study them. He described the disc as being a third of an inch in diameter and .08 inches thick "with one perfectly flat, brilliant, glassy face slightly marred by pitting. The underside is dull. Edge beveled towards face (glassy side)."[16] The other two crystals were unworked. What is especially interesting is that these were the only samples of hematite at the site except for a worked piece found on the surface of Structure 0-16 and an unworked crystal found in surface debris near Structure 0-7.

---

### Altar 1 Hematite Artifacts

In June of 2000, an attempt was made to view the hematite artifacts from Altar 1. Melissa Wagner, Assistant Keeper of the American Section at the University of Pennsylvania Museum searched the Piedras Negras collection thoroughly, but discovered that several batches of items were no longer labeled. She did spend some time sorting through the unlabeled items for artifacts that appeared to be composed of hematite, but unfortunately, to our mutual disappointment, she was unable to locate them. However, Ms. Wagner was able to locate the negative number of a photograph of the cache. We were probably lucky to find that much considering the enormous number of caches uncovered at Piedras Negras. In addition, the items were excavated almost 70 years ago and packed into storage (they were not in the displays).

Mr. Pessati from the Penn Archives Section then assisted me in locating this negative which appears in figure 99. We also located another negative of the cache shown in Figure 97 (which matches Penn researcher Coe's report. Figure 97, however, has several unusual specimens which were *not* mentioned by Coe. For example, in the 2nd row from the bottom, the 2nd item from the left was identified on the archive card as a deer antler. Its spiral shape resembles the spiral petroglyphs as well as the spiral lighting device used in the modern laser which will be discussed in the next section. Subsequent research of artifact references indicated that both pictures contain items from the Altar 1 cache.

---

There were several pyrite pieces found at Piedras Negras, as reported earlier, but only these five pieces of hematite, three of which just happened to be buried under Altar 1. Other items in the cache bowl that seem like possibilities for the firestone emblem (*fig. 98*) are a loafshaped piece of jadeite, and an eccentric flint in the shape of a flattened circle with a semicircular "bite" taken out of one side. In addition, the cache contained three unusual incised (carved) pieces of shell. Two are shown in figure 100 and seem to depict male and female figures. The third shell contains an unknown design — possibly a cosmic monster or other mythological character. However, as will be shown, hematite is the most remarkable artifact of the group since it has several characteristics which link it to Cayce's firestone emblem.

Coe noted that among the Maya "instances of hematite are quite rare."[17] As discussed previously, hematite mixed with magnetite and ilmenite were common at Olmec sites which predate the Maya culture. Some researchers have concluded that they may have been worked even earlier. Shook and Kidder believed that they were worked in Preclassic times and they cited the discovery of a crystalline hematite plate in a tomb at Kaminaljuyu, Guatemala.[18] Another unusual specimen was found in an infant burial at that site consisting of two star-shaped slate earplugs coated with thin plates of crystalline hematite. Other examples have been reported in caches found at Uaxactun by Carnegie Institution researchers as well as at Caracol and San Jose.[19, 20] Could these have been the portions Cayce said would be "carried to the Washington preservations of such findings, or to Chicago?"[21]

*Figure 95*
Another picture of workers with rope moving Altar 1 in 1931. Reprinted by permission from: University of Pennsylvania Museum Archives.

*Figure 96*
Penn excavating under Altar 1 in 1931. Reprinted by permission from: Penn Museum Archives.

*Figure 97*
Picture of cache items found under Altar 1. Note polished hematite disk (1st item in the 3rd column from left); the pieces of crystalline hematite are the two pieces directly below the polished disk (these were not labeled). The loaf shaped piece of jadeite is the 5th item down in second column from left. The round eccentric stone is the fourth item down in the first column. Reprinted by permission from: Penn Museum Archives.

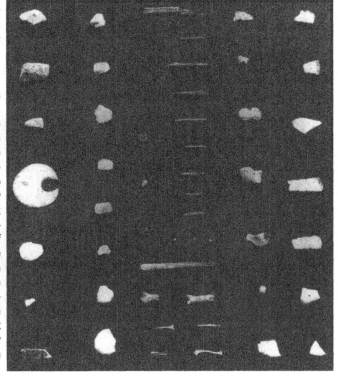

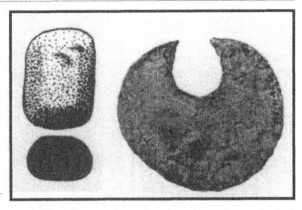

*Figure 98*
Drawing of Altar 1 cache items from left: loaf shaped piece of jadeite and semicircular eccentric flint. Reprinted from: *Piedras Negras Archaeology*, University of Pennsylvania Museum, 1959.

As mentioned earlier, the Carnegie Institution of Washington excavated at Uaxactun from 1926 to 1937 and were visited by Dr. Eric J. Thompson representing The Field Museum of Natural History of Chicago in 1929.[22] Caracol, located in south central Belize (formerly British Honduras), was initially discovered in 1938, but was not officially excavated until 1951 by none other than Linton Satterthwaite of the Penn Museum. San Jose was excavated in 1934 by a joint expedition sponsored by the Chicago Field Museum and the Carnegie Institution. Kaminaljuyu was also investigated by the Carnegie Institution for several years beginning in 1935. Interestingly, Kaminaljuyu, located in a highland valley in southwest Guatemala near modern-day Guatemala City,[23] means "Place of the Ancient Ones."

## The Hematite Crystals Fit Cayce's Clues

Now we have something that fits almost all of the Cayce clues for the firestone emblem. The hematite pieces found under Altar 1 were crystals that were taken to the Penn Museum, uncovered beneath a partially eroded monument that resembles a sundial (and is carved with mysteriously ancient dates), there was more than one (Cayce refers to them as stones - plural), similar crystals were discovered at sites with links to Washington and Chicago, and they were unearthed during the Penn expedition although before 1933. The firestone emblem is further identified in the Cayce readings not only as consisting of "stones" but, later in the same sentence, as being "set in the front of the temple, between the service temple and outer court temple or the priestly activity...in the altar that stood before the door of the tabernacle. This altar or stone, then in Yucatan, stands between the activities of the priest..."[24] The wording here seems to leave open the possibility that the firestone emblem could be stones "set in front the temple" and under an

Figure 99
Second picture of Altar 1
cache items. Reprinted from:
*Piedras Negras Archaeology*,
University of Pennsylvania
Museum, 1959.

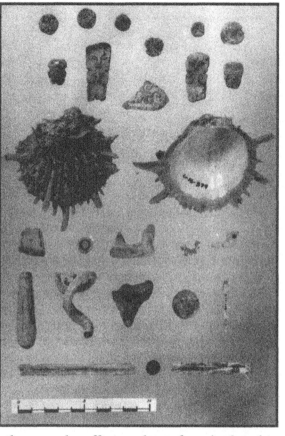

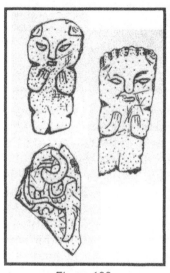

Figure 100
Drawings of 3 shell carvings.

altar as a cache offering. So, have cache offerings been found related to any other altars at Piedras Negras?

In his exhaustive study of caches from the Penn expeditions, Coe stated that 94 caches were reported with over half of them coming from Pyramid 0-13 in the East Group. He also noted that most, although not all, column altars were found to have caches beneath them. In comparison, the stelae at Piedras Negras mostly did not have caches and, when they did, they were almost always placed in front rather than underneath. There were also a few caches (3 in the Acropolis area) found under the so-called portable altars. These were actually small drum-shaped altars which showed no sign of burning and appeared to have been used domestically. None of the portable or column altar caches were reported to contain hematite or pyrite. Most of them contained some combination of jade, animal bones, shell fragments, and obsidian and flint eccentrics. The exception was a column altar on the Acropolis

*Figure 101*

Four stone (flint) "choppers" found in a cache behind Altar 5 in the East Group. *Piedras Negras Archaeology*, University of Pennsylvania Museum, 1959.

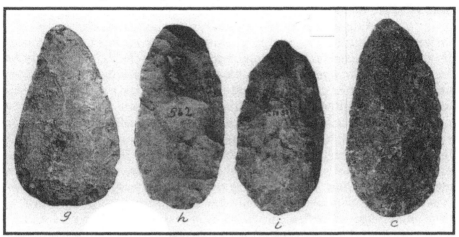

at J-29 which had an offering bowl that contained "a large lump of iron conglomerate" and "a small piece of crystalline stone."[25] Neither of these objects could be located by Coe and were listed in the field catalogs as sent to the Guatemala National Museum. Coe also reported that there were 5 flat topped table altars at Piedras Negras. All were checked for caches except Altar 2.[26] Only Altar 1, mentioned earlier, and Altar 5 contained caches. Altar 5 is the only other flat topped altar that is rounded and it is not carved. Since it is located in front of Pyramid 0-13 in the East Group, it is thought to have been constructed before 0-13 was built. The cache beneath it contained 6 eccentric flints and 5 eccentric obsidians. Behind it were found 4 "choppers" or crude celt-like flint knives assumed to be meant for a nearby stela.[27, 28] (See *fig. 101*.) So it appears that the objects discovered under Altar 1 are quite unique.

## Was the Firestone a Laser?

How could these pieces of crystalline hematite serve as an emblem for the firestone? Edgar Evans Cayce, son of Edgar Cayce, graduated with a degree in electrical engineering from Duke University and has spent the last 40 plus years as a registered professional engineer. He has noted that Cayce's description of the firestone in a 1934 reading "sounds to me like a lay person's attempt to describe a giant laser."[29] The mascr, an early form of the laser, was patented in 1958. Its inventors began working on it in the 1940s based on theories put forward by

Einstein in 1917.[30] The word maser is an acronym for microwave amplification by stimulated emission of radiation. A brief summary of the characteristics of masers/lasers demonstrates very quickly why Edgar Evans Cayce made the comparison with the firestone.

According to the *Microsoft Encarta Encyclopedia*, the maser is "a device that amplifies or generates microwaves or radio waves. A maser producing radiation in the optical region *(light is radiation that can be seen by the naked eye)* is called a laser. Masers make use of those transitions in molecules or crystals that correspond to the energies of microwave or radio frequencies." This simply means that a maser is tuned to produce frequencies located on an end of the electromagnetic spectrum which we are unable to see. In a laser we are able to see the radiation as light since the energy, or photons, being produced is vibrating at a frequency which can be processed by the human retina. This reference goes on to state that, "Paramagnetic masers use energy transitions *(photons or light created by the movement of the electrons in the medium material from lower to higher energy as they are stimulated by an outside source such as a high intensity lamp)* corresponding to the orientations of the magnetic moments of paramagnetic ions in crystalline substances *(the "medium")* placed in an external magnetic field. Different frequencies can be obtained by varying the magnetic field, thus allowing the tuning of a paramagnetic maser from less than a megacycle to several hundreds of megacycles."[31] Solid state lasers use rods of ruby crystals as a medium. Lasers can also use liquid mediums which are glass vessels containing inorganic dyes also tunable with the help of a prism.[32]

*Figure 102* Ruby laser. Note the mirrors on each end, the spiral-shaped flash tube, and the ruby crystal. Source: www.lasers.llnl.gov

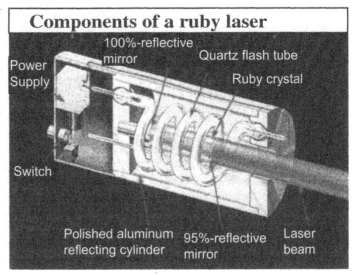

**Components of a ruby laser**

100%-reflective mirror
Quartz flash tube
Power Supply
Ruby crystal
Switch
Polished aluminum reflecting cylinder
95%-reflective mirror
Laser beam

In the field of optics, a prism is defined as "a piece of translucent glass or crystal with a triangular cross section, used to form a spectrum of light by separating it according to colors."[33]

## Comparing Cayce's Description to Scientific Definitions of a Laser

Now, let's compare the above definitions of a laser with Cayce's description of the firestone. The readings consistently stated that the firestone was a crystal: "in the form of a six-sided figure"[34] that received light from the sun's rays which were concentrated "through the prisms or glass." Cayce told one individual that he had been directly involved with the firestone in that he "directed the influences of the radiation that arose in the form of the rays that were invisible to the eye but that acted upon the stones themselves as set in the motivating forces... "[35]

In our modern lasers a medium such as a ruby emits visible or invisible photons/radiation (rays) when stimulated (acted upon) by an outside source such as a high intensity lamp (the motivating forces?). So far Cayce seems to be right on target in describing a maser/laser as defined in the previous section. The power of the firestone was initially used by the Atlanteans to attune themselves with God. Later it was used for more material purposes such as earthly communication, as well as to provide power, medical treatment and as a weapon much as we are attempting to do today. In fact, the misuse of its power was part of what contributed to one of the Atlantean destructions. In one reading Cayce indicated that the Atlantean lands were broken up in 28,000 B.C. when the forces of the firestone were "tuned too high."[36] Again, as with modern lasers, Cayce's Atlantean firestone could be tuned which may mean that it was a paramagnetic type of maser/laser device.

And now, what do hematite crystals have to do with the laser? The first similarity is that hematite crystals are six-sided (hexagonal) at the molecular level as are the ruby crystals used as medium material in laser technology. The type of crystal field in which the atomic ions are located within the medium is important in laser technology.[37] In a hexagonal crystal system, each molecule is structured with "four axes, three are of equal length and lie at an angle of 120 degrees from each other. The fourth is either longer or shorter but must be at a right angle toward the other corners."[38] Masers/lasers work by energizing the electrons in the atoms of the medium. Ruby crystals (*fig. 102*) work well because they are highly fluorescent at the molecular level and because they contain chromium atoms that are easily excited. In a side note, as discussed in an earlier chapter, calcite (found at Piedras Negras during 1933) is also highly fluorescent.

The second similarity is that hematite is paramagnetic.[39] Paramagnetic-type masers, as noted previously, are significant in that they can be tuned to different frequencies. Once again, it is worth mentioning that Cayce stated that the Atlantean firestone could be tuned.

A third connection is that hematite easily flakes off into thin sheets. In the maser/laser, synthetic ruby is applied to parallel rods in a thin layer and placed within a cylinder. The cylinder is enclosed on either end with mirrors which reflect and amplify the photons that are emitted by the excited electrons until they are emitted in a coherent, unified pattern. This pattern then creates an extremely focused beam of either visible light or invisible microwave radiation.[40]

The use of mirrors in modern maser/lasers leads to a fourth connection. Hematite was believed to have been used as a mirror by the Maya and the Olmecs. In fact, the curvature of the concave surface of the Olmec mirrors were found by archaeologists to be "almost identical to the modern practice of parabolizing optical reflectors."[41]

The fifth and most amazing similarity concerns the chemical makeup of hematite. Although ruby is often used as a medium in solid state lasers, another substance is considered more ideal for producing higher frequencies. This substance, called rutile, is a combination of titanium and oxygen ($TiO_2$). It works best if it contains impurities of iron or chromium. Hematite, as described in an earlier chapter, is made up primarily of iron and oxygen, although it often contains titanium impurities. As a result, its chemical makeup is sometimes written as $(Fe,Ti_2)O_3$. As mentioned earlier, the hematite mirrors found at La Venta were determined to be made of a combination of magnetite, hematite and ilmenite, the latter being an iron oxide containing titanium. So, hematite often contains all of the components needed to serve as a medium for a high frequency solid state maser according to current technology.[42] Perhaps the high frequency capability relates to Cayce's story that the early Atlanteans used the firestone for spiritual rather than material purposes. Regardless, the number of similarities and connections between hematite and the modern maser/laser are truly amazing. Are they simply a coincidence?

Of additional interest are the patent drawings of the first maser from 1958. It can be viewed on the web at www.bell-labs.com/history/laser. The cylindrical design of the maser contains concentric circles and has a spiral shaped piece encircling its interior. The spiral is the light source used to stimulate the electrons in the ruby crystal which is located within the cylinder.[43] Both spirals and concentric circles are important symbols found in ancient petroglyphs at Piedras Negras which archaeologists believe may have originated before the time of the Maya.

Perhaps they represent ancient stories of the firestone. If this device was as important as Cayce described, it would not likely be forgotten, although, as often happens over great lengths of time, an understanding of its true purpose may have been lost in mythology. Perhaps this explains the sacred status of hematite as a mineral found on the headbands of rulers and in cache offerings at temples where it is believed to have served to increase the spiritual power of the structure.[44] Could this mean also that pyrite, used more commonly in later years was simply an imitation of the harder to find hematite? Pyrite can be polished to reflect light just like hematite, but it is not paramagnetic nor is it hexagonal at the molecular level.

It is possible that, as time passed after Iltar's death, the true understanding of the use of hematite was lost or deliberately hidden so that it only retained symbolic value. Interestingly, modern Maya priests use clear "stones of light to discern the true location of the four corner points in an area that must be purified or made ready for a ceremony."[45] Stones were also associated with lightning among the Classic era Maya and it is believed that the shapes of some of the eccentric sculpted stones, found at Piedras Negras and elsewhere, are depictions of lightning frozen in stone. For the ancient Maya, blood contained a form of lightning and its power could be tapped during rituals involving bloodletting and human sacrifice. Modern shaman among the Quiche Maya must be able to sense the movement of the lightning within their bodies in order to communicate with the ancestors and to do divination. The lightning is said to cause "their blood to speak."[46] Could these customs be related to the more ancient Atlantean rituals of the firestone?

## Location of the Hall of Records in the Acropolis?

Assuming we have now located the firestone emblem, we are left with another possibility: i.e., does this mean the Hall of Records can be found in the Acropolis area? In our Cayce clues regarding the location of the Hall of Records we are told to look "where the temple there is overshadowing" it,[47] where these stones (that they know so little about) are now during the last few months (of 1933) being uncovered,"[48] that they are "in the rocks"[49] and can be accessed by "the entering of the chambers" in 1938.[50]

A review of the archaeological evidence from both the Penn and the BYU excavations yielded several interesting correlations. First, the Acropolis, a palace/temple complex, and one other building (a sweatbath in the East Group) were the only ones with multi-room chambers still standing in recognizable form when Penn arrived.[51]

Second, there are two temples which could be said to be over-shadowing Altar 1. Pyramid J-4 on the northern edge of the Acropolis and Pyramid K-5 which contain the huge stucco masks are both very near Altar 1. These masks on Pyramid K-5 were unearthed during July of the 1933 season and meet the Cayce clue for something being uncovered a few months before the November 1933 reading.[52]

Third, during 1931 and 1932 and later during 1939, Penn excavated extensively and uncovered sublevel, possibly "nonMaya," architecture within Pyramid K-5. (See *fig. 103* for Acropolis site locations.) During 1933, in addition to the superficial exploration of K-5 that resulted in the discovery of the giant masks, much effort went into excavating beneath all of the mounds of the Acropolis and especially those directly in front of Altar 1. At the Acropolis they found older structures underneath with evidence of burning which, according to Cayce, was an Atlantean pattern in the Yucatan.[53, 54] Although subsequent reports did not yield any evidence for discovery of a Hall of Records, this may have been due to the techniques used by Penn as well as to a lack of documentation. BYU complained that assistant Penn archaeologist Frank Cresson (field staff 1935-37) was not as meticulous in his excavations at the Acropolis and left open holes and much "rubble and heaps of earth." BYU also noted evidence that "many more, rather cursory pits and clearings were made than were suggested by their list of operations."[55]

Fourth, BYU reported finding "a bedrock outcropping and abyss accessed by steps" under Court 3 located in the upper levels of the Acropolis which they dated to the Early Classic period. How deep the steps went and if they led to a hall was not reported. Given the uncertainty of security in the area, they were understandably cautious about reporting too many details.[56]

A fifth point is simply that, given the reported potential for a large number of caves and cenotes (large underground pits) in the area around Piedras Negras, the Acropolis (located on the side of a large hill) could have been built over a natural cave formation which served Iltar as a location for storage of the Atlantean records.[57] Also, it is possible that a manmade tunnel or cavern was constructed in this area to serve the same purpose. As mentioned previously, other structures, such as the pyramids at Teotihuacan were built over manmade caverns which were highly sacred to the Maya and to the Aztec.[58] In 1933, Burial 6, containing the remains of a holy man, was found in a cave on the ridge of hills northeast of the West Group Acropolis area which means there could be more caves in the vicinity of the city center.

A sixth correlation is that the 1997 BYU report noted the presence of a "concretized, calcite layer" which they could not penetrate in the Acropolis upper Court 3 level.[59] So far, they have not reported break-ing through this layer, although the 1999 report described the discovery of "...Late Preclassic (chicanel) pottery that had been compressed into natural hollows in the bedrock."[60] The overall report on the Acropolis and the West Plaza from the 1999 season concluded that the earliest buildings found were from the Early Classic period. However, BYU noted an unusual pattern of almost complete destruction of earlier structures before new ones were added. This was especially true under the West

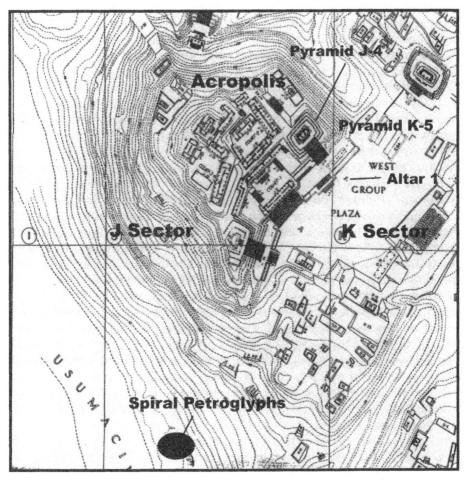

*Figure 103*
A closeup of a map of the West Group Plaza including the Acropolis (center of J-sector) Altar 1, Pyramid J-4, Pyramid K-5, and the spiral petroglyphs. Reprinted by permission from: University of Pennsylvania Museum Archives.

Plaza which they concluded was built over the earliest palace structures. Additionally, they conceded that the excavation of the Acropolis was hampered by large mounds of debris left by Penn which would indicate that they were not able to explore the entire sublevel foundation.[61] After the 1998 season, BYU had concluded that the Acropolis was initially built at the top of the hill and that subsequent renovations enlarged it down to the bottom areas and created the large complex it gradually became.[62] The structures used by Iltar could be underneath the concrete layer or perhaps any evidence of them was so totally destroyed during new construction that they cannot be identified. The 1999 report also noted that the middle Preclassic (1000 - 300 B.C.) remains found in the South Group during 1998 were under a layer of "rotted limestone" that had originally been assumed to be natural bedrock.[63] Can BYU be sure they've plumbed the depths of the Acropolis?

A seventh connection is the spiral petroglyphs which are not within any of the subareas of the city. However, they are on the cliffs which face the river just across from the West Group.

An eighth correlation is that, not only was the cache of hematite crystals found in front of the Acropolis, but almost all of the pyrite and hematite artifacts found at Piedras Negras so far have been from the Acropolis. The exceptions are a hexagonal pyrite mosaic fragment from the South Group, pyrite artifacts from BYU Burial 13 near Pyramid O-13 in the East Group and two hematite fragments discovered in surface debris in the East Group.[64, 65] Also found in the Acropolis area were several of the artifacts that partially meet Cayce's clues and which were listed as sent to the Penn Museum during 1933. For example, two pieces of polished pyrite mirrors (J-6), a pyrite ornament with an incised scroll design (J-2), and a red limestone ball with incised cross were all found at the Acropolis (J-2) in 1933 and transported to the Penn museum. Also included in this category is the fragment of the calcite vessel which shares two characteristics of the ruby used in solid state laser technology. It was found in Court 1 (J-2) of the Acropolis. An unusual carved cylindrical clay object open at both ends which is reminiscent of the cylindrical shape of both Cayce's firestone and the modern laser design was also found at the Acropolis and taken to the Penn Museum in 1933.[66] It is uncertain whether these finds point to an ancient use of the Acropolis by the early Atlanteans or simply represent treasured artifacts preserved over the generations and used at the most recent sacred structures at Piedras Negras. Either way, it seems worth noting since all of these finds fit Cayce's clues.

# Evidence for the South Group as the Location for the Hall of Records

In terms of pure age, the South Group is the most logical location for a Hall of Records deposited by Atlantean immigrants around 10,000 B.C. (See *fig. 104* for South Group site locations.) Hieroglyphic data on stelae and panels found in that area have confirmed that Pyramid R-5 was the burial place of Piedras Negras Ruler 1 who acceded to the throne around A.D. 603.[67] In addition, the oldest inscribed date, A.D. 514, was found on a broken lintel (12) which was reused in Pyramid O-13 and is thought to have originated from Pyramid R-4 in the South Group.[68] Also Lintel 11, which was found in Pyramid R-3, led Morley to state that this Pyramid was probably "one of the earliest buildings" at Piedras Negras.[69] Remains of deposits dating from as late as 1000 B.C. have been found by BYU in the Plaza area of the South Group.[70] While this is intriguing dating it is still several thousand years short of Iltar's era.

In line with Cayce's clues, Penn did excavate in the South Group extensively during the 1933 season and there are several site anomalies in the South Group with connections to the Cayce story.

First, during 1933 Penn found evidence of at least four underlying structures under Pyramid R-3, a cylindrical eroded carved stone column in front of Pyramid R-9, a large stucco head with a nonMaya forehead under the floor of Pyramid R-5, and a seemingly royal burial chamber.[71] Pyramid R-3 was one of the architectural studies done by Satterthwaite which caused him to conclude that the older sublevels of the structure were NonMaya in style, although he still did not date it outside the Classic period.[72]

Second, listed as sent to the Penn Museum after the 1933 season were objects from Burial 10, as well as a flattened spheroidal worked stone from R-1, a small hemispherical stone object from R-3 and a fragment of Misc. Sculptured Stone #11 found under the floor in Pyramid R-3. Mysteriously, the latter artifact is only mentioned in the field notes object catalog for 1933 and the field notebook for R-3. It is not mentioned in the published material that I reviewed nor is it among inscriptions used from the site for dating. This leads to the conclusion that it did not contain readable hieroglyphs although this was not absolutely confirmed.[73, 74]

Third, the Inscribed Cliff carving of the Long Nosed God/turtle/ Maize God emergence with the 5 (or 6) *Ahau* cartouche discovered by Maler and studied by Penn in 1935 is located to the east of the South Group.

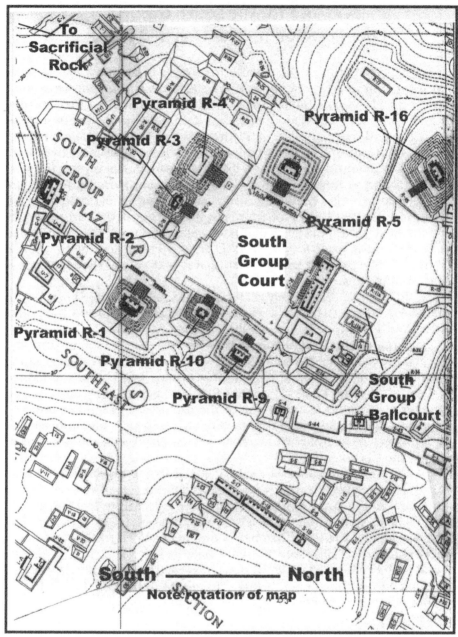

*Figure 104*
A closeup of a map of the Piedras Negras South Group Plaza including the surrounding
structures. Reprinted by permission from: University of Pennsylvania Museum Archives.

Fourth, the Sacrificial Rock is in the southern portion of the site on the river at the entrance.

Fifth, Lintel 6, a possible sundial, with its unusual six spoke design was unearthed by Mason in 1931 where it had been moved by workmen during Maler's exploration. Although its original location is unknown, Mason uncovered it 93 yards northeast of the Sacrificial Rock near the entrance to the South Group plaza.

Sixth, a hexagon shaped piece of pyrite, thought to be part of a mosaic, was found in surface debris near Pyramid R-10 sometime other than 1933 (however, it was sent to the Guatemala Museum).

Seventh, the cave where Maler reported making camp in the 1800s near the South Group was explored during the 1999 season and, although the report was not clear, it appears that burial remains were found in all caves explored during the season. No unusual finds were reported in regards to the burials, however, the overall information given was minimal.[75]

Eighth, the older levels of the South Group pyramids also contained more open ceremonial areas and nonsacrificial burned (possibly Atlantean remnant) column altars located (as Cayce put it) "in front of the temple, between the service temple and the outer court temple,"[76] but contained no flat topped altars most likely used for human sacrifice. The Acropolis had both types of altars.

Ninth, the South Group also contains the mysterious Pyramid R-16 which is the only pyramid at the site misaligned in relation to its base. Perhaps it was built to hide an entrance to the Hall of Records.[77]

Tenth, evidence for multiple episodes of water erosion were found in the South Group[78] perhaps correlating to Cayce's destruction of the original Atlantean temples of Iltar with the "changes in the contours of the land."[79]

Eleventh, in 1997 BYU reported finding a circular building from the Early Classic period in the eastern part of the South Group. This might indicate astronomical activities or might be a recreation of the Atlantean dome under which the firestone was kept per Cayce.[80]

So, as can be seen, other than a scarcity of hematite and pyrite artifacts, the South Group also has many correlations to the Cayce clues for the Hall of Records and evidence for Atlantean influences. One of the biases of the field studies is that most of the effort by both Penn and BYU have focused on the Acropolis/West Group and on Pyramid 0-13 in the East Group. The 1999 BYU season included digging a vertical shaft into the center of Pyramid R-5. They hit plaster flooring at 12, 18, and 25 feet. Unfortunately, by that time the season was over and plans had to be made to continue the excavation during the 2000 season. They were able to explore the area around the platform and found "deep deposits of early date" although they did not specify the period in their report.[81] They also reported finding 68 new structures in the southern sector of the South Group that were mostly residential and included burials.

## Where is the Hall of Records?

So, where is the Hall of Records at Piedras Negras? The jury is still out but two specific areas appear to have the highest probability. One possibility is that the first temple of Iltar was built near the South Group, maybe even underground, in the area BYU noted that seemed to have collapsed from water erosion. A second temple/Hall of Records then may have been constructed in the Acropolis area which might have been considered a safer location since it is higher in elevation. These two areas at Piedras Negras — perhaps one or the other — may, indeed, be found to contain the Hall of Records.

Even though the initial occupation dates at Piedras Negras continue to be pushed back by archaeologists to increasingly more ancient times, its origins remain an enigma. During the 1999 season BYU continued to focus on understanding the history of the site and concluded that "the beginnings of Piedras Negras, and its ending, appeared as abrupt as ever, with little evidence of gradual development or steady decline."[82] However, regarding the potential of the site, BYU was obviously still intrigued. The 1999 report noted that "...there can be no doubt that the site guards additional surprises in its buried architecture."[83] BYU planned to focus primarily on the South Group during the 2000 season. It sounds like they may be getting closer to solving the mystery of Piedras Negras. It may well be that the surprise in the buried architecture at Piedras Negras is Cayce's Hall of Records.

In the next chapter even more connections between Piedras Negras and the ancient Maya creation stories will be revealed in a fascinating look at the astronomical features of the site. These astronomical correlations provide even more evidence that Piedras Negras is the location of the lost Hall of Records.

## References

1. Reading 440-12

2. Maler, Teobert (1901). Researches in the Central Portion of the Usumacintla Valley. *Memoirs of the Peabody Museum, Harvard University*, Vol. 2, No. 1. Cambridge.

3. Reading 440-12

4. Morley, S. V. (1938). *The Inscriptions of Peten, Vol. III.* Carnegie Institution of Washington, Publication 437, Washington, p. 286.

5. Ibid, p. 285-294.

6. Thompson, J. Eric (1944) The Dating of Seven Monuments at Piedras Negras. *Notes on Middle American Archaeology and Ethnology* 2:65-82. Cambridge Mass.: Carnegie Institution of Washington.

7. Proskouriakoff, Tatiana (1993) *Maya History.* Austin, Texas: University of Texas Press, p. 84.

8. Looper, Matthew (1995) The Three Stones of Maya Creation Mythology at Quirigua. *Mexicon,* XVII, p. 24-30.

9. Bauval, Robert and Gilbert, Adrian (1994) *The Orion Mystery.* New York: Crown Publishers.

10. Sharer, Robert (1994) *The Ancient Maya: Fifth Edition,* Stanford California: Stanford University Press. p. 571.

11. Archaeology News (1999) *Archaeology Magazine,* July/August, p. 16.

12. Schele, Linda and Freidel, David (1990) *A Forest of Kings.* New York: William Morrow, p. 246.

13. Schele, Linda and Mathews, Peter (1998) *The Code of Kings.* New York: Scribner, pp. 104-106.

14. *A Forest of Kings.* op. cit., p. 252.

15. Reading 440-12.

16. Coe, William (1959) *Piedras Negras Archaeology.* Philadelphia: University Museum Press, p. 89.

17. Ibid, p. 43.

18. Shook, E. M. and Kidder, Alfred (1952) *Mound E-III-3m Kaminaljuyu, Guatemala.* CIW Publication 596, p. 116.

19. *Piedras Negras Archaeology.*, op. cit., p. 44.

20. Kidder, Alfred, Jennings, Jesse., and Shook, Edwin (1946) *Excavations at Kaminaljuyu, Guatemala.* Carnegie Institution of Washington Publication 501, pp. 493-510.

21. Reading 440-5.

22. Morley, S. V. (1938). *The Inscriptions of Peten, Vol. I.* Carnegie Institution of Washington, Publication 437, Washington.

23. Sharer, Robert *The Ancient Maya: Fifth Edition,* op. cit.

24. Reading 440-5.

25. *Piedras Negras Archaeology,* op. cit., p. 92.

26. Ibid, p. 99.

27. Ibid, p. 80.

28. Satterthwaite, Linton (1936) *Piedras Negras Preliminary Papers No. 5: A Pyramid Without Temple Ruins.* Philadelphia: University of Pennsylvania Museum, p. 13.

29. Cayce, Edgar Evans et al, (1997) *Mysteries of Atlantis Revisited.* New York: St. Martin's Press, p. 46.

30. The Invention of the Laser at Bell Laboratories: 1958-1998. http://www/bell-labs.com/history/laser/

31. "Maser," *Microsoft Encarta Online Encyclopedia 2000* http://encarta.msn.com copyright 1997-2000 Microsoft Corporation. All rights reserved.

32. "Laser," *Microsoft Encarta Online Encyclopedia 2000* http://encarta.msn.com copyright 1997-2000 Microsoft Corporation. All rights reserved.

33. *The Concise Columbia Electronic Encyclopedia, Third Edition* Copyright 1994, Columbia University Press.

34. Reading 2072-10

35. Reading 440-5

36. Readings 440-5, 877-26, 813-1, 519-1,977-1, 263-4, 877-26, 2072-101470-1.

37. Orton, J.W., Paxman, D.H., and Walling, J.C. (1970) *The Solid State Maser*. New York: Pergamon Press, p. 25.8

38. Online Mineral Gallery (http://www.minerals.net/mineral) copyright Hershel Friedman, 1997-1999.

39. Smith, George F. (1983) The Story of the Ruby Laser. Hughes Research Laboratories: Our History 1960s. On line Web site http://www.hrl.com/tradition.

40. "Laser and Maser," *Compton's Encyclopedia Online 2000* http://comptonsv3.web.aol.com/encyclopedia copyright 1998 The Learning Company, Inc.

41. Heizer, Robert and Gullberg, Jonas (1981) Concave Mirrors from the Site of La Venta, Tabasco: Their Occurrence, Mineralogy, Optical Description, and Function. In Elizabeth Benson (Ed.) *The Olmec and Their Neighbors: Essays in Memory of Matthew W. Stirling*. Washington, D.C.: Dumbarton Oaks Research Library and Collections.

42. *The Solid State Maser*, op. cit., pp. 54-55.

43. "Maser," *Microsoft Encarta Online Encyclopedia 2000* op. cit.

44. *A Forest of Kings*. op. cit.

45. Freidel, D, Schele, L. and Parker, J. (1993) *Maya Cosmos*. New York: William Morrow. p. 126.

46. Ibid, p. 200.

47. Reading 2012-1.

48. Reading 440-5.

49. Reading 354-5.

50. Reading 440-5.

51. *The Inscriptions of Peten, Vol. III*, op. cit., p. 5.

52. Satterthwaite, Linton (1933) The Piedras Negras Expedition. *University Museum Bulletin*, Vol. 4, No. 5, p. 121.

53. *The Inscriptions of Peten, Vol. I*, op. cit., pp. 99-100.

54. Satterthwaite, Linton (1939) Evolution of a Maya Temple - Part I. *University Museum Bulletin*, Vol. 7, No. 4, pp. 3-14.

55. Houston, S., Escobedo, H. and Forsyth, D. (1998). On the River of Ruins: Explorations at Piedras Negras, Guatemala, 1997. *Mexicon*, Vol. XX, pp. 17-18.

56. Houston, S. et al (1999). Between Mountains and Sea: Investigations at Piedras Negras Guatemala, 1998. *Mexicon*, Vol. XXI, p. 13.

57. *The Inscriptions of Peten, Vol. III*, op. cit., p. 8.

58. Aveni, Anthony (Ed.) (1977) *Native American Astronomy*. Austin: University of Texas Press, pp. 4-5.

59. *Mexicon XX*, op. cit., p. 20.

60. *Mexicon XXII*, op. cit., p. 4.

61. Ibid.

62. *Mexicon, XXI*, op. cit., p. 14.

63. *Mexicon XXII*, op. cit., p. 3.

64. *Piedras Negras Archaeology*, op. cit.

65. *Mexicon, XX*, op. cit., p. 18.

66. Piedras Negras Field Notes, 1933 Object Catalog, University of Pennsylvania Museum Archives.

67. *Mexicon XXII*, op. cit., p. 3.

68. *The Inscriptions of Peten, Vol. III*, op. cit., p. 28-35.

69. Piedras Negras Field Notes, Box 6, Notebook 6, University of Pennsylvania Museum Archives.

70. *Mexicon, XX* op. cit., p. 18.

71. Piedras Negras Field Notes, 1933 Object Catalog, University of Pennsylvania Museum Archives.

72. *University Museum Bulletin*, Vol. 7, No. 4, op. cit.

73. Piedras Negras Field Notes, 1933 Object Catalog, op. cit.

74. Piedras Negras Field Notes, Box 6, Notebook 6, op. cit.

75. *The Inscriptions of Peten, Vol. III*, op. cit.

76. Reading 440-5.

77. *The Inscriptions of Peten, Vol. III*, op. cit.

78. *Mexicon XX*, op. cit., p. 18.

79. Reading 5750-1.

80. *Mexicon XX*, op. cit., p. 20.

81. *Mexicon XXII*, op. cit., p. 3.

82. Ibid, p. 8.

83. Ibid, p. 3.

## Chapter 7

# Maya Astronomical Alignments:
## Another Clue to the Location of the Hall of Records?

### Astronomy and the Maya Hieroglyphs

One of the most exciting aspects of the ongoing decipherment (see highlighted box on next page) of the Maya hieroglyphs has been the discovery of certain texts carved into the various stone monuments that recount the history of the Maya going back to their creation date of August 13, 3114 B.C. In some cases the texts make astonishing reference to dates millions of years in the past. Among the monuments with inscriptions that relate this ancient history is Piedras Negras Altar 1 which may also mark the location of Cayce's firestone emblem. Since we are exploring for evidence that correlates to the Cayce story of Maya history, which linked the Maya to the destruction of Atlantis in the remote past, these ancient dates are very compelling. Of course, to mainstream researchers they are simply mythological stories with no possible basis in fact. However, as archaeologically verified settlement dates are continually pushed back for the Americas, these so-called mythological dates and stories become less and less remote. Also, the fact that some of the dates are so specific (for example, some of the gods have

# Deciphering the Maya Hieroglyphs

Tatiana Proskouriakoff's 1960 publication[1] revealing the historical meaning of the Maya stelae at Piedras Negras and the death of the authoritarian and ultra-conservative archaeologist, J. Eric Thompson, were the two primary events that allowed scholars to begin the decipherment of Maya hieroglyphs. Early researchers had concluded that the hieroglyphs simply contained calendar dates and astronomical information. This was an understandable deduction since the few Maya books rescued from the colonial Spanish destruction were known to contain detailed records of the astronomical movements of Venus and the moon. Thanks to Proskouriakoff's analysis of the Piedras Negras stelae with its "peculiar pattern of dates," it became obvious that the sculpted figures were real historical people — not mythical gods. And further, these stelae had obviously been carved to tell their story. Suddenly archaeologists were able to see the Maya in a new light and some began quietly working out a way to read the hieroglyphs. Thompson, who had opposed a phonetic based interpretation of the hieroglyphs, was such a powerful figure in Maya archaeology that collaboration and research into the decipherment of noncalendric hieroglyphs was not openly pursued until after his death.

As Michael Coe outlines in his book, *Breaking the Maya Code*, most of the credit for the breakthrough goes to the willingness of scholars from several different specialities to share their ideas in an open forum. The first of these collaborative meetings was the Palenque Round Table held at the city of Palenque, Mexico in 1973. It was organized by Linda Schele and Merle Robertson who were both artists and Maya enthusiasts. Like Proskouriakoff, they had spent a great deal of time admiring, drawing, and analyzing Maya monuments and their inscriptions. Many others in the more conservative field, or so-called "dirt" archaeologists, were resistant to the meetings and especially to the idea of receiving input from nonarchaeologists. Over time, however, many archaeologists, linguists and enthnologists were inspired by the progress made at Palenque and soon were attending as well.[2]

After writing a groundbreaking dissertation on the discovery of verbs in the Maya hieroglyphs, Schele earned a doctorate from the University of Texas where she taught until her untimely death in 1998. Even more impressive was the popularity of Schele's classes among the modern Maya. These students were particularly able to appreciate and recognize the validity of the decipherment methods. The ancient information gleaned from the inscriptions provided connections between their own belief systems and customs and those of the ancient Maya. In return, attendees who still spoke the old Maya languages often provided assistance to the archaeologists through their knowledge of the meaning and context of the ancient information being revealed.[3] Using drawings and photographs from the early twentieth century explorers, such as Teobert Maler, as well as information from the Maya books or codices from the time of the Spanish conquest, an index of different glyph symbols was created. Many of these glyphs have now been at least partially translated and breakthroughs continue to be made.[4]

*Figure 105* — Example of hieroglyphic writing on Piedras Negras Altar 1. By John Montgomery.

actual birthdates) seems to hint that these stories could be based on the actions of real people.[5]

## The Orion Connection

Also of significance within these historical inscriptions are references to astronomical phenomena which could be especially useful in our search for Atlantean evidence. Schele and others have concluded that these references were not accidental. The movement of the sun, as well as certain planets and constellations, both reflected and served to recount the story of the last creation for the Maya. And, of even further interest, both the sky and the creation story are believed to be mirrored in the architecture and layout of many Maya cities.[6] For example, in 1921, Hagar proposed that the major buildings in the Maya city of Uxmal were designed and laid out to represent the constellations we currently call the Zodiac.[7] Archaeologists Jose Fernandez and Robert Cormack reported that the ceremonial center of Utatlan, a Postclassic Maya city in Guatemala, was designed in the shape of the constellation Orion. In addition, they found that some of the major temples there were aligned to view the heliacal rising of Orion.[8] The word "heliacal" simply means that the stars in the constellation were seen to rise in the eastern sky just before the sunrise occurred to blot them out. This is similar to the astronomical relationship which occurs with the three great pyramids of Giza in Egypt as described by Robert Bauval and Adrian Gilbert in their book *The Orion Mystery* .[9] Given Cayce's story of Atlantean migrations to Egypt as well as to the Yucatan, this Orion connection may be more than coincidental. In this chapter, we will review the current theories on the relationship between the sky and Maya architecture and how it could relate to Piedras Negras and the location of the Hall of Records.

## As Above, So Below:
## The Maya Creation Story In the Stars

As will be described in more detail in the final section of this book, many Mesoamerican native groups, such as the Maya and the Aztecs, related ancient stories that include multiple creations. According to the Maya, the world has been destroyed and recreated four times. They believed that the last destruction/creation occurred on August 13, 3114 B.C. Other civilizations have similar creation dates in the distant past, for example, the modern Greek Church uses the date 5509 B.C., while the Hebrew date is 3761 B.C.[10] Given Cayce's story of a Hebrew migration to the Yucatan in 3000 B.C., this latter date is quite interesting. It is not far from the date chosen by the Maya for their most recent creation.

As with many ancient stories, the terminology can sound strange to our modern ears. It is helpful to think of them as metaphors that contain levels of hidden meaning. For example, the primary event of the 4th creation was the resurrection and emergence of the Maize God (another aspect of the First Father, Itzamna) which was said to have occurred from the cracked shell of a turtle. (See *fig. 106.*) Maize or corn was very important to the Maya and represented life. Also, the Maize God, who is an aspect of Itzamna/the First Father, is said to have paddled across the sea from the east to arrive at the place of the three stones where he was resurrected and created the world. This story is not unlike Cayce's story of the immigrants from Atlantis.

## Five Monuments Commemmorate 3114 B.C.

There are five Maya monuments known to have inscriptions commemorating the 3114 B.C. creation date. These include the Temple of the Cross at Palenque, Coba Stela 1, Copan Stela 23, Quirigia (pronounced Kee-ree-gwah) Stela C, and Piedras Negras Altar 1.[11] Hieroglyphic decipherment has determined that these monuments consistently tell of three important events that occurred during the 4th millennium B.C. The first happened on May 28, 3149 B.C. and relates to the

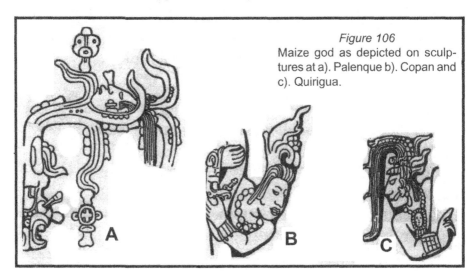

*Figure 106*
Maize god as depicted on sculptures at a). Palenque b). Copan and c). Quirigua.

Hero Twins of the *Popol Vuh* (the Bible or Council Book of the ancient Quiche Maya compiled by the Spanish in the 1700s from the Maya originals). On this date, the twins overcame the character Seven-Macaw whose vanity caused him to equate himself with the sun. Only when he was subdued could the next creation occur.[12]

The second important event described on the various monuments is the beginning of the 4th creation which occurred on the date 4 Ahau 8 Cumku (August 13) in 3114 B.C. On this date, one inscription is read, "was manifested the image." Another monument elaborates that, "On 4 Ahau 8 Cumku it was seen, the first image of the turtle, great holy lord." The turtle image is said to have "appeared at Lying-Down-Sky, First-Three-Stone-Place" an earthly location where the records tell us that three stones were set in place. (See *fig. 107*.) Then, 542 days later, on Feb 5, 3112 B.C., the third important event transpired. The First Father/Itzamna (called Raised-Up-Sky-Lord or Six-Sky-Lord) entered the sky and created a house in the north that was made of 8 partitions (believed to represent the 8 directions). He "raised the World Tree out of a plate of sacrifice" which, in turn, raised up the sky. Before that point, the Maya believed that the sky and the earth were pressed together. By raising this so-called World Tree (*fig. 108*), the Maya believed that the First Father created the sky and the 8 directions, which includes the 4 cardinal directions (N,S,E,W) plus the 4 intercardinal directions(SE, NE, SW, NW).[13]

During the raising of the sky the three stone image that had been placed on the earth was also imprinted in the heavens. The Maya often referred to the sky as the house to the North and for them it was centered on an axis that aligned near the North star. Since the Maya were located in the tropics, the North axis was not directly over their heads, but was, instead, closer to the northern horizon. The monumental inscriptions tell that when the World Tree

*Figure 107*
The turtle carrying the three stones — the Belt of Orion. From the *Madrid Codex*.

was raised a place called "black is its center" was "brought into existence." Polaris, the North Star, which was called the heart of heaven, was located in a dark place in the sky which the Maya saw as a black void around which they witnessed the rotation of the planets and constellations.[14]

Stela C at Quirigia recounts in more detail the setting of each of the three stones in their earthly locations. At the time the three stones were placed on the earth it is suggested that the sky was pressed into the earth. The *Books of Chilam Balam*, written by native Maya seers and priests shortly after the Spanish conquest, recounted this precreation period: "When the world was submerged, when there was neither heaven nor earth..." The three stones on Stela C are identified as the jaguar, snake and water thrones, the latter of which being of higher status. The first stone, called the Jaguar throne, was set up by two characters called the Stingray Paddler and the Jaguar Paddler at a location called "House-Five-Sky." These two deities were said to have *accompanied Itzamna across a large body of water* and were identified as lords of a supernatural location. The second stone was set up as the snake throne by some other unidentified supernatural entity. Regarding this stone the passage reads, "He set up a stone, Black-House-Great-?, it happened at Earth-Place, snake-stone-throne." The third stone was called the water throne and it was set up by Itzamna at Lying-Down-Sky, First-Three-Stone-Place. On Piedras Negras Altar 1 and other monuments the symbol for the Lying-Down-Sky place is three Kwak glyphs placed in a triangle. This pattern is mimicked in the Maya's traditional placement of three stones to make a hearth or central house fire. It is a pattern known to have been used by both ancient and modern Maya.[15] Just as the hearth is the center of the home, the three stone thrones form the center of the cosmos.

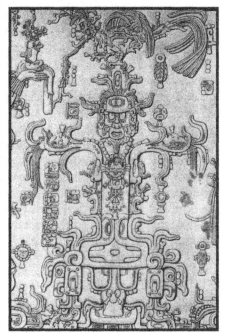

*Figure 108*
World Tree as depicted on one of the panels found in the Temple of the Foliated Cross at Palenque. Reprinted from Maudsley, *Achaeology:Biologia Centrali-Americana*, 1902.

# Following the Movement of The Stars:
# The Creation

What has been discovered most recently is that the ancient Maya's preoccupation with astronomy related directly to this story of creation. The Maya saw the creation story reflected in the movement of the stars and planets through the sky. First, the researchers found evidence from drawings on an ancient mural that the Maya referred to the three stars in the belt of Orion as the turtle's back. The next question they wanted to answer was the location in the heavens of the triangular three stone/thrones of the creation.[16] A clue was provided by a Maya drawing from the Madrid codex depicting three symbols suspended from the heavens and arranged in a triangle above the back of a turtle. Schele, Looper and others have since concluded that the triangular hearth is represented in the sky by stars in the constellation of Orion. ***Alnitak (one of the outer stars in the belt of Orion), Rigel, and Saiph make up the triangle of the three stone/thrones of the creation story.*** The M42 Nebula, that can be seen in the middle of the triangle, was considered by the Maya to represent the smoke from the fire in the hearth. (See *fig. 109.*)

*Figure 109*
Picture of turtle in probable conjunction with Orion. Actual constellation formation is below left for comparison. The top of the turtle's back was believed to have cracked allowing the "creation" to have emerged.

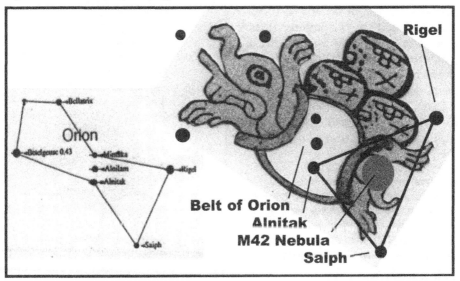

Using computerized star charts, Linda Schele replayed the movement of the stars on August 13, A.D. 690 (which was the year the Palenque creation inscriptions were dedicated). What she discovered amazed both her and her colleagues. The star charts revealed that the movement of the Milky Way, the Big and Little Dippers, and the constellations of Gemini, Orion, the Pleiades, and Scorpious seemed to mirror the images used in Maya art to depict the creation story. It begins at sunset when the Milky Way aligns north-south to resemble the Crocodile Tree (*fig. 110*). In Maya art this is a common image and is depicted as an open mouthed crocodile standing on its head with body and tail extending straight up to form the trunk and branches of a tree.[17] An image of the villain, Seven Macaw, is also visible in the sky, represented by the Big Dipper according to the *Popol Vuh*. It appears to be attempting to land in the top of the crocodile tree. Over the next 4 hours or so the Big Dipper begins to move up and out of view symbolizing the Hero Twins subduing Seven Macaw. Once the Big Dipper disappears the creation story begins.

At this point the Milky Way moves into an east-west orientation and seems to form a canoe complete with paddler type figures moving from east to west. The canoe eventually dips below the horizon and into an area of the Milky Way between Orion and Gemini. This scene represents the Maize God becoming immersed in the primordial sea of creation. Several examples of Maya art work depict the paddlers and Itzamna in a long canoe that is shaped like a crocodile and seems to be sinking headfirst into the depths. Around 4:00 A.M. Schele noted that the Milky Way begins the final stages of a rotation back into a north-south position in the sky. As it does this, it takes on the form of the World Tree, a different image from the crocodile tree. It then appears to raise up the other con-

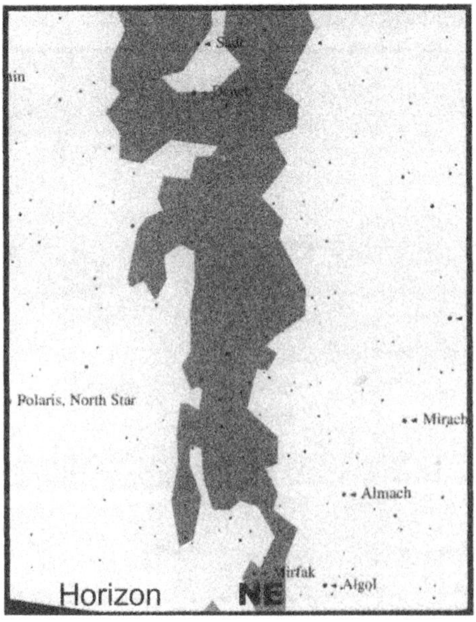

*Figure 110*
Recreation of Schele's idea using the Starry Night computer chart. The Milky Way in position as the Crocodile Tree. Polaris is on the left middle portion of the picture with the Big Dipper in the upper right hand corner representing the vain Seven Macaw. (8:47 p.m.; August 13, A.D. 690)

ORION

*Figure 111*
The Milky Way in its final position near the dawn as it the World Tree. Note the constellation of Orion is located to the upper right near the zenith position in the sky which depicts the raising of the sky.

stellations. By dawn the constellation of Orion, containing patterns for both the turtle's back and the three stones of the hearth, is positioned directly to the east of the Milky Way where it has been raised to its zenith in the sky (*fig. 111*). And thus the Maize god has emerged, centered the sky with the stones of the triangle, and created the world. As the Maize god is reborn, his umbilical cord stretches across the sky on the ecliptic which will become the pathway of his sons: the sun, moon, and the planet Venus. On Feb 5 the story is repeated, only in reverse. This movement of the stars is believed to relate the story of the Maize god spreading the maize seeds of the Pleiades down to the earth to be planted, thus completing the process of creation.[19]

Is it really possible that the Maya were able to witness the details of this story unfolding in the night sky? It is not only possible, but highly likely since it is well known that the Maya were excellent and attentive astronomers. In fact, their meticulous documentation of the cycles of Venus and of the moon has gained the awe and respect of those who have studied their culture. For this reason, it does not seem unreasonable to assume that the Maya were well aware of the movement of the stars as seen by Linda Schele on her modern computerized star charts.

Anthony Aveni, an expert in the field of archaeoastronomy, has studied ancient civilizations throughout the Americas for over 30 years. He has found tangible evidence of the importance of astronomical observation among Native Americans at many major sites. Over the years, the scientific approach he and his colleagues have used has resulted in the acceptance of archaeoastronomy by mainstream archaeology as a respected and complementary discipline.[20] From this relatively new field of study we know that the Maya culture focused much attention on the varying positions of the sun, moon, and the planet Venus. They not only developed techniques for predicting the eclipses of the sun and moon, but they also understood the 583.95 day cycle of Venus and its role as both a morning and evening star. They were concerned with the movement of the constellations especially those which followed the path of the ecliptic (the path of the sun). These included Orion, the Pleiades, Scorpious and Gemini as well as the planets Mars, Jupiter and Saturn.[21]

Through our understanding of the Maya calendar, as well as from the evidence of their rituals, we know that they were very much aware of the cycles of nature. For the Maya, everything was part of a great cycle and there were many cycles within cycles. They even viewed time as a cycle. As Freidel put it, "To the Maya time only *appears* to move in a straight line. The Creation date is a point on ever larger circles within circles within circles of time."[22] In this way, time, for the Maya, resembled the concentric circles or spirals pecked into the rock at San Lorenzo and Piedras Negras. Day and night were part of a daily cycle, but the monthly changes in the moon, and the seasonal changes in the movement of the sun across the horizon from the summer to the winter solstice were also recognized. They identified multiple year cycles such as the 52 year cycle, the 256 year cycle and the 5128 year cycle, the current version of which began on August 13, 3114 B.C. and ends on December 22, A.D. 2012. It is believed that some of these cycles were used to assist the Maya in planning agricultural activities, but others seem to be related only to spiritual and ceremonial considerations and to their understanding of the nature and history of the cosmos. This understanding formed the basis of their political and ceremonial lives and greatly influenced their architecture.[23]

## Astronomy and Architecture

In a 1993 article, Aveni and Hotaling conceded that, "Major sky events likely played a role in the architectural planning of Mayan ceremonial centers."[24] In fact, the field of archaeoastronomy has revealed the presence of astronomical relationships in the design of many ancient sites not only in Mesoamerica, but in North and South America as well. Hartung identified three types of astronomical alignments used with architecture. First were those that were made in conjunction with an element of nature such as a mountain top, a large rock, or sightings from the mouth of a cave. The pecked cross located on a mountain near Teotihuacan is an example of this type of alignment. As mentioned earlier, it was used to mark the heliacal rising of the Pleiades constellation which heralded one of the solar zenith days. A second relationship involves the use of sculptural or other manmade elements such as stelae as a line of sight to view particular astronomical events.[25] At the 13th century Native American mound site of Cahokia in eastern Illinois, archaeologists discovered what some call a wooden Stonehenge. Postholes were found at the site indicating that large wooden poles had been arranged in a circle 400 feet in diameter. The poles were subsequently discovered to have been placed to mark the solstices and equinox as well as various planetary and star risings.[26] (See *fig. 112.*) At the Maya site of Copan the positions of several of the stelae align to astronomical points which were referred to on the monuments themselves.

The third type of astronomical architecture involved a deliberate city-wide design of buildings. This type may involve not only the position of a single building, but also the relationship between a number of buildings. The layout may be used as a means of viewing certain astronomical events or as a symbolic reproduction of important star patterns. For example, a group of buildings may be arranged so that an individual could stand at a point on one building and view a particular point in the sky from a line of sight created by one or two adjacent buildings.[27] Little has reported that mounds at the early 1st century A.D. ceremonial site of Pinson, TN were aligned to each other to allow for accurate astronomical observations similar to those at Cahokia. Interestingly, Native Americans throughout the Northern hemisphere seem to have been concerned with the same astronomical events as their counterparts in Central and South America.[28] In Maya architecture the doorways of buildings were often made to accomodate these observations. In particular, the central doorways of temples and other buildings were primarily involved.[29] In his analysis, John

*Figure 112*
Illustration of Woodhenge at Cahokia in eastern Illinois as it was used to make astronomical sightings. The summer solstice sunrise is seen in this depiction. The large mound in the background is Monk's Mound, the largest mound in the U.S. at 100 feet tall. Reprinted from *People of the Web* (1990).; drawing by William Iseminger.

Carlson determined that the Temple of the Sun in Palenque was built to face the winter solstice sunrise while the doorway to the Temple of the Foliated Cross aligns to allow sighting of the setting position of the star Capella. From the doorway of the Temple of the Cross on the summer solstice the sun can be viewed setting over The Temple of Inscriptions which is the burial place of the great Palenque ruler, Pacal.[30] Even more intriguing, as we shall see, is the discovery that, at some sites, multiple buildings were arranged in a particular pattern in order to imitate the positions of various constellations.

# Maya Architecture and The Creation Story

### Examples of the Triangular Creation Hearth

Matthew Looper and others believe that the constellations involved in the creation story of the *Popol Vuh* are reflected in the layout of

*Figure 113 & 114* Two views of sculpture Zoomorph B from Quirigua which along with Stelae A and C were erected in a triangular formation to replicate the cosmic hearth. Reprinted from: Spinden, *A Study of Maya Art*, 1913.

many Maya sites. For example, at Quirigua he has noted that Stela C, upon which is written the creation story, was strategically aligned with another stela and a zoomorph sculpture to form a cosmic hearth triangle. (See *fig. 113 & 114.*) Each of the three monuments contains drawings with characteristics that link it to one of the three stone thrones of the creation story. For example, according to its dedication date, the zoomorph sculpture, which resembles the cosmic monster design often associated with Itzamna, was the third stone to be placed. As stated in the creation story, this was the last of the stones placed on the earth. The zoomorph sculpture is located at the apex of the triangle and, in imitation of Alnitak in the constellation of Orion, is the monument closest to the north and west. Thus, these three monuments appear to have been deliberately placed to recreate the creation hearth. Looper believed this arrangement served as an architectural spiritual center and as a way for the ruler who commissioned it to associate himself with the power of the ancestor gods.

Even more impressive is Looper's hypothesis that the three temples in the Cross grouping at Palenque (*fig. 115*) were built and arranged to represent the creation hearth. First of all, the three temples are correctly oriented so that they assume the same directions as in the

*Figure 115*
The three temples in the Cross grouping at Palenque. From Corel Galery.

star pattern. Following that pattern, it means that the Temple of the Cross, which sits on the highest and northernmost mound, was deliberated located to represent the water throne placed by Itzamna in the creation story. In the sky, the water throne/stone, represented by the star Alnitak in the Belt of Orion, is located opposite of the other two stars/thrones and forms the apex of the triangle. Similarly, the Temple of the Cross forms the apex of the three temples in the grouping. Decipherment of the many inscriptions in the Temple of the Cross have indeed confirmed that it was dedicated to GI (God One) who is considered to be the Palenque version of Itzamna. The Temple of the Foliated Cross, located southeast of the Temple of the Cross, is decorated with snake icons and is also known to have been dedicated to GII or God K, the serpent footed god. This temple represents the star Rigel and the snake throne. And falling right in line with the creation story star pattern is the Temple of the Sun located due west of the Temple of the Foliated Cross. Completing the pattern, amazingly, this temple was dedicated to the jaguar sun god, GIII. It therefore appears to have been placed in its present location to represent the jaguar throne and the star Saiph.[31]

Although not mentioned by Looper, it is also interesting to note that directly to the west of the Cross temple group is a small stream running northward which serves to separate this group from the other major temples and palaces. In *The Orion Mystery*, Bauval and Gilbert were able to show that the pyramids of Giza were aligned in such a way as to mirror the three stars in the belt of Orion. They were astonished to further discover that the Nile, on its northern route to the Mediterranean just to the east of the pyramids, also lined up perfectly with the Milky Way.[32] (See *fig. 116.*) If the temples in the Cross group at Palenque have been built to represent the creation triangle, was the stream meant to represent the Milky Way? It certainly appears that way since it is aligned in the correct position in relation to the temples. In Linda Schele's astronomical replay of the creation story, the constellation of Orion and the three stars of the triangular hearth ended up located directly east of the Milky Way which was oriented on a north/south axis. This matches the temple group placement at Palenque. Coincidence? Possibly, but not likely. The hieroglyphic inscriptions not only identify these temples with the correct gods, but also contain a great deal of information about the creation story. In addition, it is obvious from their art, rituals, and texts that the ability to replay the creation story and thus to connect themselves to the ancestor gods was very important to the rulers of Palenque and other Maya sites.

*Figure 116*
The three great pyramids at Giza which are aligned like the three stars in the belt of Orion. For the Maya, these same three stars form a crack in the turtle's back through whih the Maize-god emerged. A triangular "creation hearth" is formed by the three stars. From Corel Gallery.

## The Quincunx Design of the Four Sacred Directions

Freidel noted other aspects of ancient Maya city plans that seemed to relate to the creation myth. For example, many cities are laid out with four pyramids facing into a central plaza. The four sides represent the four directions and the center is the plaza which thus becomes the primordial sea from which the Maize God raised the World Tree and created the sky. Thus, the plaza was a sacred and powerful place. Modern-day Maya residing near Copan follow a related ritual as they prepare for the agricultural year. In the ritual four stones are placed to form the corners of a square around a center stone (see *figure 117*) resulting in an ancient Maya five point design called a quincunx (pronounced, keen-coonsh). The first two stones are placed to correspond with the eastern sunrise and the western sunset positions of the summer solstice. The remaining two corner stones are placed at the eastern sunrise and western sunset positions of the winter solstice.[33] Rafael Girard, who studied the modern Maya of Copan, wrote that the participants believed this ritual reenacted the creation of the world. They further explained to him that this was how the gods did it "at the beginning of the world" by "measuring the space and squaring their measurements." In this way the Maya today continue to make the world "as it was made by the gods the first time."[34]

Gods that measure and square? It sounds like they had some very practical skills. According to Cayce, the Atlanteans were skilled builders and their technological abilities were critical to the building of the pyramids in Egypt.[35] If Cayce's Atlantean immigrants to the Yucatan were perceived by the resident natives as gods, they may be the deities described in the Maya creation story. If so, then perhaps the earthly stone/thrones placed at the time of creation are descriptions of the temples they built. Interestingly, in the Maya creation story the Jaguar throne stone is placed by the paddlers at a location on the earth called House-Five-Sky. Could the five point quincunx design be related to that placement and, if so, could it be referring to a real earthly place? Or perhaps each of the three stone/thrones are references to different earthly locations.

*Figure 117*
The basic quincunx design.

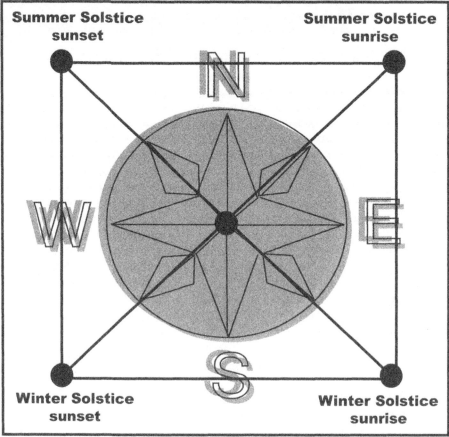

Summer Solstice
sunset

Summer Solstice
sunrise

Winter Solstice
sunset

Winter Solstice
sunrise

## Iltar's First Temple & The Three Stones

Cayce indicated that the first temple built by Iltar in the Yucatan was destroyed "when there were changes in the contours of the land."[36] Earlier we proposed that this could have been referring to a collapsed underground cavern in the the South Group at Piedras Negras. The second temple would then have been moved to higher ground in the Acropolis area. However, Cayce's statement could instead be describing changes to a shoreline as if the first temple was located closer to the Gulf or Caribbean coasts. From evidence uncovered so far it is believed that the Olmec culture was centered in the Gulf Coast area in the Mexican State of Tabasco. This is not far from the place where the Usumacinta River empties into the Gulf of Mexico (*fig. 118*). However, Cayce also hinted at British Honduras (now Belize) as a possible starting place for Iltar.[37] Could Iltar and his group have set up a second stone/throne after migrating inland to a more stable and remote site — a site such as Piedras Negras where they could better store and protect the records?

Another point mentioned by Cayce is that the Atlantean groups eventually left the Yucatan area gradually migrating into North

*Figure 118*

Map of Maya area showing Piedras Negras and the Usumacinta River in relation to the Olmec settlements on the Gulf Coast. Adapted from Stirling (1943) and Morley (1937).

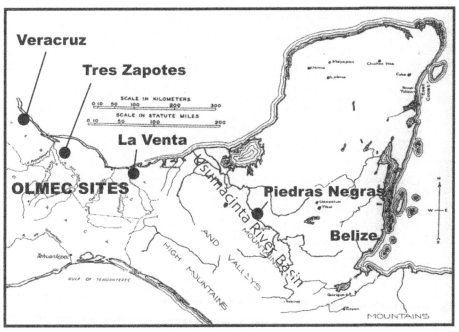

America. This could mean that the third stone throne represents a location in North America reflecting Cayce's story of the movement of the Atlanteans. Given the Maya nonlinear philosophy regarding the cyclic nature of time, the creation story could reflect the Atlanteans' activity within a single site and at the same time their movement over the continent. In the next section we will look at the astronomical evidence for the existence of Cayce's Atlantean immigrants in the architecture of Piedras Negras.

## Architecture and Astronomy at Piedras Negras

Just as the Maya near Copan continue to create the quincunx form in their fields, Maya shaman of today use spider stones which contain the 8 cardinal and intercardinal directions to map out the four corners within which they can open a portal to the spiritual world. It is also known that the ancient Maya performed similar rituals. Once a portal was opened, it was reused generation after generation. It is believed that the Maya built new ceremonial structures over older ones for this reason. In some instances, as discovered by BYU in the Acropolis at Piedras Negras, the Maya found it necessary to totally remove the previous structure which must have been a very time-consuming undertaking.[38] What a contrast to our modern world where we think nothing of abandoning older buildings for new ones built on the outskirts of town. For us the time and monetary costs of demolition are too high, but not for the Maya. A location became increasingly sacred for the Maya over time and especially after many centuries of ceremonial use. For this reason, it seems logical to assume that if the ancient Atlanteans did indeed settle and deposit their records at Piedras Negras sometime around 10,000 B.C., it is very likely that the current ceremonial center is built over a sacred space used in the early days.

As mentioned previously, Satterthwaite believed that the earliest versions of the main buildings at Piedras Negras were all constructed around the same time. He acknowledged that they were updated periodically, but, among the major structures he excavated in all three of the main subareas, he reported ceramic (pottery) evidence indicating a common start date which he estimated to be around A.D. 435.[39] BYU identified even older settlements primarily from dating ceramic deposits uncovered by test sampling at much deeper levels than Penn had reached. But, significantly, BYU discovered that underneath some structures, such as in the Acropolis and the West Group Plaza, there were signs of renovation that had occurred in two shifts. The last of these seemed very sudden and involved the whole site. BYU called this the Great Shift and indicated that it was not in line with what was being done at other Maya sites. The first shift they believed happened during the Early Classic period when the site was transforming itself from a small village to a large city. The second occurred during the Classic period and was marked by evidence of burning and an almost total removal of previous structures. What seemed strange to BYU, however, was that the ceramic evidence did not mirror these dramatic shifts and seemed to proceed as would be expected for a Maya site. They also did not find evidence to support the theory that these changes were the result of warfare since they were obviously deliberate and complete.[40]

If scientific analysis of the site is correct, then the structures remaining at Piedras Negras are definitely not the ones used by Iltar or the Atlanteans. Buildings erected by that group would have been removed long ago as hinted at in the Cayce readings. According to Cayce, the Atlanteans deliberately set about removing evidence of their settlements and burials primarily through cremation. It's possible that this tradition remained at Piedras Negras and contributed to its tendency to burn and remove old structures. So, what we are looking for at Piedras Negras primarily is the influence of the ancient Atlanteans on the Classic era Maya. Fortunately, Piedras Negras is considered to be a conservative site which was reluctant to change and may be more likely to have retained older, possibly Atlantean inspired, traditions. Since the creation story occurs at a very ancient date and may be based on the actions of the Atlantean immigrants, it is important to take note of the traditions and customs at Piedras Negras related to it. Astronomy provides us with just that opportunity. Maya cosmology is closely connected to the sun, moon, stars and planets and includes dates that may be contemporary with the Atlantean migrations. Perhaps we can to look at Piedras Negras' relationship to the skies for clues to the past. For example, does the complex have structures that appear to be aligned to resemble any of the constellations, particularly Orion and the Milky Way? Is there any evidence for quincunx or cosmic hearth type groupings? Amazingly, as will be shown, the answer to all of these is yes!

## Orion and the Milky Way

Despite the fact that we cannot expect to find the actual buildings constructed by Iltar's group, it is still likely that later residents of the site remained committed to the original settlement ceremonial sites. Locations within the ceremonial center which were already considered to be sacred probably continued to be used for religious ritual. The center at Piedras Negras may have had special significance since it was located on the eastern bank of a major river which could have served as an earthly representation of the Milky Way. Certain structures within the complex may also have been built to mirror the position of the stars in the Belt of Orion. This is especially noteworthy since during the 1990s, Bauval and Gilbert made a similar discovery in Egypt. Their research revealed that the Nile was correctly oriented in relation to the three great pyramids of Giza to represent the Milky Way. The three main pyramids at Giza, located on the western bank of the Nile, were found to line up in relation to each other in a manner identical to the alignment of the three stars in the Belt of Orion (*fig. 119*).[41] One of the so-called ventilation shafts in the King's Chamber of the Great Pyramid was reported to to be aligned to the Belt of Orion. As will be discussed later, Orion symbolized the important god, Osiris, to the ancient Egyptians.[42] In addition, Bauval and Gilbert found that the face of the Sphinx is oriented to view the heliacal rising of the various constellations of the zodiac. Since the Sphinx has the body of a lion, they theorized that it would have been built at a time when it would align with that particular constellation. To their

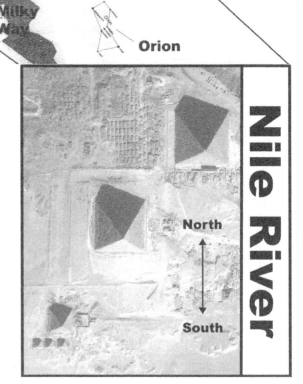

*Figure 119*
Drawing of the three Great Pyramids of Giza in relation to the Nile reflecting the positions of the three stars in the belt of Orion and the Milky Way.

According to Bauval & Gilbert and Bauval & Hancock, in 10,500 B.C. the Belt of Orion was at its lowest point in its movement up and down the meridian in the 26,000 year precession of the equinox. The three pyramids were built to mimic this arrangement. The Nile River represents the Milky Way.

surprise, the heliacal rising of Leo, which occurs over a 2,000 year period only every 26,000 years, was in the correct position around 10,500 B.C. Of course, this is the period which coincides with Cayce's Atlantean migrations to Egypt and Yucatan. Bauval and Gilbert concluded that this was no accident and may be a signpost for the importance of Giza as the location of the Hall of Records. At the very least, it indicates the presence of a very technologically advanced civilization.[43]

It seems possible that a similar argument could be made for Piedras Negras' location on the Usumacinta. The Usumacinta river resembles the Nile in Egypt in that it begins in the south and empties in the north. The ceremonial center at Piedras Negras is located on the eastern banks of the river just as the constellation of Orion is located directly east of the Milky Way. This is significant since the star movements of the Maya creation story, like the cosmology of ancient Egypt, focus on Orion.

There are four groupings in the ceremonial center of Piedras Negras where a triad of structures have been placed in a straight line (with one offset) like the stars in the Belt of Orion. However, the current structures do not line up quite as closely as the Pyramids at Giza. For example, as shown in *figure 120*, in the Acropolis, Pyramids J-3, J-4, along with Court 1 are built side by side with one structure, J-3, slightly off center. The other three examples occur in the South Group among Pyramids R-4, R-5, and R-16 as well as Pyramids R-1, R-10, and R-9. Pyramids R-2, 3, and 4 also seem to closely resemble Orion. (See *fig. 121.*) Another possibility is the R-3/R-4 platform, the R-11 ballcourt structure and Pyramid O-12. This one is oriented the most correctly to the river to simulate the relationship between the Milky Way and Orion's Belt as it was seen to rise in the east at Piedras Negras on August 13, 3114 B.C. Since we know that these structures may not be oriented as the oldest structures were, this could account for the lack of a more exact alignment. However, the tendency of the Piedras Negras builders to create so many of these type of triad alignments is worth noting especially since the river orientation and flow direction so closely matches that of the Nile.

## Evidence for the Five Point Quincunx Design

Piedras Negras has an interesting relationship to the quincunx symbol. In 1940 Heinrich Berlin reported the discovery of what he called Emblem Glyphs within the hieroglyphic inscriptions of the Classic Maya. These Emblem Glyphs contained signs that represented the primary patron gods of a city and/or the names of the ruling dynasties. He identified ten different city glyphs and Piedras Negras' was one of these.

**Figure 120**
Close up of the Piedras Negras Acropolis and West Group Plaza showing Pyramids J-3, J-4, and Court 1 as reflecting the positions of the three stars in the belt of Orion. Reprinted from the Parris map courtesy of the University of Pennsylvania Museum Archives.

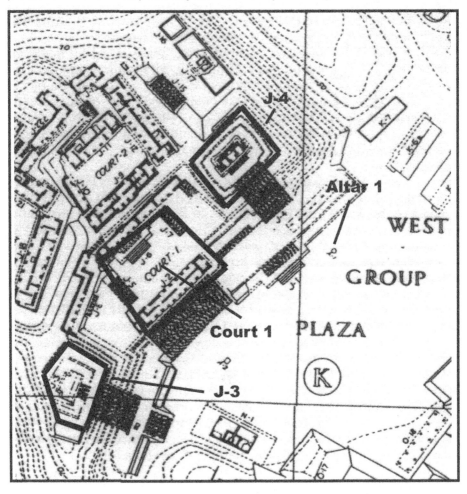

*Figure 121*

Closeup of the the Piedras Negras South Group showing two different triad building arrangments that may reflect the three stars in the belt of Orion. a). Pyramids R-4, R-5, and R-16. b). The R-4, R-3, and R-2 alignment strongly resembles Orion. Reprinted from the Parris map courtesy of the University of Pennsylvania Museum Archives.

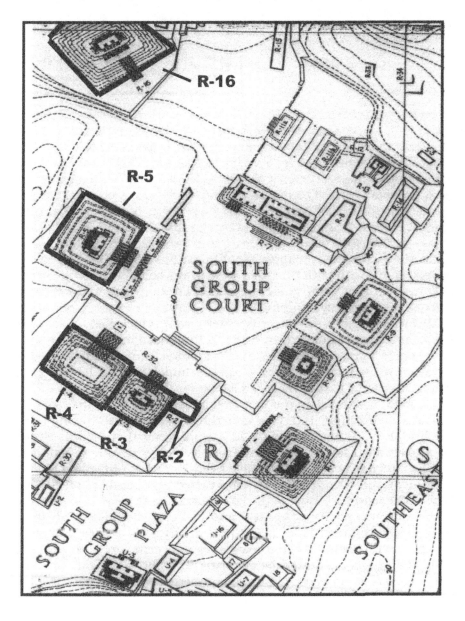

*Figure 122*
The Emblem Glyph used by the Classic era Maya to denote the city of Piedras Negras. Note Quincunx symbol in lower right hand corner. From Berlin.

Although the Emblem Glyph for a particular city had a consistent structure, it could vary somewhat depending on the location where it was found and its relationship to the text.[44] What is particularly interesting is that the Emblem Glyph for Piedras Negras (*fig. 122*) always included the quincunx design.[45] Often it also included a symbol for the turtleshell which probably related to the most prominent of its two ruling dynasties, the Turtleshells.[46] As mentioned earlier, it is curious that a ruling family of Piedras Negras had the name Turtleshell since it is the sacred symbol for the place where the Maize god/Itzamna emerged during his resurrection at the last creation. What this means is that Piedras Negras was associated with both the three stars in the belt of Orion (the turtle's back) and the five point quincunx which are both important creation symbols. It is certainly tempting to look at these as possible connections to a distant past at Piedras Negras which perhaps included Cayce's Iltar as a founding ancestor. It also leads to the question of whether these two symbols mirror something in the architectural design at Piedras Negras. If so, it must have some special importance to have become such a consistent part of the city's Emblem Glyph.

Also of interest is the fact that Proskouriakoff stated that the quincunx symbol (*fig. 123*) was sometimes used in inscriptions to denote burials.[47] Although this could simply mean that Piedras Negras was a place associated with mortuary activities, it does not seem to be the case. Relatively few burials have been identified at Piedras Negras. Penn uncovered 10 and BYU has since raised that number only to 49 as of the 1999 season.[48] Most of the BYU burials were located in two cemeteries, one behind Pyramids R-3 and R-4 and one located in the U sector.[49] This number is far below that of other Maya sites and is not consistent with Piedras Negras being a regional cemetery or funeral site. Could the quincunx design be referring to some other sort of burial such as the Hall of Records? Could a quincunx perhaps mark the spot of the location of the records? In order to attempt to answer these questions, we will look at the evidence for this pattern in the architectural design of the Piedras Negras ceremonial complex.

As discussed earlier, there is evidence at Piedras Negras of older pre-Maya occupation. For example, the spiral petroglyphs and the Inscribed Cliff were specifically identified by Satterthwaite as evidence of an earlier, more primitive settlement.[50] In addition, these features do not fit into the overall scheme of the structural portion of the site. BYU proposed that the renovations of the Great Shift, which created the present Acropolis, were part of an overall plan to provide the greatest emphasis to the pageantry of the ruler's ceremonial activities. Each of the three subareas, the South, East, and West Groups, were carefully connected to create a smooth flow for a ritualistic procession that would rise ever higher in elevation as it moved from the South to the West Groups.[51] Compared to such a sophisticated ceremonial technology, a crudely pecked inscription on a cliff in an area southeast of the center would seem to be out of place or perhaps just out of date. And yet, ceramic remains indicate that the Inscribed Cliff was still in use during the Classic period. The Maya, true to form, continued to honor their sacred heritage. However, for some reason, they did not build their main temple complexes around the cliff.

---

*Figure 123*
Examples of the quincunx symbol in Maya hieroglyphs. Reprinted from: *Carnegie Institution of Washington*, Publication 528, Vol. VII, No. 39, 1942.

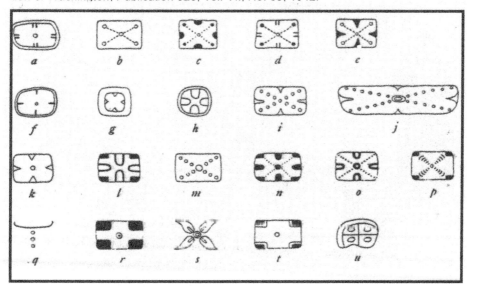

The spiral petroglyphs on the river are another matter. In the first place they are not visible from the city and can only be seen from the river at a location far north of the South Group entry point. In addition, since a piece of it was used as a vault stone in the Acropolis during the Classic period, it appears that its sacred status was either forgotten or abandoned. Or perhaps it was not meant to be a sacred symbol at all, but was instead a cryptic signpost of Atlantean occupation and of the Hall of Records. It is interesting that these two primitive remains are located on opposite corners of the site. The spirals are near the northwest corner facing toward the southwest while the Inscribed Cliff is located in the southeast corner of the site and faces northwest. Combined with the locations of the Sacrificial Rock (southwest corner) and the cave in which the holy man of Burial 6 was found (northeast corner) these features form a square around the site not unlike the quincunx. Nearly in the center of the square, which would represent the most sacred area, are Ballcourt R-11 and Pyramid R-5, both located in the South Group. (See *fig. 125*.) The center is an important part of the quincunx symbol since it is the area in which the Maize god (Itzamna) raised the sky and created the 8 directions.

The R-11 Ballcourt at Piedras Negras is one of only 2 in the ceremonial center. The other ballcourt, K-6, is located near the Acropolis and Altar 1. Of the two, only R-11 contains three round stone markers embedded within the center of the playing field. Satterthwaite described them as being inscribed, but so badly eroded that their designs could no

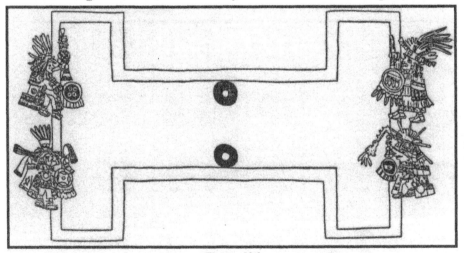

*Figure 124*
Example of the basic "I" shape of the Maya ball courts. Reprinted from Seler, *Collected Works in Mesoamerican Linguistics and Archaeology,* 1902-1923.

*Figure 125*
Map of Piedras Negras ceremonial center showing approximate locations of the spiral petroglphs, the Inscribed Cliff, the Sacrificial Rock and the cave Burial 6 which may form a quincunx layout which would put Ballcourt R-11 in the sacred center spot. Reprinted from the Parris map courtesy of the University of Pennsylvania Museum Archives.

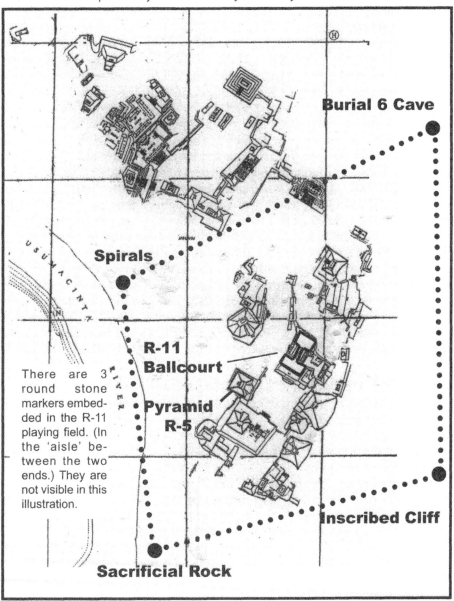

longer be determined.[52] The manner in which these three markers are placed resembles the three stars in the Belt of Orion except that none of them are offset. From information provided by hieroglyphic inscriptions, researchers have determined that the ballcourt was a sacred site. It appears to have been used to replay the creation story and for ritual human sacrifice. The Maya believed that the ballcourts actually opened into the supernatural world. Interestingly, different ballcourts provided access to different locations in this other world. Some ballcourts were believed to provide transport to the time and space of the last creation. As will be described in the next section, much of the precreation activity described in the *Popol Vuh* occurred among ballplayers on a ballcourt.

Ballcourts were usually built in an "**I**" shape and thus have four corners as in the quincunx. The turtleshell from which the Maize god emerged also is depicted with four corners and it is believed that the Maya built ballcourts with three marker stones to represent the crack in the shell. This would also provide support for the idea that these markers represented the three stars of Orion. According to hieroglyphic inscriptions, the ancient Maya word for ballcourt means "grave" to the modern Quiche Maya and "chasm" or "abyss" to the Yucatec Maya.[53] Could this be another clue to the location of an underground Hall of Records? Penn excavated R-11 during the 1931 and 1932 seasons and did not report any underground chambers. However, their main concern seemed to be uncovering the surrounding structures and determining how deeply the markers were embedded in the court. They were not looking for sublevel structures or chambers.[54] BYU has not reported any excavations in the R-11 Ballcourt, but did spend time studying the nearby R-13 sweatbath which they dated to the Early Classic period.[55]

## Pyramid R-5 and the Orion/Creation Date Connection

A computer star analysis of alignments related to the other centrally located (within the quincunx) structure, Pyramid R-5, using the third edition of the Parris map of Piedras Negras, revealed some very significant correlations. (The program used was the Starry Night Deluxe version with LiveSky®.)

First of all, Pyramid R-5 is aligned so that a person standing on the central stairway could sight Orion rising in the eastern sky at 12:06 A.M. on August 14, 3114 B.C. On this date, the three stars in the Belt of Orion rise one on top of the other in a vertical column above the space between Pyramids R-9 and R-10. (See *figures 126, 127, & 128.*) In addition, the winter solstice sunrise, which occurred around January 13 during the year 3114 B.C., could have been viewed from the same point between these two pyramids. (Although the date of the solstices vary

*Figure 126*

Map of the South Group at Piedras Negras showing a few of the alignments our computer star analysis uncovered. Alignment **A** from Pyramid R-5 sighting between Pyramids R-9 and R-10 showed the vertical rise of Orion's belt at 12:06 a.m. on August 14, 3114 B.C. Alignment **B** from Pyramid R-5 is the equinox sunrise. Alignment **C** from R-5 through the center ballcourt is the summer solstice sunrise. Alignment **D** from Pyramid R-10 across the side of the top of Pyramid R-4 will show the setting of Orion's Belt at 4:31 a.m. on December 22, 2012. The alignments at Piedras Negras showing the rise of Orion on August 14, 3114 B.C. and its setting on December 22, 2012 may well be a key to understanding the beginning and end of this age.

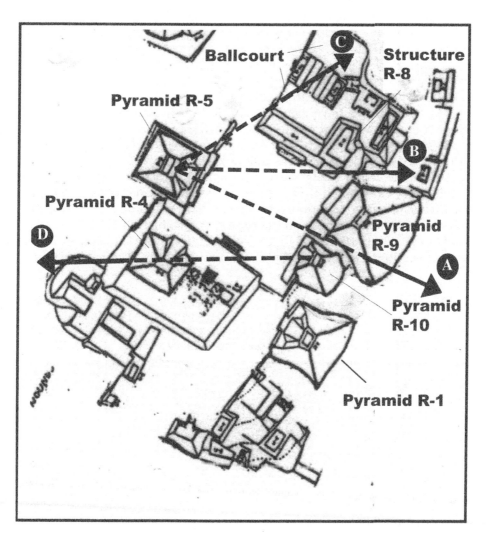

somewhat over time, the viewing location does not and would still be accurate today). The equinox sunrise also occurs in the space between Pyramid R-9 and Structure R-8. And finally, from Pyramid R-5 the summer solstice sunrise appears on a line to the northeast that crosses over the southernmost marker in the R-11 Ballcourt. (See *fig. 126*.)

However, an even more astounding correlation will occur on December 22, A.D. 2012 (the end of the current Maya era) involving different, yet nearby, structures. At 4:31 A.M. on this date, Orion is one of the last visible constellations in the sky and can be seen to set on the western horizon. From the center of the staircase of Pyramid R-10, this will be observed to occur over the top of Pyramid R-4. (See *figures 129 & 130*.) At sunrise the last visible star in the sky will be Sirius located on the western horizon. This means that, at the end of the Maya era, Orion will have completed almost a 180 degree flip in its orientation in the sky. In A.D. 2012, Alnitak, one of the outer stars in the belt, is the last to set, while in 3114 B.C. it was the last to rise.

So what we have are monuments in the South Group that are aligned to astronomical events which symbolize the "birth" ( the rising in 3114 B.C.) and "death" (A.D. 2012 setting) of both Orion and the current 5,128 year Maya era. It is especially notable that Orion, the constellation which depicts the emergence of Itzamna, the Maize god, can be seen emerging from the horizon to the east on the date identified as the last creation. Itzamna, like Cayce's Iltar, was said to have paddled his way to Mesoamerica from the east. It is also interesting that the last star in the Belt to rise in 3114 B.C. is Alnitak which has been identified as representing Itzamna and the third and last stone/throne to be placed

---

*Figure 127*
12:06 a.m., August 14, 3114 B.C. Sighting from the top of Pyramid R-4 at Piedras Negras between Pyramid R-9 (on left) and Pyramid R-10 (center), the Belt of Orion rose straight up from the horizion. The Milky Way appears to be emerging directly out of Pyramid R-4 (due East). Note: Pyramids are not to scale - representations only.

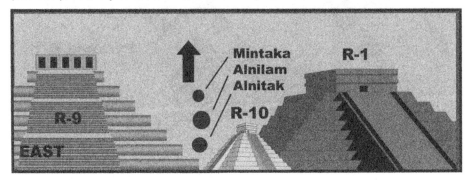

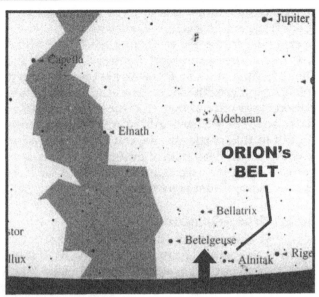

*Figure 128*
Computer star program printout of eastern horizon (bottom) at Piedras Negras on August 14, 3114 B.C. at 12:06 a.m. Note the Milky Way and how Orion's Belt rises straight up.

*Figure 129*
Orion will set in the western sky at 4:31 A.M. on December 22, 2012 as seen from Pyramid R-10. Orion will appear to set directly above Pyramid R-4.

Figure 130
Computer star printout of Orion setting due West on 12/22,2012.

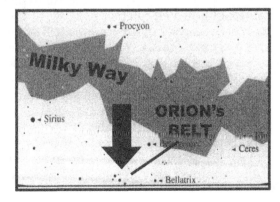

in the creation story. It is also the apex of the cosmic triangle. And, even more amazing, is that in A.D. 2012, on the morning the current era or cycle ends, Orion will be among the last stars to set in the western sky just as the rising sun blots them out. On this date, Alnitak is the last of the three belt stars to set. Was the South group designed deliberately to take advantage of these astronomical events? If yes, how would the Classic period Maya have known that these important Orion events occurred on dates so far in the past and future? Were Ballcourt R-11 and Pyramid R-5 built in this particular area in order to represent the sacred center of a complex-wide quincunx design? If not, it is certainly an interesting coincidence that astronomical events of such importance to the Maya can be viewed from structures in this particular location.

### South Group Quincunx?

It also appears that the South Group Court may have been set up in a deliberate quincunx pattern. It is the only group in the city center that contains a square shaped plaza totally surrounded by large structures. In his analysis and comparison of the architectural patterns among various Maya cities, Andrews noted that most sites contain at least one temple grouping similar to the South Group at Piedras Negras. These temple groups usually consist of three temples facing each other in a U-shape with one side open. At Piedras Negras and Copan the open side is occupied by another nontemple structure.[56] In order to be a true quincunx, the corners of the South Group Plaza would need to point to the intercardinal directions since they are normally set to relate to the solstices. The solstice sunrises and sunsets do not occur exactly on the intercardinal directions, but do approximate them. For example, the winter solstice sunset occurs south of west, while the summer solstice sunset occurs north of west. As it turns out, the points at the corners of the South Group Court, if squared off, are aligned almost exactly to the cardinal directions. This means that the pyramids and ballcourt surrounding it are all aligned roughly to the intercardinal directions. We have seen already that Pyramids R-5 and R-10 have solstice alignments and there are others. Satterthwaite reported that Pyramids R-3 and R-4, which are located on the southwest side of the South Group Court, face 30 degrees east of north.[57] Our computer calculations using the third edition of the Parris map show that all of the structures surrounding the South Group Court are oriented 30 degrees off the cardinal directions. Pyramid R-9 is aligned to face the solstice and equinox sunsets. Standing on top of its central stairway, an individual would view the winter solstice sunset near the north corner of Pyramid R-5, the equinox sunset over the space between Pyramid R-5 and the R-4/R-3 base, and the summer solstice sunset over the corner of the R-3 temple. Although these calculations may not be exact and should be verified in the field, they do lend support to the possibility that the South Group is a deliberate quincunx design.

Since we are proposing that the quincunx design could mark the spot of the location of the Hall of Records, it is important to know what archaeology has revealed about the South Group Court. Is there anything under the center area of the court? It does not appear that Penn excavated in the court area itself, but, during the 1997 season, BYU uncovered both Protoclassic and Preclassic deposits there. These are among the oldest dated finds at the site and they link Piedras Negras to a period that goes back as far as 1000 B.C.[58] Pyramid R-5, which has been identified as the burial place of Ruler 1, was excavated by both Penn and BYU. Penn cleared the temple on top during the 1933 season and discovered an almost life size stucco head with traces of red paint under the temple floor.[59] BYU dug a vertical shaft from its top level down to its fourth sublevel in 1999, but had to leave before completing their exploration. They also dug into the base of the pyramid and reported finding "a well preserved cache, a fragmentary human burial, and, in front of the platform, deep deposits of early date." They don't elaborate further. Drawings of the cache reveal various eccentric shaped worked stones, shells, and two carved pieces, probably jade, incised with similar grotesque faces in the Maya style.[60] It therefore appears that nothing out of the ordinary has turned up within the center of the plaza, but one reason is that most of the effort has been directed toward the structures around the perimeter.

Besides having characteristics of the quincunx design, the South Group Court is also unusual in that it has two pyramid temples on its southeast side and two on its southwest side. As stated earlier, the pyramids opposite Pyramid R-5 may have been placed to serve as a means of sighting the rising of Orion and the solstice sunrise. The northwest side of the court contains only one pyramid temple while the northeast side is filled with a base structure that contains one of only two ballcourts (R-11) in the ceremonial center. This means the South Group Court is surrounded by five pyramids which also brings to mind the creation story placement of the first stone at House-Five-Sky. If the South Group was designed to resemble House Five Sky then perhaps the theory that the Hall of Records was first placed in the South Group is correct.

Andrews reported that at several Maya cities there is a grouping he called "a special astronomical assemblage" in which a pyramid is placed on the west side of the group facing three temple-like structures to its east. He stated that only the one at Uaxactun has been shown to be of definite astronomical use (*fig. 131*). From the vantage point of the western pyramid, the sun could be seem to rise over the tops of the three eastern temples during the summer and winter solstices and the equinoxes.[61] At Piedras Negras this pattern may have occurred with Pyramid R-5 facing east toward Pyramids R-9, and R-10 which are located side by side across the plaza. The third temple would be Pyramid R-1 which is located in the southern corridor leading into the South Group Court. This temple is not part of the plaza square, but is located in line with R-9 and R-10. Its unusual location puzzled both Satterthwaite and Morley. Using Parris' map we could find only one computer star correlation to support Pyramid R-1 being used to align to the solstice positions as at Uaxactun. From the center of the stairway of Pyramid R-4 (not R-5) the summer solstice sunrise would appear near the northeastern corner of Pyramid R-1. Perhaps R-1 aligns to some other astronomical event which would certainly explain its unusual placement.

## Acropolis Quincunx?

Although the East and West Groups both have Plazas, neither of them take on a true square shape. The West Plaza near the Acropolis is actually more of a rectangle. There are square shaped structures in the

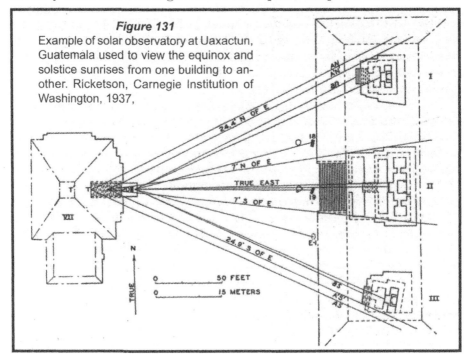

**Figure 131**
Example of solar observatory at Uaxactun, Guatemala used to view the equinox and solstice sunrises from one building to another. Ricketson, Carnegie Institution of Washington, 1937,

West Group, but unlike the South Group, they are not part of the public area. The only square shapes are the different courts and rooms within the Acropolis building complex itself. Interestingly, as in the South Group the corners of these squares are pointed in the cardinal directions. Could it be that the sacred portals at the center of these newer quincunx de-signed structures became less a place for public access and more of a special holy place accessed only by the ruler and nobility? As discussed previously, this seems to be exactly what happened over time with the pyramid/temple structures. Satterthwaite called this "a tendency to-ward priestly exclusivity."[62] In Cayce's story this would probably equate to an increasing tendency toward self indulgence as the influences of the Sons of Balial took greater hold of the rulers and the people. Some archaeologists have speculated that the demise of the great Maya cities occurred as a result of the decadence of the rulers and a turning away or even a revolt of the common people. BYU noted that at Piedras Negras the sweatbaths seemed to have evolved from relatively single occupancy to group occupancy. They theorized that one of the reasons could be that group sex became a part of the sweatbath experience as depicted on the art work on some Maya vases.[63]

So what we have is several possible quincunx patterns among the architectural layout of Piedras Negras. The largest of the patterns is created by a sacred cave site and petroglyphs, two of which are thought to be among the oldest carvings at the site. Also, the South Group ap-pears to have been designed in a typical Maya quincunx court design. This section of the site contains the oldest of the dated monuments and, from inscriptions so far deciphered, were among the first to be con-structed. Satterthwaite identified Pyramids R-3 and R-4 as the oldest.[64] These two patterns could be the reason for the quincunx symbol show-ing up in the Piedras Negras Emblem Glyph. And, if so, they may signal that the Hall of Records is located in the South Group.

## Evidence for the Cosmic Hearth Pattern

Another architectural grouping to look for at Piedras Negras is the triangle or the cosmic hearth. As mentioned, there are three stars in the constellation of Orion - Alnitak, Saiph, and Rigel - which form the Maya cosmic hearth. This triangle is important since it symbolizes a key concept in the story of the last creation which may, in turn, be a de-scription of Iltar and the Atlantean migration. The First Father, Itzamna (Iltar?), was resurrected through the center of the cosmic hearth. Per-haps the resurrection of Itzamna is also a metaphor for the future dis-covery of the Hall of Records. If so, could this mean that it is located within the center of a triangle? Interestingly, the star that forms the apex of the triangle, Alnitak, is the same star which the Great Pyramid of Giza is said to represent according to Bauval and Gilbert's theory.[65] This is especially significant since Cayce stated that an identical set of Atlantean records is buried near the Great Pyramid and the Sphinx.[66]

There are several structures within the Piedras Negras ceremonial complex that could be connected to form an equilateral triangle resembling the Orion pattern. If we follow the directional positioning of the stars as they appear when Orion reached it zenith on August 13, we would look for a grouping in which the single pyramid/structure that forms the apex is in a northwesterly position. It would then have two structures, one due east and the other southeast of it, creating the base of the triangle. At Piedras Negras this pattern is first met on a small scale by the grouping of three table top altars in front of Pyramid 0-13. In 1997, BYU found what may be a royal burial in front of this building. As described earlier, the occupant was buried with several carved shell and jade pieces and an inscribed pyrite disk containing the portrait of a lord from the lost city of *Hix Wits*. Much digging has been done by both Penn and BYU in this location and, although many caches have been unearthed, so far no chambers have been reported.[67]

The triangle grouping also occurs on a larger scale among three different pyramid/temple combinations. First is a grouping of structures in the South Group. The apex of the triangle (Alnitak) would be represented by Pyramid R-5, the position of the star Saiph would be mirrored by Pyramid R-1, and Pyramid R-9 would serve as the easternmost star of the triangle's base, Rigel. (See *fig. 132.*) In this case, the center of the triangle would be a point within the South Group Plaza. The second grouping would include the Acropolis Pyramid J-3 or J-23 as the apex, Pyramid 0-13 as Rigel and Pyramid R-16 as Saiph. (See bottom of *figure 132.*) This grouping is the most accurate in terms of the directional orientation of the 3114 B.C. rising of Orion, but its center covers a largely unexplored area that is devoid of major structures. In fact, the very center point would occur within a finger shaped ravine that separates a portion of the West and East Group Plazas. Satterthwaite described this ravine as containing "two or three broad platforms, and one low mound or platform, Structure 0-6."[68] He conceded, however, that most likely there were similar structures located up and down the sides of the ravine and extending out toward the river. BYU concentrated on the sweatbaths on the east side of the ravine and the so-called servant's quarters on the west side. No discoveries significant to our search were reported. However, it should be noted that the mysterious petroglyph spirals are located on the river only slightly north of the ravine.

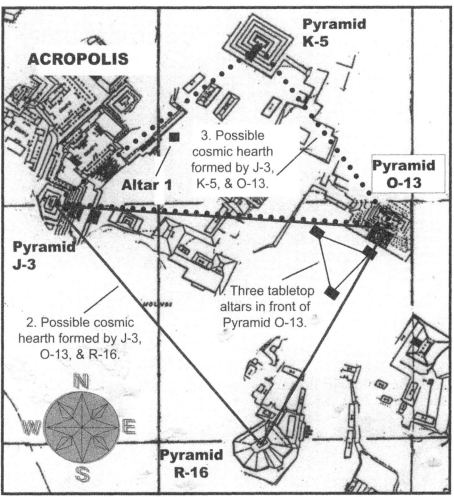

**ACROPOLIS**

**Pyramid K-5**

3. Possible cosmic hearth formed by J-3, K-5, & O-13.

**Altar 1**

**Pyramid O-13**

**Pyramid J-3**

1. Three tabletop altars in front of Pyramid O-13.

2. Possible cosmic hearth formed by J-3, O-13, & R-16.

**Pyramid R-16**

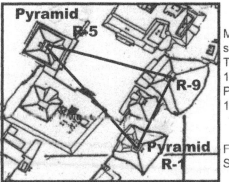

**Pyramid R-5**

**R-9**

**Pyramid R-1**

*Figure 132 (above)*
Map of Piedras Negras showing three possible cosmic hearth triangle patterns. #1: Three table top altars in front of Pyramid 0-13; #2: Acropolis Pyramid J-3, East Group Pyramid 0-13 and South Group Pyramid R-16; #3: Pyramids J-3, K-5 and 0-13.

Figure 133 (left)
Fourth possible cosmic hearth formed by South Group Pyramids R-5, R-1, and R-9.

The third and most interesting triangle is the combination of Pyramids J-3 (Alnitak), K-5 (Rigel), and 0-13 (Saiph). (See top of *fig. 132.*) Since we are concerned with what may be within the triangle, this one is significant because Altar 1 was found within it. In addition, Altar 1 has another triangular link. While looking at pictures of Maya pottery, my (Lora) husband noted that a large number of them were made to rest on tripod legs which form the points of a triangle (*fig. 134*). Aware that we were looking for triangular groupings among the monuments, he asked whether any of the altars at Piedras Negras were supported by three legs. A quick review of the altar descriptions revealed that, of the five major platform altars at Piedras Negras, all had four supports expect for two.

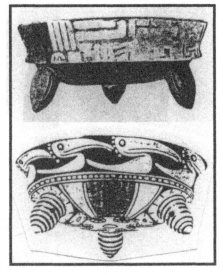

*Figure 134*
Examples of pottery with tripod supports. Reprinted from: Carnegie Institution of Washington, Publication 596, 1952

These two were also the only round table tops, the others being rectangular. And of course, in case you have not already guessed, one of these was Altar 1. There it was again. Was the cache containing the hematite crystals deliberately placed under a tripod altar and within the sacred triangle of these three pyramids because of its special significance as an emblem of the firestone? Could this placement be additional evidence that the Maya priests had retained some Atlantean knowledge and were aware that hematite could be used as a means of communication with the spiritual world?

Since these pieces of hematite may be Cayce's firestone emblem, it seems appropriate for them to have been placed with a cache in a location that represented a portal to the supernatural world. In fact, archaeologists believe that caches in general were used as a means of focusing spiritual energy. In this way an opening could be created that would join the material and spiritual worlds. In many examples of Maya art it is obvious that the cache plate or bowl was to function "as the holy of holies."[69] Often these plates and bowls were used during the vision serpent rituals to collect the blood of the ruler which was then offered along with other objects to the Maize god. The cache found under Altar 1 included not only the hematite stones, but several jade pieces and stingray spines used in bloodletting. It also contained bird bones to represent the upper world and salt and fresh water shells to represent the underworld. Three of these shells were carved with one seeming to represent a male figure and another a female. The third carved shell is a strange design that resembles a crocodile or "cosmic monster" with an open mouth. The male and female characteristics are also seen in the loaf-shaped jadeite piece which may be a phallic symbol. The crescent-shaped circular eccentric may be a moon goddess-female symbol. Caches were to serve as the portal just as the center of the cosmic hearth triangle was the portal through which Itzamna, the First Father, emerged at the last creation. As Linda Schele wrote "People and gods opened the portal in the plate with sacrificial offerings, and through this heart of heaven flowed the miracle of birth and life for both gods and people. The souls of infants came through the Ol portal to find the bodies growing for them in the wombs of Maya women, making them the progeny of the plate of sacrifice at the heart of everything."[70]

# References

1. Proskouriakoff, Tatiana (1960). Historical Implications of a Pattern of Dates at Piedras Negras, Guatemala. *American Antiquity*, Vol. 25, No. 4, pp. 454-475.

2. Coe, Michael (1992) *Breaking the Maya Code*. New York: Thames and Hudson.

3. Freidel, D, Schele, L. and Parker, J. (1993) *Maya Cosmos*. New York: William Morrow.

4. *Breaking the Maya Code*, op. cit.

5. Schele, Linda and Freidel, David (1990) *A Forest of Kings*. New York: William Morrow, pp. 250-251.

6. *Maya Cosmos*, op. cit.

7. Hager, Stansbury (1921) The Zodiacal Temples of Uxmal. *Popular Astronomy*, Vol. 79, 1921, 96.

8. Fernandez, Jose (1992) A Stellar City: Utatlan and Orion. In *Time and Astronomy at the Meeting of Two Worlds, Proceedings of the International Symposium*, 27 April-2 May 1992, 72 and 74.

9. Bauval, Robert and Gilbert, Adrian (1994) The Orion Mystery. New York: Crown Publishers.

10. Sharer, Robert (1994) *The Ancient Maya*. Stanford, California: Stanford University Press, p. 568.

11. Kubler, George (1973) Mythological Ancestries in Classic Maya Inscriptions. In Merle Greene Robertson (Ed.) *Primera Mesa Redonda De Palenque Part II*. (pp. 23-43). Pebble Beach California: Pre-Columbian Art Research.

12. *Maya Cosmos*, op. cit., p. 71.

13. Looper, Matthew (1995) The Three Stones of Maya Creation Mythology at Quirigua. *Mexicon*, XVII, pp. 24-30.

14. *Maya Cosmos*, op. cit., pp. 71-74.

15. *Mexicon*, XVII op. cit.

16. Miller, Mary (1986) *The Murals of Bonampak*. Princeton: University Press.

17. *Maya Cosmos*, op. cit.

18. Tedlock, Dennis (1985) *Popol Vuh*. New York: Simon & Schuster.

19. *Maya Cosmos*, op. cit., p. 112.

20. Aveni, Anthony (1977) Concepts of Positional Astronomy Employed in Ancient Mesoamerican Architecture. In Anthony Aveni (Ed.) *Native American Astronomy*. (pp. 3-19) Austin Texas: University of Texas Press.

21. Vogt, Evon (1997) Zinacanteco Astronomy. *Mexicon XIX*, pp. 110-116.

22. *Maya Cosmos*, op. cit., p. 63.

23. Ibid

24. Aveni, Anthony and Hotaling, Lorren (1993) Monumental Inscriptions and the Observational Basis of Mayan Planetary Astronomy. In Merle Greene Robertson (Ed.) *Eighth Palenque Round Table*. San Francisco: The Pre-Columbian Art Research Institute, p. 364.

25. Hartung, Horst (1979) The Role of Architecture and Planning in Archaeoastronomy. In, *Archaeoastronomy In the Americas*, Ray A. Williamson, (editor) pp. 33-41, Los Altos California: Ballena Press.

26. Little, Greg (1990) *People of the Web*. Memphis, TN: Eagle Wing Books, Inc.

27. *Archaeoastronomy In the Americas,*, op. cit.

28. *People of the Web*. op. cit.

29. *Archaeoastronomy In the Americas,*, op. cit.

30. Carlson, John (1976) Astronomical Investigations and Site Orientation Influences at Palenque. In *The Art, Iconography and Dynastic History of Palenque, Part III*, Merle Greene Robertson (editor), pp. 107-122. Pebble Beach (California): The Robert Louis Stevenson School, PreColumbian Art Research.

31. *Mexicon*, XVII op. cit.

32. *Orion Mystery*, op. cit.

33. *Maya Cosmos*, op. cit.

34. Girard, Rafael (1966) *Los Mayas: Su civilizacion, su historia, sus vinculaciones continentales*. Mexico: Libro Mexicano, p. 33.

35. Reading 378-13.

36. Reading 5750-1.

37. Reading 364-3.

38. *Maya Cosmos*, op. cit., p. 126.

39. Coe, William (1959). *Piedras Negras Archaeology: Artifacts, Caches, and Burials*. Philadelphia: The University Museum, pp. 149-156.

40. Houston, Stephen (2000) Among the River Kings: Archaeological Research at Piedras Negras, Guatemala, 1999. *Mexicon*, XXII, pp.8-17.

41.*The Orion Mystery*, op. cit.

42. Hancock, Graham and Bauval, Robert (1996) *The Message of the Sphinx*. New York: Crown Publishers, p. 243-244.

43. *The Orion Mystery*, op. cit.

44. *Breaking the Maya Code.*, op. cit., p. 177-178.

45. Proskouriakoff, Tatiana (1993) *Maya History*. Austin: University of Texas Press, p. 27.

46. Ibid, p. 102.

47. Ibid, p. 126.

48. *Piedras Negras Archaeology,* op. cit.

49. Houston Stephen, et al (1998) Between Mountains and Sea: Investigations at Piedras Negras, Guatemala, 1998 *Mexicon,* XXI, op. cit. p. 15.

50. Satterthwaite, Linton (1935) The Black Rocks. *University Museum Bulletin,* Vol. 6, No. 1.

51. *Mexicon,* XXII, op. cit.

52. S atterthwaite, Linton (1933) *Piedras Negras Preliminary Papers No. 2, The South Group Ball Court.* University of Pennsylvania Museum.

53. *Maya Cosmos,* op. cit., p. 351-352.

54. *Piedras Negras Preliminary Papers No. 2,* op. cit.

55. Houston, Stephen (1997) On the River of Ruins: Explorations at Piedras Negras, Guatemala, 1997.*Mexicon XX,* p. 20.

56. Andrews, George (1975) *Maya Cities.* Norman Oklahoma: University of Oklahoma Press, pp. 56-59.

57. Morley, S. V. (1938). The Inscriptions of Peten, Vol. III. *Carnegie Institution of Washington, Publication 437,* Washington.

58. *Mexicon, XX,* op. cit. p. 18.

59. Satterthwaite, Linton. Piedras Negras Field Notes, Box 6, Notebook 6, R-1 to R-10 University of Pennsylvania Museum Archives.

60. *Mexicon,* XXII, op. cit., p. 3.

61. *Maya Cities.* op. cit. p. 71.

62. *The University Bulletin,* Vol. 7, No. 4, op. cit., p. 7.

63. *Mexicon, XXII,* op. cit.

64. The Inscriptions of Peten, Vol. III., op. cit.

65. *Orion Mystery,* op. cit.

66. Reading 5750-1.

67. *Mexicon XX,* op. cit.., p. 18.

68. *Inscriptions of Peten, Vol. III,* op. cit., p. 15.

69. *Maya Cosmos,* op. cit., p. 217.

70. Ibid, p. 218.

# Section III

# The Akasha & the Archaeological Record

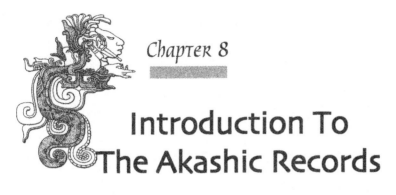

## Chapter 8

# Introduction To
# The Akashic Records

### The Akasha – Recorder
### of Every Thought and Action

Scientists find the records of life in the strata of the Earth, layers upon layers of fossils, bones, and shards telling a tale of ages long ago. This is the record of material life, of matter left behind. But life is more than matter. To fully understand the ancient history of Yucatan we need to journey beyond the physical. The records of non-material life are not in the Earth's strata; they are in the *Akasha*.

The ancient term *Akasha* has its origin in the oldest body of religious literature yet discovered in the world, the *Rig Veda*, circa 1300 B.C., a collection of more than a thousand hymns written in an archaic form of one of the oldest languages on Earth, Sanskrit. The central myth in the *Rig Veda* is the myth of creation, told in several different ways. "Akasha" refers to the essence of life and the records of its activity since creation began. According to Vedic philosophy, life consists of two types: 1) formed or corporeal life (with which we are so familiar) and 2) unformed life. Unformed life possesses no substance whatsoever, yet is the fundamental condition for any corporeal existence and is the container for all matter. Formed and unformed life are comparable to matter and energy. All life is matter and energy. Matter is formed. Energy is unformed. Energy possesses no substance but is the fundamental condition for matter to exist and the container in which all matter is manifest. Matter is equivalent to our bones and tissue; energy, to our minds and *élan vital*, or life force – that spark or spirit that is so obviously missing in dead, decaying matter. Mind and spark affect the whole of life as much as or more than matter, but they do not leave their record in soil strata. Instead, thoughts and actions leave imprints upon an etheric wave, the Akasha.

In order to read the Akasha one has to tune in to its frequency, like tuning a radio to a specific wavelength and converting that wavelength to one that can vibrate a speaker and, in turn, vibrate an ear drum. The Akasha may be a bit more difficult to tune in to than a radio station, but the same basic principle applies. Since the Akasha is essentially energy "records" recorded on formless ether, much like radio waves are in the air around us, one can use the mind to read them, a very deep portion of the mind.

In many of the indigenous tribes along the Amazon River, shamans enter into altered states of consciousness using various plant extracts found in the jungle. In these states they say that they can "see" beyond the normal physical world into the essence behind manifested life. For example, in his book *Cosmic Serpent*, Jeremy Narby explains: "Amazonian shamans have been preparing ayahuasca for millennia. The brew is a necessary combination of two plants, which must be boiled together for hours. The first contains a hallucinogenic substance, dimethyltryptamine, which also seems to be secreted by the human brain; but this hallucinogen has no effect when swallowed, because a stomach enzyme called monoamine oxidase blocks it. The second plant, however, contains several substances that inactivate this precise stomach enzyme, allowing the hallucinogen to reach the brain. So here are people without electron microscopes who choose, among some 80,000 Amazonian plant species, the leaves of a bush containing a hallucinogenic brain hormone, which they combine with a vine containing substances that inactivate an enzyme of the digestive tract, which would otherwise block the hallucinogenic effect. And they do this to modify their consciousness."[1] When asked how they know which plants to select, they simply reply, " The plants tell us." This is difficult to accept. These shamans have an *inner knowing* that comes from depths of the mind-body or energy-matter relationship that yields information which would be difficult to discover using our powerful, external, scientific research alone. Interestingly, the shamans' insights that come from chemically-induced altered states of consciousness have been experienced by others without the use of drugs. Seers have been recorded throughout human his-

---

[1]. *The Cosmic Serpent* by Jeremy Narby, G. P. Putnam's Sons, a division of Penguin Putnam, Inc., 1998.

tory, from the ancient oracles, of which the Mayans and Aztecs had their share, to modern psychics. The mind's ability to perceive complex information from beyond physical dimensions can provide insights into the origins and destiny of humanity.

## Cayce, the Akasha, and the Yucatan

Over a period of forty-three years Edgar Cayce showed a remarkable ability to read the akashic records and interpret them. (For more on Cayce's abilities see the section entitled, "About Edgar Cayce" in Chapter 1.) The tale Cayce tells of Yucatan adds so much to our overall understanding that it is worth telling. As you might expect, correlating the akashic records as read and interpreted by Edgar Cayce with the physical records as excavated and interpreted by archaeologists and paleontologists is a challenge. But rather than begin with this, let me just tell the tale as conveyed through Edgar Cayce, and my interpretation of his interpretations. Due to their syntax and the presence of archaic terms and style, Cayce's readings can be difficult to read. Also, they are *written* records of a *verbal* process, which occasionally does not carry the full intent that was expressed, and punctuation can significantly change the meaning or intent of the voiced statement. Sometimes Cayce covers so many concepts and relevant issues that it can be difficult to determine just which one he is referring to in complex paragraphs. Despite all of this, with practice, one can become familiar enough with the syntax and the complex thought pattern to read and understand the Cayce readings fairly well.

Cayce explains the Akasha this way: "That upon the film of time and space, or that between time and space, makes or carries the records of the activities and thoughts of individuals in their sojourn through any realm of experience. And as to how well the record may be given depends upon how well [they are] interpreted by one who may read such records."

Cayce's history of humanity from the Akasha begins with the creation and its unfolding to the point that Central America becomes a meaningful stage in the human journey. As Cayce reads these records, Middle America is one of the "new lands" to which humans migrated from the sinking legendary lands of Mu (Lemuria), Atlantis, Oz, Og, Zu, and Ohum. Yucatan, Egypt, and China were the new lands where culture was going to make another effort to realize its full potential and escape from the many dangers and threats on this planet in those ancient times. Although Cayce's dating of these times is older than most archaeological dates, scientific data is moving closer and closer to Cayce's timeline with each new discovery.

His tale is not just the evolution of matter but an *involution* from dimensions of energy *into* matter, followed by an entrapment or possession by matter, and then the evolution up through matter. In his reading of the Akasha, the realms of the collective subconscious mind, even unconscious, are significant in understanding the people of Middle America because they lived in these states of consciousness far more than we do today; a condition that makes it difficult for us to understand their language, mythology, tales, ceremonies, and abrupt abandoning of magnificent temples and cities. Another handicap is our fundamental belief that everything old is primitive and that we are evolution's progeny. From our perspective, ancient cultures live in superstition and myth, but we live in reality, the "real" world. Few Ancient Mayans would consider the world of matter to be the real world. For them the real world lay behind the conscious one, and the more one was in the outer, projected world, the further in their unconscious lay the real, true world. This is a very difficult perspective for many modern minds to accept.

Here's the tale Cayce tells of the forces leading to and the development of Yucatan's many fascinating cultures, magnificent temples and pyramids, and amazing cities as he reads and interprets the akashic records:

# The Beginning

Our story begins in the womb of the Creator's mind, an infinite expanse of consciousness that was perfectly still, formless, absolutely clear, with no thought prior to the creation, but with all the latent potential to conceive. At some immeasurable moment, this universal consciousness moved within itself and creation began. As ideas form in our little minds, so this first mind conceived, expressing its creativity and innate sense of beauty, harmony, and movement. The idea of light came forth from the Creator's mind; playing with light, stars were conceived; playing with stars, galaxies emerged; and the primordial stillness was alight with activity. But it was all in thought, in the mind of the Creator, which we would consider formless and not real; only matter is real. In a wondrously surprising moment of love, the one mind conceived of countless individual points of mind within itself, each given freedom to experience the creation and to co-create with the Creator. In the one were now many.

It was the first dawn, when the morning stars sang together and all the children of God shouted for joy (Job 38:7), to have found themselves awake and astir with wonder and excitement. In this early morning light their virgin minds were so like the infinite, omnipotent mind of their Creator that they were virtually one and the same. The Creator had put a piece of itself in each of them. Each innately possessed their Creator's desire for expression and companionship. Flush with life, their minds ablaze with wonder and imbued with the dynamic spirit of their Creator, these godlings began to reach out with their minds and experience the endless cosmos. As children explore everything, they peered into the many mansions of their father's house where wonders upon wonders were to be found in every direction their young minds turned. It was a glorious beginning, but there were dangers. Paramount among these dangers was freedom, for it included the potential to rebel, even against the very source of their freedom.

As the godlings used their freedom they began to develop uniquenesses that made them less homogeneous and more individual. Each was building a personal story, with unique memories and desires. The Creator's ultimate goal was for them to know themselves to be themselves yet remain cooperatively one with the whole of life, one with the Creator and all of creation. In order to know themselves they had to experience individualness; but the individuation process had a dangerous side to it, a danger that was soon to cause all manner of trouble in paradise.

Consciousness allows such a sense of self that the awareness of the underlying oneness may be lost. Some among the godlings lost their sense of oneness. They saw only individualness or multiplicity. As they continued to give strength to this perspective, they became self-focused, uncooperative, and motivated by their own self-interests. The ultimate impact of this would not be fully realized until the

*Figure 135*
The Individuation process led to a loss of consciousness of oneness. From DigitalVision.

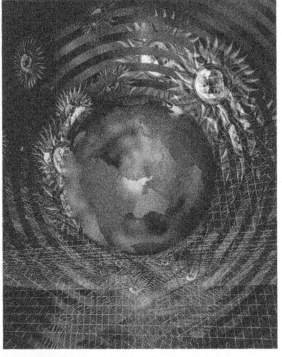

*Figure 136*
Earth became the location holding the promise of return to wholeness. From DigitalVision.

godlings moved out of the realms of the mind and into those of matter, particularly into the third dimension of the little, blue planet Earth.

The Earth was still cooling and life was just beginning to stir in its gases and waters when some of these godlings descended out of formless mind-spirit dimensions and into matter. At this early stage they were little more than whispers in the breeze, voices in the wind as their minds swept across the steaming planet, foretelling their coming into matter. Earth was not the only planet they visited, nor was the third dimension their primary level of consciousness. All the planets in this star system provided their minds with opportunities. Indeed, the entire universe with all its dimensions was theirs to enjoy. It was hoped that by doing so, they would grow to be fit companions for the Creator, the universal mind within which all of this was taking place.

# Chapter 9

## Maya-Aztec Legends and the Akashic Records

### Sun, Venus, and the Moon: Creation and the Cycle of Life, Death, and Rebirth

In the Quiché Mayan manuscript *Popol Vuh*, literally "Book of Counsel," we find a legendary tale that is best read as one would read a dream. In this tale the Sun and Venus go through recurring cycles of entering the Underworld to face its shadowy challenges to life and consciousness. The Sun represents the strength and weakness of the mind, and Venus the strength and weakness of the heart. Over and over they engage or are engaged by the dark forces of the Underworld. They fail, recover, and rise again to face the challenges over and over. This cycle — this pattern — is an underlying truth about life in and around Earth, a life that the ancient ones knew and understood well. The tale goes like this:

The Sun (*Hunhun-ahpu*) and Venus (*Vukub-hunhun-ahpu*) are called by the Lord of Death (*Vucub Caquix*, "7 Macaw") who appears in the form of a macaw, a large parrot with brilliant plumage indigenous to subtropical America. He wants them to come into the realms of Darkness in the Underworld (*Xibalba*, the "place of awe"). When they enter the Lord of Death captures a part of the body of the Sun which must be recovered. In an attempt to retrieve it the Sun is defeated by Death and Darkness. They decapitate the Sun and hang his head on a tree. The head of the Sun calls to the Moon who, in the personage of the virgin *Zquic* or *Xquiq*, represents another level or aspect of the mind. The Sun has learned from its failure and teaches the Moon that behind the face of all flesh is only a fleshless, bony skull (see *figure 137*); real life is in the mind and spirit, the essence of the being, not the face or appearance.

Following this lesson the Sun impregnates the Moon with its saliva (symbolically a life-giving liquid that is magically made from within one's head — not one's loins). The Moon returns to Earth pregnant with this new wisdom and gives birth to powerful twins, who are, in fact, the resurrections of the Sun and Venus (this time in the forms of *Hunahpu* and *Xbalanque)*. The Lords of Darkness are so upset by this magic that they demand the virgin's heart on the funeral fire. After being captured by the dark forces, the Moon convinces her guards to spare her. They replace her heart offering with the heart-shaped fruit of a rubber tree. When the pretend heart is put upon the funeral fire it creates an enchanting fragrance, amazing the Lords of Darkness. With the birth of this second set of twins and the preserving of their mother's heart, the cycle begins again.

In going about their work of putting the world in order, the Sun and Venus decide that order will not be achieved until they descend into the Underworld to face and overcome all the dark forces. As they attempt this they are again defeated by the Lords of Death (now called *Hun Came*, "Universal Death," or *Vucub Came*, "7 Death") and the other Lords who are called by the names of a host of illnesses, misfortunes, and evils. In the depths of the Underworld (symbolic of the darkness of the subconscious mind's shadowy urges and fantasies) the Lords of Darkness appear to triumph again and again, only to witness the resurrection of the Sun and Venus again and again. Remember, the Sun and Venus represent the mind and heart of

Figure 137
Engraved skull found at Kaminaljuyu.

each godling, each human, that has to struggle through the challenges of individual development. For example, in the next cycle, the twins are called again to the Underworld, challenged to a ball game by the Lords of Darkness. As reviewed earlier, ball courts appear all over ancient Central America, recalling the primal game played between the forces of good and evil, light and dark, life and death.

During the sojourn in the Underworld to play the game, the Sun and Venus face seven trials. The 1st Trial requires that they discern the false from the real lords or forces of the Underworld (the subconscious mind), and name these forces; which they do. The next six trials deal with sleeping in various "houses of torment," or dimensions of thought that can possess one's consciousness and limit it. Of course, there is no surer way to get into the subconscious than by sleep and dreams, so they sleep.

The first night's sleep begins the 2nd trial which is in The House of Shadows, where they are to keep a torch and a cigar lit throughout the night, yet each item must be returned the next morning in its original, whole condition. The torch represents the light of the cosmos and macrocosm, the cigar the light of the individual and microcosm.

The 3rd Trial is in the House of Spears where they are to defend themselves against constant attacks from warriors with spears while preparing four vases of rare flowers without leaving the temple to gather the flowers. The spears represent the free-will assaults of others that can cause one to retreat from the challenges of life. But even in the face of such challenges, one must bring forth goodwill, as in the beauty and fragrance of flowers. Yet, these rare flowers must be gathered from within oneself, not from outside.

The 4th Trial is in the House of Cold where they must conquer the icy cold in order to survive through the night. As Jesus warned (Matthew 24:12), the hearts of many will grow cold and bitter, giving up hope and faith that good will overcome evil. In this house of torment, the mind and heart had to keep the warmth of hope and faith alive throughout the night.

The 5th Trial is in the House of the Jaguar where they must elude the beast in the dark night in order to live to the next morning. The Jaguar is a complex influence in ancient Yucatan. Its night cries recall a beastly, deadly nature latent in all humans, a nature that could spring out of the darkness of one's mind at anytime and rend the outer self and others to pieces. Subduing this dark, beastly nature is important to survival and ultimate victory over the dark forces.

The 6th Trial is in the House of Fire where they have to endure the furnace of the fire. Fire is a symbol of the greatest of tests, "the test as by fire." In this trial our mind and heart endure the greatest form of purification. Fire also represents rage and fury, which must be mellowed if one is to cooperate with others and the Whole.

And finally, the 7th Trial is in the House of Bats where they have to enter a subterranean labyrinth with many strange and odious creatures of destruction and find their way through to the next morning. In this house we meet the shadows in the dark corners of our mind and heart. Each must be faced and tempered.

Through cleverness and enlisting the cooperation of creatures and forces within each of these houses of torment, the Sun and Venus survive them all except for the very last, the House of the Bats. Here the Sun, the Mind, loses its head. Fortunately, Venus, the Heart, makes it through untouched. Celebrating their triumph over the Sun, the Lords of the Underworld place the Sun's newly decapitated head in the ball court. However, Venus, as the caring Heart, evokes the gods, fashions a temporary head for the Sun, and then (as god of war) takes command of the field and eventually conquers the Lords of Darkness, sacrificing most of them by "limiting their power and lowering their rank." The dominion of Death and Darkness is no longer absolute, and humanity can now survive their trials.

Through these trials the Sun and Moon become Father and Mother of Humanity, and Venus is now the helper who understands the struggles of humans.

In his book *Lacandon Dream Symbolism: Dream Symbolism and Interpretation Among the Lacandon Mayas of Chiapas, Mexico*, Robert D. Bruce explains how the Sun and Venus lived the heavenly cycle in all its various dimensions and challenges as a preparation for humanity, and that each human's life is a repetition of the same cycle, reflected in the cycle of a day. Man, like the Sun, rises in the morning of his or her life (dawn) to the height of one's power (noon), then is called to descend to the realm of Death and Darkness, and cannot escape that destiny, dying like the Sun at dusk. Then, ever seeking to rise again, one's mind begins the journey through the night world or underworld, rising to another dawn, wiser and stronger for having made the journey through the whole cycle. According to ancient legends, the journey and its struggles are also reflected in the movement of constellations, specific stars, and planets through the heavens and the ages of the Sun's passage through the ecliptic. Strikingly similar cycles are found in the manuscripts and on the walls of tombs and temples in Ancient Egypt, Persia, India, and China.

# The Role of Bird-Serpent

In the Nahua manuscript known as *The Legend of the Suns* (*Leyenda de los Soles*) the god *Quetzalcoatl* invents and molds humans (the god's name is *Gucumatz* in Quiché-Mayan and *Kukulcan* in Yukatec-Mayan). Quetzalcoatl (pronounced, *ket-sel-ko'-tel*) is a fascinating god. Its name in Nahua (the language of the Aztec and Toltec) refers to the *quetzalli*, a specific bird of magnificent emerald green, blue, and scarlet plumage (see *fig. 138*) and *coatl*, literally meaning *serpent*. In the Quiché-Mayan language *guc* refers to this same beautiful bird and *matz* to the serpent, thus the god's name is *Gucumatz*. In Yucatec-Maya, *kuc* is the word for "feather," and *can* means serpent. However, Kukulcan may be a misspelling by the Spanish of *Cuculcan*. If so, *cuc* means "wave," *cucul* means wave-like or back-and-forth motion, a motion the quetzel bird makes as it flies, again identi-fying the god with this specific bird. The quetzel bird (*pharomachrus mocinna*) is about a foot long but with two more feet of tail feathers. It is the national bird of Guatemala (land of Quiché-Mayans) and is found in both South and Central America. Quetzalcoatl is often interpreted as "feathered-serpent" or "plumed-serpent," an idea that may come from

*Figure 138 (right)*
Quetzal bird.

*Figure 139 (right)*
Huge stone statue of feathered serpent. Internet photo.

*Figure 140*
Left: Quetzalcoatl seen emerging from serpent's mouth. From Dover's American Indian Design. Above: Feathered serpent painted on rocks in Nicaragua. From: Squier, E. G. (1851) *Serpent Symbol.*

*Figure 141*
Various images of feathered serpent from Egyptian designs. From: *Egyptian Motifs*, Dover.

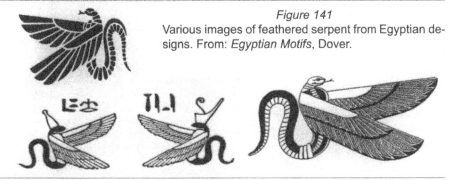

*Figure 142*
The feathered serpent was a common theme of America's Moundbuilders. Left: from Alabama; Right from Georgia. From Spinden (1913).

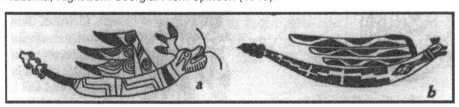

spelling Cuculcan as Kukulcan, and because the statues and depictions of this god give the impression of a feathered serpent. (See *fig. 139.*)

Ancient mystical legends around the world contain images and tales of a "bird-serpent" or "winged-serpent" and, in some cases, of a bird carrying a serpent. (See *figures 140, 141, & 142.*) In mysticism the bird can be a symbol of wisdom; with its higher-flying, higher-perspective mind. A bird flying above the ground would have a better perspective of the world than those who live only on its surface. In ancient Egypt, the messiah god *Horus* is presented by a falcon or hawk. Horus is depicted in the same way that Ra is, but with a new, wiser view than the original god. On the other hand, the serpent is often a symbol for the knowledge and power of the mind, occasionally misused knowledge and power, even evil. When the mind is raised with wisdom, then good growth, good change can occur. Therefore, the ability to lift one's mind (serpent) up to wisdom (bird) may be the deeper meaning behind the bird-serpent or winged-serpent symbols found in the ancient world. In deep trance Cayce interprets these two key icons as mind and wisdom. Therefore, henceforth we will use "Wise Mind" as a meaningful name for this important, active god in Central America, a name that each initiate in these ancient times would have known and understood.

Interestingly, the Nahua term *quetzal* may also be interpreted to mean "twin," another worldwide concept found in ancient legends. Twins in the form of intertwined serpents or struggling siblings is a powerful symbol for two aspects of consciousness.

## Struggling Twins or Siblings

There are two distinct parts in every human being; one dominant, projecting into the physical world, and the other lying just behind daily consciousness. Even though most modern humans are not readily aware of the twin aspects of consciousness, they often experience them and interact with them. For example, we have all at one time or another awakened with a dream that was so dynamic we wanted to remember it, perhaps write it in a journal, but as we came closer to consciousness we noticed that the bladder was full and went to empty it. Upon returning to the bedside to write down the dream we realized that we had completely lost the content of this significant dream. We remember having dreamed but not the dream. How is this possible? It is possible because our outer self, our daily conscious mind, does not dream the dream. Dreams come from the deeper self, the deeper consciousness. And we are very familiar with this inner self because, while dreaming, each of us clearly feels that our normal, personal self is dreaming. We say, "I'm dreaming" or "I had a dream." This deeper self is so natural to us, such an integral part of ourselves, that we don't even sense that it is a different portion of our being until we move into the outer self and lose the dream completely.

What we today call the subconscious mind is the inner twin to our outer self. Moving through the thin veil of consciousness to stimulate the physical body to empty the bladder is so subtle a shift of consciousness from inner to outer self that we normally do not sense it. As we engage the somatic nervous system to move the physical body, we completely engage the outer mind, the outer physical self, losing conscious connection with the inner mind, the inner self. Even so, when we were in the dreaming mind, we felt that we were in our personal self; a normal, natural part of our being. We know our inner selves but **the veil between the two is so delicate that we do not normally notice our shifting between the two, and the veil is so opaque that we cannot normally see back through it once on the other side of it**. We need to work to make this veil more transparent and our sensitivities more acute to subtle shifts in consciousness. In this way we can connect our inner self with our outer self, and become whole again.

This type of work — connecting the inner and outer self — was being conducted in the temples of Mu, Atlantis, and eventually in Yucatan, at a time when the changes of energy into matter were still new and not so firmly established as they are today. The minds of heaven were fast becoming focused on the world and its challenges. This created another self, an earthly self.

Many of the spiritual teachings throughout the ages contain this two-part self in curious tales of two siblings or twins. One pursues the world, the other lingers behind, staying close to the parents or the original home. In some of these legends, the worldly one kills the other. Sometimes, it only seems as though the other is killed. In ancient Egypt we find tales of Osiris and his brother

*Figure 143*
The veil between the inner self
and the outer self is delicate.
Photo: DigitalVision.

Set, in Mayan culture the legend of two godly brothers against two earthly brothers, in the Old Testament we find Cain and Abel, Jacob and Esau. In the New Testament Jesus tells the parable of two brothers, a prodigal son and his brother who stays home and helps their parents. The tales contain the elements of deep truth about ourselves. Let's review them:

In the creation legend of the Quiché Maya as recorded in the manuscript *Popol Vuh*, both the heavenly self and the earthly self are depicted as twin brothers. In the beginning, the one named *7 Macaw* comes to life in the world. He has a self-exalting nature, magnifying and glorifying himself. 7 Macaw claims a place in the Cosmos for himself that he does not deserve. He acts and talks like a god — but he is not one. Therefore, two real gods, *twins* from "the Heart of Heaven," come to destroy him. Here the tale repeats the struggle in a series of battles. In one of the series, the twins are named *Blowgunner* (representing the breath of God) and *Jaguar Deer* (the fleeting magic of God), who decide that the self-glorifying 7 Macaw must die because he has neither a heritage nor a legacy with the Heart of Heaven. But 7 Macaw gives birth to two sons who continue in the ways of their father. These two brothers are symbolically named *Alligator* (one who attacks from beneath the surface) and *Two-his-leg* (one who stands upright and stomps mountains underfoot). They are just like their bragging father, taking upon themselves undeserved glory and attacking life for self-satisfaction, self-gratification. Now the godly hero twins plot to destroy them all, father and brothers. 7 Macaw is destroyed when the godly twins draw his *pride* from him, for all he was was pride. Alligator is destroyed by magic made by the godly twins. Two-his-leg is destroyed when he eats a bird cooked by the godly twins. The bird is symbolic of a higher, lighter influence that can fly above the earth and its mountains. Ingesting this influence took Two-his-leg's strength from him, leaving him unable to stomp mountains.

In the Egyptian legend of Osiris and Set we have twin brothers who come out of the heavens into the world together. They marry twin sisters, Isis and Nephthys. Osiris proves to be good, just, loving, and cooperative with all life. But Set seeks to exalt himself and satisfy his desires. Set becomes so jealous of the praise his brother receives from the people of the world that he kills him, cutting him into pieces. Osiris, upset by the terrible deed his brother has done to him, rejects the world as fundamentally evil and leaves it to those who pursue it. Osiris chooses to remain in the Netherworld between the outer world and the heavens and will weigh the heart of any who attempt to pass from the world to the heavens. Eventually, his brother Set is subdued by the Egyptian's version of a messiah, Horus, the immaculately-conceived son of Osiris' widow, the goddess Isis.

In the biblical story of Cain and Abel we have the two offspring of the fallen Adam and Eve. In Hebrew, the name *Cain* literally means "acquired one" and *Abel* means "a breath." Their names give an insight into their symbolic roles. "Cain" has been acquired in the pursuit of earthly desires. He is the outer ego-centric self. "Abel" denotes the breath that was received from the Lord in the Garden. Cain becomes a tiller of the soil, while Abel becomes a shepherd, a "keeper of flocks." In this we see the further distancing of Cain from the Lord, following in the curse of his father Adam: "cursed is the ground because of you; through painful toil you will eat of it all the days of your life. Both thorns and thistles it shall grow for you; and you shall eat the plants of the field; by the sweat of your brow you shall eat bread, till you return to the ground, because from it you were taken; for you are dust, and to dust you shall return" (Genesis 3:17-19). When the two brothers bring their offerings before God, Abel's is pleasing to God, while Cain's is not. (See *figure 144*.) This causes Cain to become angry and his countenance falls. Yet, when the Lord sees Cain's anger and low countenance, He instructs him, "If you do what is right, will you not be accepted? But if you do not do what is right, then sin is crouching at your door; its desire is to have you, but you must master it" (Genesis 4:7).

In another Bible story we find twins Jacob and Esau who are very different in their interests and pursuits. Jacob lingers around the tents and talks about life and people's needs. Esau hunts and adventures in pursuit of life's many pleasures, gratifying his appetites. In a defining moment, Esau's desire to satisfy his hunger causes him to give away his inheritance to Jacob for a pot of lentil soup. Jacob becomes the heir to all their family's wealth. The story spins on the premise that even though Jacob came out of the womb first, his twin brother Esau stuck his foot out first making him the eldest son and inheritor of his father's kingdom. But it was not to be so. Fate and Esau's own nature played a role in passing the kingdom onto Jacob.

These stories have meaning for us because they reflect a deep truth about us. We are two. If we read Genesis carefully we will see that there were two creations. In the first (Gen. 1:26-27) we were created in the image of God, which is *spirit* – "God is Spirit," John 4:23-24. In the second creation we were made of flesh (Gen. 2:5-7), from the dust of the earth. Hence, there are two parts to us, one godly and the other human. Here are those passages from Genesis:

Gen. 1:26-27

So God created man in his own image, in the image of God he created him; male and female he created them.

(our original androgyny)

Gen. 2:4-8

This is the account of the heavens and the earth when they were created. When the Lord God made the earth and the heavens – and no shrub of the field had yet appeared on the earth and no plant of the field had yet sprung up, for the Lord God had not sent rain on the earth and there was no man to work the ground, but streams came up from the earth and watered the whole surface of the ground – the Lord God formed the man from the dust of the ground and breathed into his nostrils the breath of life, and the man became a living being. Now the Lord God had planted a garden in the east, in Eden; and there he put the man he had formed.

In the Mayan *Popol Vuh*, people (the outer twin) were made to provide nourishment for the gods (the inner twin) in the form of prayers and sacrifices. It is, after all, the godly portion that will live beyond death, and this portion is nourished by prayers, good deeds, and sacrifice of earthly pleasures that possess the mind after death of the physical body.

Returning to Quetzalcoatl (Wise Mind), the *Popol Vuh* records that before anything was created "only the sky alone is there; the face of the earth is not clear. Only the sea alone is pooled under all the sky. There is nothing else. It is all at rest, not a single thing stirs." Coiled within the still water is Wise Mind, with green and blue feathers this serpent lies still. In the sky above is the Heart of Heaven, who appears as three forms of lightning. Out of the stillness the Heart of Heaven and Wise Mind begin speaking to one another. Their words form the creation. As they discuss the creation it appears. The first dawn, the people,

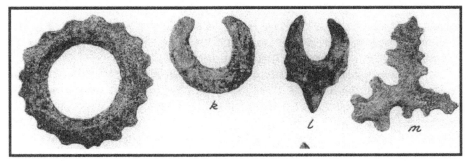

*Figure 145*
Examples of some of the thousands of "eccentrics" found at Piedras Negras.

the food, the mountains and the earth, magically rise from the deep, silent, sea of consciousness as the Heart of Heaven and Wise Mind conceive them in their discussion.

In looking at the eccentric shapes found at many Mayan sites, one could easily associate the disk-shaped objects with the Heart of Heaven and the jagged-shaped pieces with the Wise Mind (see *figure 145*). Certainly the Mayans gave these two gods characteristics and roles that reflect the interplay between inner and outer, female and male, unseen and seen, formless and form. These two common eccentric shapes found at their sites reflect these dual forces. They are the yin and yang of Maya.

## Into Matter, Ready or Not

All of these fascinating stories refer to a time in the mind, in the heavens, long *before* the story of matter and flesh. This particular aspect can be confusing to those encountering the stories for the first time as well as for many trying to understand Cayce's Akashic story of humanity; thus, it bears repeating. The mythical tales recounted in many ancient texts reflect heavenly events prior to the physical incarnation of humans on earth. The beginning of the journey into matter and the cycles through physical reality are recorded in the Akasha as an *unintended* side-trip for the godlings that turned into an extended sojourn. We now turn our attention to that story.

Before incarnating, many of the free-will godlings had already become so self-centered and self-motivated that they lost their spiritual purpose and began seeking self-gratification and self-exaltation. Movement from the realm of energy to the realm of matter served their new

*Figure 146*
Self-glorification became the focus of many of the free-will godlings before they incarnated. From DigitalVision.

self-gratification purpose. So they pushed their way into matter without regard for the consequences.

Since there were no humanoid bodies, they attempted to experience three-dimensional life through the senses of the existing animals and plants (entangling their minds with these forms in the process). From this very ancient time came our mythological legends of creatures that were part man and part animal.

A fundamental principle of creation was that each life-form should give seed to itself, to its own kind: dogs should produce dogs, fruit trees should produce fruit trees, and so on, but the godlings had pushed their minds into these life-forms, creating mixed creatures. This careless entrance into matter produced semi-human beings with feathers, scales, fur, claws, hooves, and tails. Their minds, though still powerful, were possessed with animal features: satyr and faun (human and goat), centaur (human and horse), sphinx (human and lion), merman and mermaid (human and fish), minotaur, (human and bull), gorgon (human and snake), geryon (human and cow), chimera (human mixed with lion, goat, and serpent), and so on. These creatures were known for their vanity, idle fancy, lust, drunkenness, and cruelty. Virgil's depiction of the Gates of Hell touched on this in his poem in *Aeneas*: "Of various forms, unnumbered specters more; centaurs and double shapes besiege the door; before the passage horrid Hydra stands and Briareus with all his hundred hands; Gorgons, Geryon with his triple frame; and vain Chimera vomits empty flame."

In addition to beastly mixtures there were grotesque giants: titans, cyclopes, and gigantes (huge beings with the heads of men and the bodies of serpents). Even entire forests were enchanted by spirits, godling minds trapped in tree forms. It is important to understand that these were not so much physical as they were mental. That's difficult to comprehend given that life today is predominantly physical. But at this ancient time life existed more in energy or thought than in matter. Thought *forms* existed before physical forms, and the contamination first occurred in the mind. We like to call this "mythology." Odd blends of gods, humans, and animals are mythology. They are imaginative tales of the origin and nature of the world told by primitive people. Yet these myths exist in all of the world's societies (Africa, Asia, India, Persia, the Middle East, the Mediterranean, Europe, Scandinavia, the Americas, and the Pacific) and are considered by each to be sacred. Myths are in prescientific legends of the past. (See *figure 147*.)

The Akasha contains the great story of a pre-evolutionary fall from heaven of great beings, angel-like beings made in the image of God. Prior to the evolution of matter there was an involution into matter from formless energy, or from mind and spirit. Hindu teachings of transmigration were founded upon these ancient legends. And though transmigration does not occur today, it once did. Beings we would consider to be humanoid were

*Figure 147*
A few mythological creatures blending human and animal characteristics. Top/down: Winged creature (Java); Garuda (India); Manticore (Europe); Griffin (Egypt); Minotaur (Greece); bottom left, Siren (Greece). From: *Treasury of Fantastic and Mythological Creatures*, Dover.

incarnating in non-human forms. But this was all about to change. A human form or body was needed and through a series of prototypes, one was developed.

## Mu

According to the akashic records, the first place godlings incarnated in large numbers was not in Africa, that came much later when we were more deeply immersed into matter. The first place was in Mu, or what is often referred to as Lemuria (an ancient continent in the Pacific Ocean), about 12 million years ago. The minds of the godlings had been entering the realm of Earth since about 4.6 billion years ago, but much of this time passed in the realm of the mind. True incarnation into carnal forms did not begin until Mu. Here's where human evolutionary theory and akashic tales part company. According to evolutionary theory, humans were still wandering around in primitive forms only a few thousand years ago. Cro-Magnon man (Homo-sapiens) was very active in Europe and the Middle East about 40,000 years ago. The first city wasn't built until Jericho, about 10,000 B.C. Egypt and China didn't begin their spectacular cultures until 3,000 B.C. However, scientists have found humanoid or, as they call them, "hominid" remains dating back millions of years.

During the latter stages of the involution into matter the godlings were highly attuned to the forces of the Universe *and* Nature, capable of amazing feats of creativity and building. According to the akashic records the megalithic structures we find around the world from antiquity were indeed built by these godlings. It was a time of power that we can only imagine. For example, today there are just two cranes in the world that can lift the stones in the Great Pyramid of Giza. In order to build it we would have to perfectly lay 63 of these huge stones each day for 100 years (no days off) – not likely. Everything old is not primitive, yet where are the physical remains of these powerful beings?

The Akasha records that the tools of the ancient builders were not as physical as ours, their "bodies" not dense; therefore, no remains are in the layers of Earth to be discovered. Another curious indicator that ancient times may not have been as we believe is that even the physical evolutionary records reveal unexplainable jumps in development. For example, the time for evolution from monkey-men to Cro-Magnon is millions of years, but the time for evolution from Cro-Magnon to Queen Hatshepsut ruling over the glories of golden Egypt is only 37,000 years. Her granite obelisk in the temple at Karnak weighs approximately 100 tons and is carved with a level of skill that would be hard to find today. In fact, raising her obelisk is impossible today. And there are many similar megalithic structures around the world. According to the akashic records, the descending godlings used their powerful minds and intuitive understanding of the forces of the cosmos and Nature to build and survive. They projected themselves into this world using thought-form rather than matter, yet they could influence matter and its evolution. For example, their minds affected the breeding of animals, especially monkeys. They created what Cayce called, "things" to labor for them, zombie-like creatures of physical form, some of which were actually humanoid. However, the forces of Nature occasionally reacted with such force and violence to their disturbing presence that dramatic cataclysms occurred in the Earth. These cataclysms were so dramatic that the godlings would sometimes withdraw or be forced out of Earth, leaving life here to evolve untouched by them for long periods. During these times of turmoil and change the "Things" were left to their own evolution following the laws of Nature. They wandered the Earth, evolving along with the plant and animal life. These zombie-like creatures had primitive minds, without souls, and were used by the godlings as we today use domestic animals. They bred and multiplied.

The godlings always returned. Each return was like a new creation or era with major changes in life on earth. Cayce sees almost the identical record in the Akasha as in the Central American legends of the four major creations or ages.

## The Four Ancient Creations Within a Fifth

A belief in multiple creations is found in most of the ancient legends around the world. These ancient legends tell of several attempts to create carnal, humanoid beings that were well-acclimated to the dimensions of Earth yet would remain aware of the gods and honor them by magnifying good rather than giving strength and power to the forces of darkness, death, and evil.

In Nahua (Aztec and Toltec), Maya, Mixtec, Zapotec, and Otomi legends there are normally four creations, "world ages," or "suns." We find the same number among the Navaho and Pueblo of North America and the Quechua in Peru. The age we currently live in is the fifth world age and is the sum of the previous four ages, resulting in the concept of five in four, as carved in the magnificent Aztec Sun Stone currently on exhibit in the National Museum of Anthropology in Mexico City. It is a 25-ton, basalt, circular monolith, almost 12 feet in diameter, called the *Cuauhxicalli* or "Eagle Bowl." It illustrates both mythological and astronomical messages. (See *figure 148*.)

*Figure 148*
The Sun Stone
as it is dis-
played today in
Mexico City.
Photo: Lora
Little.

On this magnificent stone the sign that names the present "sun" or age, called *Movement* (*Nahui Olin*), is composed of the signs that name the previous four suns or ages which, interestingly, correspond to the four elements (earth, water, fire, and air). The order of these ages is in question and varies from record-to-record, but the Akasha would dictate that these go in clockwise order around the Sun Stone beginning in the upper right. Therefore, the order of the suns or ages is: 1) Jaguar Age (*Nahui Ocelot*), 2) Water Age (*Nahui Atl*), 3) Fiery Rain Age (*Nahui Quiahuitl*), and 4) Wind Age (*Nahui Ehecatl*).

In each age humans assumed a different form: In the first age they were giants who became like wood; in the second, like fish; in the third, like birds; and in the fourth, like apes. The fifth age is indicated in the very center of the circle by the face of the Sun god (*Tonatiuh*) and the four other ages in a process of *movement* or change, and is the final age. The Mayan calendar indicates that the fifth age ends December 22, 2012 A.D. After the fifth age the legend indicates that the original state prior to the creations returns. Whether this occurs through gradual change or by a sudden cataclysmic event is unclear in the legend. But, as Cayce reads the Akasha, a gradual change is indicated.

These ages are enclosed in the unending ring of the Twenty Signs or "day names," each composed of thirteen numbers, resulting in a calendar of 260 days (13 x 20 = 260), matching Venus' journey with the

Sun through the sky. The Twenty Signs run counterclockwise on the Sun Stone, and two huge serpents encompass the outer rim, meeting at the bottom of the circle. (See *figure 149.*) Out of the mouths of the two serpents appear the face of the Sun god (right serpent) and the Fire god (left serpent). The four points of compass directions (north, east, south,

*Figure 149*
Detailed drawing of the Sun Stone. From: *Symbols, Signs, Signets. Dover.*

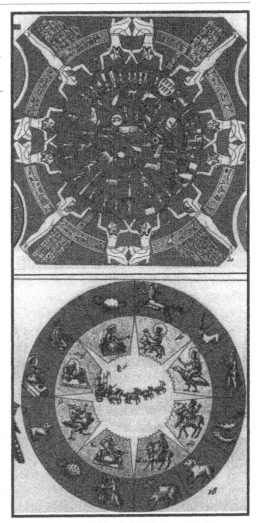

and west) and the four seasons of the year (spring, summer, fall, and winter) are also indicated by pyramid-like cones that represent beams of sun- and moon-light. Very similar designs can be found in other ancient cultures, showing the ages, zodiac, seasons, and compass points (See *figure 150*).

## Interpreting the Ages

When we combine the Aztec and Maya versions of the creation story through the four ages or suns, we have the following story. Again, it is helpful to read these as one would a dream.

### 1st. The Age of Jaguar *(Element: Earth)*

In the Jaguar Age the people were giants, with great power, but became like wood. The wooden people were stiff-necked and heartless, no longer listening to the gods and not seeking the light of the gods. Therefore, the gods caused the light of the Sun to be eclipsed, and in the resulting darkness jaguars and other beasts of the world ate up the wooden people. So repulsive were the wooden people that even things like grinding stones and cooking pans attacked them, saying: "We have been shattered by you every day, every day, night and day, all the time; crunch, crunch, scrape, scrape, on our faces you went." This same tale is found in the Quechua myth from Peru but with slightly different animals.

Seeing this terrible situation, the Wise Mind became the morning and evening star, Venus. Its illumination would reduce the darkness of the Jaguar Age. To soften the darkness, Wise Mind, as Venus, heralds the coming of the Sun in the morning for 260 days and lingers after the setting Sun in the evening for 260 days. In Genesis 1:14-15, we find a correlating reference to this,

> "And God said, Let there be lights in the firmament of heaven to divide the day from the night; and let them be for signs, and for seasons, and for days and years; and let them be for lights in the firmament of heaven to give light upon the earth, and it was so."

This extra light, and the other lights of the night (the moon and stars), cured the curse of the Jaguar Age. The wooden people were destroyed but the *Popol Vuh* says that their descendants are the monkeys.

## 2nd. The Age of Water *(Element: water)*

In the Age of Water the people were made of mud (Aztec) or clay (Maya). They were created to be conscious, aware of the thirteen heavens, nine levels of earth, and nine realms of the underworld, and to nourish the gods (symbolic of the godly portion of themselves) with prayers and offerings. However, the people lost their consciousness, blending so completely into the watery world that they turned into fish. This was unacceptable because they were to be fully conscious people — not fish lost in one dimension of life. Keep in mind that this is not to be understood in a literal sense but, like a dream, it is the imagery and symbolism of the deeper levels of the mind. The story is trying to convey the essence of an event that was only barely physical yet so important to gaining an understanding of our origins.

The water represents a less dense aspect of matter into which the descending godlings moved. Once in it they so merged with it that they became lost. For all intents and purposes they were like fish in the sea, unaware of the worlds beyond the water. The Mayan *Popol Vuh* talks about this being a time of the creation of animals who could not praise and worship the gods because they could not speak: "They just squawked, they just chattered, they just howled. It wasn't apparent what language they spoke, each one gave a different cry." For the companions of the Creator of the cosmos, this was an intolerable condition and could not be allowed to go on eternally.

In an attempt to correct this confusion, the celestial water merged with the waters below to create a great flood that cleansed the world of fish-like people. But the flood made things worse. Wise Mind saw that the horizon was lost due to the flood waters, and because of this no one could determine which direction to go or where they were. Therefore, Wise Mind separated the waters above from the waters below by again becoming the planet Venus. The legend says that Venus "wounds the sources of water," keeping the rain-gods from bringing the flood again. Now the waters above are separated from the waters below. This same tale is recorded in Genesis 1:6-8,

> "And God said, Let there be a firmament in the midst of the waters, and let it divide the waters from the waters. And God made the firmament, and divided the waters which were under the firmament from the waters which were above the firmament: and it was so. And God called the firmament Heaven. And there was evening and there was morning, a second day."

### 3rd. The Age of Fiery Rain (Element: fire)

In the third age people are made like birds, more like turkey birds than high-flying birds. They could walk on the earth and fly a little. In the *Popol Vuh* this age ultimately causes our Heavenly Twins (Sun and Venus) to determine that the Earth will never be an inhabitable place until evil and darkness are defeated. As a result, the Twins decide to enter the Underworld and defeat darkness. *Xibalba* is the legendary underworld or netherworld for the Maya, *Mictlan* for the Aztec. As presented earlier, it is representative of the uncentered, unenlightened mind where all manner of darkness and death abide. It is considered by the Maya to be a "watery place."

As we have seen, the Heavenly Twins go into the Underworld where they experience many trials, tests, and challenges. They die but rise from it again and again, continuing to face every challenge that is brought against them by the Lords of the Underworld, representing the forces within the minds of the godlings who are struggling with the challenges of independent consciousness and free will. Ultimately, the Twins subdue the forces of evil and darkness, taking away the power of the Lords of darkness, death, and evil. Now the Earth is finally ready for a more perfect creation: the Maize People. This portion of the Yucatan creation story corresponds almost exactly to the Akasha's creation story of the first Eden in Atlantis – a story we will get to in a moment.

In the *Popol Vuh* Wise Mind created maize people from yellow and white maize (corn) with the help of the aged goddess Xmucane (Maya) or Cihuacoatl (Aztec; literally, *woman serpent*). In this story the corn is identified with the bones of the fish people, which Wise Mind retrieved from the Underworld. The serpent goddess Xmucane grinds the bones or corn into meal that she then places in a sacred bowl, around which the gods gather and shed drops of their blood in order to turn the meal into a substance that can make maize people. These maize people become god-like, able to see visions, read thoughts, perceive the secret of the four world-ages and know instantaneously what is happening anywhere in space. Wise Mind and the Heart of Heaven realize that these maize people are too perfect and will establish an eternal home in matter on the Earth, never seeking the heavens of pure energy and consciousness again. In order to preserve the heavens as the true realm and the gods as the true nature of humanity, the gods decide to "chip the eyes of the maize people," causing them to lose some of their vision and thereby deprive them of establishing an eternal kingdom in matter on Earth. This loss of vision humbled the maize-people. Now they needed to seek deeper understanding, to seek the light of truth in their darkness. Powerful beings who lose power is a theme found in many ancient legends; even the Bible recounts that "The Nephilim were in the earth in those days" and God repented having created them. (Genesis 6:1-4)

To compensate for this loss of vision and power, the gods create beautiful wives for the maize people. This corresponds with the creation of the feminine and the Atlantean story of the creation of Lilith, which we will cover in detail in a moment.

In their darkness the first tribes of the maize-people journey to the place of the Seven Caves and Seven Canyons (*Tulan Zuiva*) – a possible metaphor for entering the physical body with its seven hidden chakras or lotuses. There they received their patron gods, including Tohil, a patron god of the Quiché and the source of fire, the element of this age. When the people finally leave the Seven Canyons, they no longer speak one language and now travel in five different groups and directions, exactly as the Akasha describes the original five races, five nations, and five senses separating and going to specific locations on the Earth (more on this in a moment).

The Fiery Rain Age was ended by volcanic fire and ash.

### 4th. *The Age of Wind* (Element: air)

The fourth age was the age of the Wind with its hurricane, when people became like apes, simians. It would be an age of strong winds against which the people would have to hold on tightly. Therefore, their hands were made for powerful gripping, hence the prehensile thumb. Rather quickly the age proves no better than the three before it. It ends by devastating hurricanes, tornadoes, and wind storms. Once everything is swept away, the four ages are ready for the process of movement and change, and the fifth age begins.

## 5th. The Age of Movement

For the Aztecs, this age begins in the city of Teotihuacan, literally "the place of those who became gods," considered the place where current time began. Here the gods came together in a great meeting to determine who would be the new sun to light the new age. They are faced with two choices, represented by two gods who volunteer for the mission: *Tecuciztecatl* and *Nanahuatzin*. The first god is showy, proud, and offers the finest raiments of quetzal plumes and golden balls, with awls of jade tipped with red coral, and incense of the rarest fragrance. The second god is sickly, and offers bundles of reeds, maguey spines dipped in his own blood, and for incense burns scabs picked from his body.

The gods prepare a great fire to test which of these two choices will make the best sun. As the test proceeds it turns out that the showy choice cannot withstand the heat of the fire and retreats, but the second lowly choice jumps straight into the white hot fire and is consumed immediately. So taken by the bravery of this act, the retreating showy god returns and follows the lowly one into the fire. So taken by these brave acts the eagle and the jaguar also jump into the fire. The company of gods waits to see where these gods will reappear. Slowly the sky reddens and the new sun appears, red hot in the eastern sky. Shortly thereafter the moon also appears in the eastern sky. Worried that the two lights will make the Earth too bright, the gods dim the moon's light.

These two choices are symbolic of the way of self-glorification, self-exaltation versus humility, meekness, and sacrifice. It is decided that the latter will guide all people to the deeper truth and higher achievements.

In the Aztec tale, the new sun and moon are stationary in the sky. This isn't good because it does not reflect the cycles of growth through trials, tests, failures and resurrections that all the gods have come to know as requirements to overcome darkness, death, and evil. Movement must begin. But, the new sun (now called, *Tanotiuh*) demands that the company of the gods shed their blood also before movement begins. He insists that all must help this great effort. After initial resistance, the gods finally comply with the sun's demand and begin to sacrifice themselves to join in the long journey of life through matter. One by one, Wise Mind cuts the hearts out of each god with a sacred knife. From this legend one finds the source of the distorted understanding that led many ancient Central American priests into the brutal, bloody practice of cutting hearts out of human bodies. They had lost so much attunement to the higher, finer understanding that they could no longer perceive the metaphorical meaning behind the legends. The symbolism of this heart-removing act among the gods matches the Old Testament of circumcising the hearts so they are more compatible with the Heart of Heaven or God. Here are a few examples:

"Circumcise therefore the foreskin of your heart, and be no more stiffnecked," Deuteronomy 10:16. This is reminiscent of the wooden people in the Jaguar Age who became stiffnecked and no longer listened to God.

"And the Lord thy God will circumcise thy heart, and the heart of thy seed, to love the Lord thy God with all thy heart, and with all thy soul, that thou mayest live," Deuteronomy 30:6.

"Circumcise yourselves to the Lord, and take away the foreskins of your heart, ye men of Judah and inhabitants of Jerusalem; lest my wrath go forth like fire, and burn so that none can quench it, because of the evil of your doings," Jeremiah 4:4.

Unfortunately, the later priests were so out of touch with the deeper truths and inner sources of insight that they could not understand this.

## Family gods, Bloodletting, and Death

As individuation continued, and awareness of the Oneness became more difficult, the people turned increasingly to themselves and to those among them that appeared powerful or simply more dominating. Before long, the one god was replaced by many gods and goddesses. But the descent continued until even the gods were of no help. Then, one's dead ancestors became a source of worship. It was believed that discarnates were nearer heaven than incarnates, so seeking their attention, guidance, and help became important. Altars to family or community gods were built. Early on, discarnate souls did prove to be helpful, often speaking to their incarnate loved ones during ecstatic ceremonies designed to create altered states of consciousness among the incarnates.

*Figure 151*
The human sacrifices of the Aztecs was a misinterpretation of earlier ideas. From: *The Complete Encyclopedia of Illustration*, Gramercy Books.

However, the deeper one descended into matter, the more one needed physical help and protection. It became increasingly difficult for discarnates to provide this help. But, due to the distortion of the deeper truths, many attempted to gain the gods' attention by sacrificing grains, animals, and even humans on the altars. A variation on this was the idea that the soul of a recently killed person could rise up into the heavens and get help for the people left behind in Earth. Initially, enemies were the best candidates for sacrifice. But eventually, as the gods proved more difficult to contact, the priests began to teach that sacrificing a loved one, a virgin, or a young one would get the greater response from the discarnate, family gods – so reminiscent of Abraham attempting to sacrifice his son Isaac to gain God's favor.

Some ancient ceremonies were actually designed to take a pumping heart out of a sacrificial person, keeping them semi-alive in this world while they were becoming semi-alive in the next world. (See *figure 151*.) Some victims actually offered themselves, believing that they could help their families. Even among the less violent tribes, blood was believed to be magical, with a "smell" that not only attracted animals but the gods in the borderland or netherworld to this world. In these communities the priests and priestesses would cut themselves or those seeking help, dripping their blood upon the altar to attract discarnates of their family or tribe. If anyone received help in this way, then the spot upon which it happened became sacred, honored by all and returned to many times in an effort to repeat the experience. Since blood had been a part of the ceremony, then much more blood would be shed trying to recreate the experience. In some cases, so much blood was shed that channels were built to carry it away, making room for more.

This happened with most ancient people, not just those in Yucatan. Even the Judeo-Christian religions have their legacy in blood sacrifice; from Abraham offering his son Isaac to the blood of Jesus Christ offered up for the sins of the world.

## Lost Tribes

According to Cayce's reading of the Akashic records, members of the Lost Tribes of Israel actually landed in Yucatan, bring their blood sacrifice ceremonies with them and influencing the religious ceremonies in Yucatan. Some of these migrating Hebrews eventually ended up joining the Mound Builders in North America. Cayce also reads that many who migrated to Yucatan refused to accept blood sacrifice and migrated northward to escape these aberrations of true spiritual ceremonies. Some of these headed to Chaco Canyon, others up the Mississippi Valley. Some were powerful leaders who simply abandoned their positions of authority to live humbly among the earth and trees of North America.

## Death

Death is another issue of some importance. Early on there was no death. These were immortal minds that descended from the heavens. They did not become mortal humans until much later. The beginning of death as we know it today was a major change, as you can imagine. In order to die, a mind has to so lose awareness of its connection with the Source of Life that it actually *believed* that it was dead. This is easier to do if the mind completely identifies with matter. In other words, identify "self" with the physical body thereby losing awareness of the spark. And this is what happened. However, Cayce states that there is no reason for a physical organism to age and die. With proper assimilation of nutrients and eliminations of drosses and toxins, a physical organism should continue to regenerate, rejuvenate, and live; that is if the *élan vital*, the kundalini, the life force runs through it. As soon as the mind loses contact with the Life Force, then the body slowly deteriorates, until it gives up the soul or ghost, and the mind and soul depart.

Once death became a part of life all kinds of problems and concerns developed. Ceremonies were developed to prepare for death, to take care of the corpse after death, and even to contact the deceased soul-mind in the worlds beyond. Two excellent examples of ceremonies preparing one to die to this world, then enter the borderland or netherworld, and successfully traverse it to the heavens above are found in two different books, both entitled the *Book of the Dead*, one Tibetan, another Egyptian. Both of these ancient texts outline the journey through various gates and realms of the Underworld up to the Heavens.

## Chapter 10

# Edgar Cayce's Reading of the Akashic Records

## The Four Creations from the Akasha

The Maya-Aztec Four Suns or Ages and the 5th Age of Movement correspond fairly well with the four creations and a major change described by Cayce as he reads the akashic records. He lists these ages in order as: 1st & 2nd in Mu, the Motherland; 3rd in Atlantis, 4th in Eden, and 5th as the change indicated by the story of Noah. In each of the first four creation periods Cayce identifies a new body-type or "root race," as he called them. Then, the Noah period was the being of movement that would result in a new, fifth body-type or root race that is to appear during the early centuries of our present new millennium. Here are Cayce's creations from the akashic records:

### 1st & 2nd in Mu, The Motherland

Up to this point in time much of the involvement with matter and the Earth was in the mental dimensions (the realms of thoughts and ideas), but about 12 million years ago, halfway through the Neocene period, the minds of the godlings moved into matter to *incarnate*, in the purest sense of that word. The first group focused their attention on the Pacific continent of Mu. Here the self-seeking godlings pushed their minds into whatever forms appealed to them. The resulting forms were the half human, half animal or plant bodies, the first "root race." These intermingled forms existed for about 2 million years. The godlings who remained in the formless realms did not impress their minds and hearts in matter but attempted to help from their better vantage point, like guiding or guardian angels. The legend of the fallen angels originates here. According to this legend, an angel named Lucifer – literally "light giver" – considered to be the "bright morning star," or Venus, with a rebel army of angels numbering 133 million were defeated by the archangel Michael and his army of 266 million. Acting under God's orders, Michael removed the rebels from the heavens and cast them down into Earth and Hell until they had repented of their sins. The principle sin leading to this battle was pride. Lucifer, who had once been the mightiest of the *seraphim*, and his angels had come to think of themselves with such "hubris," as Dante writes in his *Divine Comedy*, that by the sheer weight of their self-centeredness they fell out of the gossamer-like realms of heaven into the depths of matter, becoming stuck there in a vast tomb called Hell. The descending godlings were the falling angels.

In Cayce's reading of the Akasha, the fallen angels were redeemable, and many enlightened "angels" attempted to help them. But those that had become too terrestrial were difficult to communicate with or were no longer listening. For Cayce, the chief motivation for the fall was a heightened sense of self, with little to no sense of the Oneness, and increasing desires for sensual gratification, in many cases, of the basest kind. This led to the push into matter. He explains that there is only one energy, and it may be raised to enliven and enlighten life or lowered to levels that allow one to sensually intermingle with the beastly influences. After such intermingling, the mind is contaminated with these influences and cannot easily rise up to the higher levels of consciousness and energy, leaving the individual bound to the lower realms.

It was time for another creation, a second root race form, one that would allow more awareness of the higher realms of consciousness and the oneness. Despite the dangers to one's own consciousness, some of the more enlightened godlings decided to incarnate in order to help those who had become trapped in lower realms of selfness and matter. Among these incoming helpers was one called Ouowu. The name was not exactly that of an individual as we have today. Rather, it was the collective name for a soul group, all of whom were called "Ouowu." Individuality was not nearly what it has become today. Differentiating one soul or mind from another wasn't done; many were still very much a collective. Names were also the sound of the *vibrations* of the group rather than simply a label. To say the name was to evoke the vibration, energy, or spirit of that group. Eventually, however, Ouowu became individualized, associated with a single soul and mind as the individuation continued its course. In such cases, other soul members of the original group took on variations of the original name that best expressed their own individualizing qualities, such as Ouo, Ouo-tu, Ouo-mu, and so on. Ouowu became the individualized leader of this enlightened group of souls, dedicated to helping the lost ones without losing grasp on the truth themselves. Many other groups were involved in this mission, notably Io and Lala-mu, which we will meet later. Collectively, the groups of enlightened ones were called "The Children of the Law of One" because of their insistence that there was only one force in the universe, and all life came from and lived within that One. They taught that matter may be diverse but there is only one energy. They also taught that actions and thoughts produce reactions that must be met, an idea that the Children of Darkness considered absurd and just another attempt to keep them from doing whatever they wanted. In Vedic philosophy this law of action-reaction is called "karma," and affects everyone, whether one is aware of it or not.

Ouowu and her soul group perceived how the self-driven godlings had become dense and heavy; their minds narrower, less universal. As she and her soul-group studied this phenomenon they realized that the self-driven ones were moving so deeply into the Earth's dimension that they were separating from the higher, lighter dimensions of the cosmos and taking on the forms of creatures indigenous to this little planet. Out of energy and into matter, they were becoming terrestrial and solid, and communication with them was increasingly difficult. Their essence was the same, but just as water is vaporous in the clouds but can harden to ice, these once vaporous, cloud-like godlings were crystallizing into separated, solid forms. Their minds seemed trapped in these forms. But Ouowu knew this began long ago with their willful desire to separate from oneness and experience self without regard for the consequences. There was no greater sense of separation than to be in one single body, all by yourself. It was the ultimate impact of an out-of-control individuation process which had so much promise yet so much danger. Self was the evil – a self with no sense of or concern for the rest of life.

To Ouowu's amazement, these Earthly beings had developed a hierarchy among themselves, setting some souls above others, something that was totally alien in the celestial spheres where they were all children of the same family and parentage, equals. To add to this fall from paradise, the leaders of the terrestrial groups were expounding a belief that there actually was no central universal consciousness to whom they need remain attuned; their source of life was not a formless Creator but simply the visible forces of Nature. They encouraged all to take what they wanted from life. Successful survivors deserved to live better and use the labor of the others because it would improve the species. Power, superiority, force, strength, and survival of the fittest were among their new ideals and teachings. Ouowu and her soul-group considered this to be nonsense. They reasoned that some great distortion of perception had come over these minds, and, in order to see the truth again, they needed to regain their finer nature. However, in order for the soul-group to communicate with these Earthbound minds they would have to move deeper into the Earth's dimensions themselves, a move few of them wanted to make. Yet, they couldn't just leave these lost souls in such a ridiculous state of awareness.

Obviously, things had gotten beyond a brief flirtation with the Earth. It was now time to develop a long-range plan for dealing with the situation. On this point, many of the Children of the Law of One disagreed or had other ideas about how best to deal with the problem. For the first time a difference of opinion arose within the ranks of the Children of Oneness. Some felt that they had done enough to help the lost ones and, since they wanted to stay lost, let them go. Others felt that sending good minds after bad was a waste. But some felt that they only needed to find safe, isolated locations on the planet's surface and build centers to maintain a light presence in this dimension to which any mind could turn when one had enough of self-seeking and wanted to rediscover one's original purpose and nature. Ouowu, Io, and Lala-mu

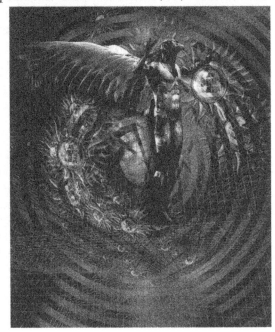

*Figure 152*
These Earthly beings had developed a hierarchy among themselves, setting some souls above others, something that was totally alien in the celestial spheres where they were all children of the same family...The leaders of the terrestrial groups were expounding a belief that there actually was no central universal consciousness to whom they need remain attuned; their source of life was not a formless Creator but simply the visible forces of Nature. From: DigitalVision.

were among those, and prepared their collective selves to enter. In order to do this a body type more suited for corporeal manifestation or physical incarnation would have to be developed. The semi-forms employed up to this point were either too ethereal to be useful in this world or too contaminated with selfish vibrations to be of help to the incoming enlightened minds. A new form was needed, one that would allow the incarnate mind and spirit to maintain its attunement to formless life while in this world of form. According to Cayce's reading of the Akasha, this second body type was created about 10 million years ago in Mu, termed the "second root race" body. Souls that entered these bodies were coming to keep the balance in the realm of material life, not to satisfy or gratify their appetites or egos. Though these bodies were not like bodies today, they had human-like form but were more comparable to focused fields of energy, light, and thought rather than flesh and bone. The second body type was powerful compared to our bodies, bridging the spiritual with the material. Whereas today we have seven endocrine glands secreting hormones, these bodies had seven whirling energy centers, known in the Vedas and Yoga Sutras as "chakras" or "padmes." (See *figure 153*.) In these centers a powerful electromagnetic interplay of positive and negative charges, yin and yang, generated energy. This was not an arbitrary selection of seven. The bodies were being developed according to what the godlings saw as natural characteristics of this world. As sunlight is refracted by matter into seven primary parts: red, orange,

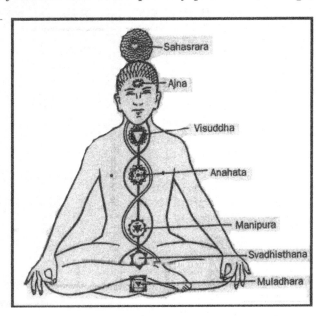

*Figure 153*
The Chakra System.
From: Edgar Cayce on
the Revelation (2000)
by J. Van Auken.
A.R.E. Press

yellow, green, blue, indigo, and violet, so these light beings manifested with seven energy centers: root, naval, solar plexus, heart, throat, forehead, and crown of the head.

7 Macaw, the prideful Lord of Death, may correspond to the chakras in the physical body when under the influence of selfish desires and ego-exalting urges, with little regard for the concerns and needs of the higher mind. In these early days, their whirling centers generated enough *élan vital* or electrical energy to light a small modern town. Every atom contains both positive and negative charged particles, so electricity cannot be separated from matter. Magnetism, conductivity, and crystal structure are all phenomena of electrical fields. The space around charged particles is an electrical field. Thus, "bodies" were fields of focused electricity. From thought-forms these beings had moved closer to materialization by becoming dynamic matter. Of course, this was the form of the godlings — the gods. Others were so immersed into matter that they were more animal than god. It was the age of gods and monstrosities.

The consistency of the godlings' second root race bodies was not fixed or set. Their powerful minds could concentrate these forms at a specific place, walk and talk, and then shift to ethereal formlessness, disappearing completely. But this was during the very early periods when they still had their heavenly connections. As time went on and the godlings lived more and more in this dimension, their bodies became more structured and three-dimensionally defined because their minds gradually lost a sense of the formless reality. What was originally an idea, a thoughtform, was crystallizing into matter. They became what we call today "real." You see, in these ancient times imagination was not illusion or idle daydreaming but *actual creation*. Actually, it still

*Figure 154*
Movement from spirit to matter involved separation from oneness — but it doesn't have to be that way. Photo: DigitalVision.

is, but few believe it, so it lies dormant within us. As the mind conceived, so it manifested. Imagination was and is the power behind creation, even creation of "real" matter.

As the increasing descent into matter took hold on these minds and hearts, they became heavier and less free to move between form and formlessness, between the realms of matter and those of pure energy. Egypt's famous "weighing of the heart" scene may harken to this, a light heart indicative of one's ability to pass through the darkness of the Netherworld on up to the heavens. Despite Ouowu's high ideals and purposes, she and her soul group eventually could not easily shift the conditions of their bodies into the infinite state. They learned instead to place their physical forms in sleep-like states while their minds and spirits sojourned in the higher dimensions. This required that their bodies be cared for in order for them to take possession of them upon returning from the ethereal sojourns. Temples were constructed for these periods of cosmic attunement. The temples were designed to accentuate electrical energy within the body, within the planet, around the planet (the magnetosphere), and beyond the planet, especially in relation to the Sun's energy. (See *figure 155.*)

*Figure 155*
The sun and earth are intimately connected. The earth's magnetosphere is greatly affected by the solar winds constantly bombarding us. NASA illustration.

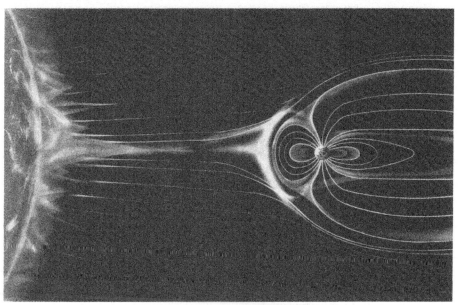

## A Time of Many Dangers

As the two sides became more clearly defined, the Children of Darkness became more rebellious and war-like, attacking the more vulnerable Children of the Law of One. And though the Children of the One were powerful, they were not war-like. Ouowu knew that she and her group needed to find remote, isolated places to avoid these constant confrontations with the terrestrials, and to carry on their work assisting in the re-enlightenment of any who wanted to recapture the glory that was theirs before the world was.

In addition to raging Children of Darkness, there were other dangers on this planet. At this time in the Earth's evolution the dinosaurs were long gone (occurring between 70 million to 220 million years ago - Mesozoic era), but it was still the Neocene period. Large mammals were increasing in size and number and posing serious danger to incarnate beings. This was not a concern in the early stages of human incarnation because they retained so much of their powers, but as they became more a part of the Earth, losing their connections to Nature and the source of power, they became very vulnerable to physical damage. However, at this time in the human journey, death was not yet a cyclical experience. As difficult as it may be to understand, Cayce notes that these beings, even the evil ones, did not die, but lived for as long as they wanted or as long as their bodies were not damaged; that could be hundreds or even thousands of years. One of the key characters in Cayce's readings of the Akasha is an Atlantean priestess named Alyne. She lived for six thousand years, leaving of her own accord to sojourn in the deeper meditations of the realms of Jupiter. This strange statement recalls that these are children of the cosmos, not just this little, blue planet that has become so important to us, and there are many realms beyond this world. Yet, while incarnate, one was vulnerable to physical laws and physical damage, which could lead to the soul having to abandon the body.

The enlightened ones also chose to abandon their magnificent temples rather than contend with the negative influences of invading terrestrials. Raising the energies of contention, confrontation, and war within their bodies and minds was abhorrent to the enlightened ones. They would just as soon leave the material structures and build new ones elsewhere. Eventually, Ouowu and her companions moved to an island off the eastern coast of Mu in the land of the morning sun and there built another center. Life at the center consisted of spending long periods of time in the formless life of pure energy and oneness, then coming back into the formed life of physical manifestation with wisdom, understanding, and power, and then conveying these to any who would listen. During their periods of physical manifestation they would teach and heal those who had become entrapped in matter and whose minds could not connect with formless life. The terrestrially trapped ones also had to be sustained with food, shelter, and clothing, and protected from the assaults of the Children of Darkness and the large animals. Ouowu and her companions became caretakers of these people. By virtue of their attunement, they could use the forces of Nature, the Sun's energy, and the Earth's magnetic fields (both internal and atmospheric) to generate power that could be used to light, heat, and protect those in and around the center. The few who retained high levels of attunement to Nature and the One could affect the temperature, atmospheric pressure, and winds in order to affect weather and thereby grow food year-round. Unfortunately, these abilities attracted many terrestrials that were not so much seeking enlightenment as sustenance. But Ouowu reasoned that it was better to have them under her influence even if their motivations were less than the highest.

Other enlightened groups built centers throughout Mu. In the South the collective group known as "Io" built a large temple complex. As this group became more individualized, the high priestess Io manifested as their leader. And, on the Western shores of Mu, the priestess Lala-mu developed a huge center and taught all who came that all power, all glory, all happiness is from the One original Mind, and all entities are of that Holy One, whether they still knew it or not. Lala-mu's teachings spread across Mu, uplifting many who were growing tired of the limitations and confusions of matter, but raising the ire of the leadership of Children of Darkness, who sought to destroy her. But she and her soul group were clever and powerful, in gentle ways, such as creating visual illusions that confused the physically-powerful terrestrials who hunted but never found her. There were several other centers, all in out-of-the-way places.

Work in the various light centers was in two fundamental areas: First, animal characteristics had to be removed from the minds and bodies of the intermingled or contaminated ones. One of the primary methods for diminishing these influences was through music. The music of the spirit in its activity through a physical body would quell the breast of many a tortured soul or tortured body that was warring within itself with the-spirit-that-is-willing but the-flesh-that-is-weak. The music, using reed instruments or flutes, would help minimize the body's desires and elevate the spirit's. Through this sacred music some terrestrials saw visions of their former selves, and once their minds perceived their truer selves, their physical forms responded in kind, losing many or all of the animal features and urges. Second, the temple needed to provide training and assistance for regaining attunement to the finer, lighter realms of formless life and the underlying Oneness. This required experiences in the dimensions of mind and spirit. The more one experienced these, the less matter possessed one.

Many were helped at the light centers, but Mu would not survive the discordant energies of the Children of Darkness. In addition to breaking the natural laws of procreation and phylum order, they carelessly toyed with the forces of the atom and gravity. The disharmony became so great that even the Earth revolted and began to shake and explode from the discordant vibrations. Mu broke into pieces, into islands. The misapplied, misdirected energy had shakened matter. Earthquakes, volcanoes, and weather changes transformed the Motherland Mu. Many of the contaminated bodies were destroyed in these cataclysms. Those who were attuned foresaw the coming changes and the signs that the end to this era was upon them. Some of the enlightened ones willingly left the carnal life (they "died" to their projected forms) to sojourn in other dimensions until the Earth was ready for another try. But others did not leave their bodies, choosing to join in a great migration to safer lands.

*Figure 156*
Colossal stone head at La Venta has features similar to Samoan characteristics. Photo: Corel Gallery.

*Figure 157*
Another stone head uncovered at La Venta with Samoan characteristics. Photo: *Stone Monuments of Southern Mexico*, Stirling (1943).

Ouowu and her band of light bearers abandoned their center and sailed east into the rising Sun, coming to what is today Arizona and New Mexico, becoming the mysterious cliff-dwellers in these areas. Io and her group migrated to the lands known today as Peru, becoming the predecessors of the Incas. Lalamu and her followers migrated to one of the island remnants of Mu, called La Mu, or simply La, and there continued their work until more changes forced them into the Indochina areas. Much of the wisdom and work of Mu was scattered throughout the Pacific to Tonga, Samoa, Fiji, Nan Madol on Pohnpei Island, the Marianas, Palau, Kosrae, Guam, Tahiti, and so on. Some of these peoples and their wisdom moved on further, entering into Peru and the western lands of Mexico and Guatemala. For example, some early Olmec statues and altar images match the Samoan people's appearance perfectly.

Unfortunately, self-seeking was not the sole possession of the terrestrially-bound minds. Free will and independent consciousness were God-given gifts, yet with just the slightest shift in intent, these sublime gifts could become weapons of devils. Every companion had to struggle to subdue their self-only desires in order to remain in harmony with the Creator and the other companions. Ouowu struggled hard to maintain her attunement and to aid those who sought her guidance and counsel. But she could feel herself assuming more and more the substance of the Earth, and as she struggled with the leaders of the Children of Darkness, she found herself becoming more determined to force her views upon them. This righteous and well-meaning desire was subtly giving strength to forces of self-interest. Although aware of this she seemed unable to stop herself.

The first and second ages were coming to an end and the third was about to begin. It would lead to the first true Eden of the World. The hope of everyone was riding on a new potential for healing, enlightenment, and victory over the forces that had taken such strong hold of the godlings.

### 3rd. Atlantis: Eden of the World, Male & Female, and the Five Races

About 210,000 B.C., many souls began a fresh incarnation in legendary Atlantis, a continent in the Atlantic Ocean. Mu was now many islands scattered throughout the Pacific Ocean, and though some temples were still providing help, the age of Mu was ebbing. It had gone on for an amazingly long time, nearly 12 million years, but by 50,700 B.C., it would be only a legend, a myth. Atlantis was the new hot spot for dynamic life, transformation, and new hope. The incarnations in Atlantis would be purely second root-race bodies; no mixed animal forms. The Children of One and the Children of Darkness both began to use these bodies. These bodies were androgynous, hermaphroditic, having both sexes in one (as do many plants, some animals, and the mythological Hermaphroditus, the bisexual child of Hermes and Aphrodite). Therefore, godlings, good and bad, could conceive new bodies within themselves, attracting fellow souls to inhabit them, often from their soul group. Even though these bodies were androgynous, souls tended to accentuated one sexual aspect, and feminine was the predominant aspect during the early periods in Earth. It was an age of feminine rule. All the major leaders were predominantly feminine in their expression. Although Ouowu, Io, and Lala-mu were predominantly feminine, they had male energies as well. Because of this they could conceive within themselves; no coupling with another body was required. To build their communities, they would often conceive new bodies, gestate them in the wombs of their minds, and then bring them forth into the form world to be inhabited by souls coming out of the unseen realms of formless life. But Atlantis would be a new era, one in which many amazing changes would bring about better conditions for all – at least that was the intention. Sexual unity may appear to be a good thing, but this world was a lonely place for souls in separate, individual bodies. The oneness and community that was always present in the boundless dimensions of mind and spirit were difficult to experience in the world. Each mind was isolated in a separate body. But that was about to change.

According to the Akasha, Eden, that garden with God, first occurred around 106,000 B.C. in a paradisiacal portion of Atlantis called Poseidia (possibly identified with Poseidon, the Greek mythological god of the sea; the Romans called this god Neptune). According to the Akasha, it wasn't until about 12,000 B.C. that the Eden spoken of in the Bible was created, between the Tigris and Euphrates rivers with Adam, Eve, and the troublesome serpent. The Eden of Atlantis was as important as the Bible's. In this first Eden the Logos of God incarnated among the Children of God to help all the godlings find their way out of matter and selfishness. The Logos is the essential mind or consciousness of God *individualized* in order to be among individualized beings. The disciple John in the first verses of his Gospel refers to the Logos as "The Word" that became flesh and dwelt among us. This was a momentous entry into matter, into the world of form. The infinite was now among the finite, the universal among the individualized. The One had come among the Many in a form that they could relate to and learn from.

Upon entering this world the Logos quickly determined that it would be helpful if the two sexual aspects were separated into two unique forms or bodies, not just for companionship but to be *helpmeets* to one another (see Genesis 2:18). This world required a different arrangement of being in order to overcome the sense of loneliness and separateness. In many ways this separate feeling contributed to the selfishness and lack of cooperation with or attunement to the oneness. The Logos, God incarnate, divided its hermaphroditic self into the legendary Lilith, the first individually manifested female, and Amilius, the first male. These two were the first Eve and Adam. They were twins of the same being, halves of one mind, one spirit. According to Cayce's reading of the Akasha, it took eighty-six years to accomplish the separated projection of the complementary male-female aspects of soul into separate body types. Once this was accomplished, the complementary qualities could come together in a union that reflected the oneness in the heavenly dimensions, and the two would feel comforted and united. Oneness of the two was the emotional, mental experience that was hoped for. And it worked well for a while.

These new bodies were the third creation, the third root race for the godlings. Once the Logos had shown the way, most souls repeated the process, separating their male and female qualities, and manifesting them individually. Word of this spread around the world. In these ancient times the world still spoke one common language, so communication was easy and fast. The news that God's Logos had come among the people of Poseidia and created a new body type drew visitors from around the world. Some came driven by skepticism, some by wonder and hopefulness, some to challenge and confront, and some because it was their last hope. Poseidia was the center of the world. Even Lala-mu came from the far side of the planet to experience in the physical what she had in the mind and spirit

Now union could occur between males and females, creating love, companionship, families, and home. The concept of home was one of the most fascinating to incarnate godlings. Prior to this, people lived in groups and community structures. The idea of sharing a special place with your companion and any offspring from that union was new. It quickly became apparent how comforting this arrangement was to incarnate souls. Sexually matched partners also fit with Nature's arrangement of this world. A sense of balance now existed. The godlings became harmonious with Nature's ways. It is repulsive today to accept that these early couples were halves of themselves, or incestuous brothers and sisters. At that ancient time genetics was not an issue among the Children of the One because their bodies were not yet completely physical structures like today, subject to genetic mixing and the strengths and weaknesses that we've come to understand. They were coupling with their spirits, minds, and hearts in oneness with God, the Oneness, not copulating with their physical bodies (except for the Children of Darkness which had been copulating using animal forms and later humanoid forms). Our mythologies reveal this situation, containing numerous stories of brothers and sisters married to one another. For example, in Egyptian mythology the great god Osiris is married to the great goddess Isis, who is also his sister, or in truth, the feminine half of his whole soul. The god Ra (pronounced *ray*) is married to his feminine half Rat (pronounced *ray-t*). The god Thoth (pronounced *tote* or *tothe* with a long "o") or, as the Greek's called him, Hermes, is married to his feminine half Maat (pronounced *mate*). It was the way of things in these early times. Later, as genetic forces became more important and more lessons needed to be learned, it became evident that marriages would gain by uniting with other than one's other half (in the ancient sense of "other half").

### Lilith – The First Eve

Though Lilith may seem an obscure figure in history, we have physical artifacts showing her image, written records, and even a Bible passage. The oldest work in which she appears, under the name "Lillake," is the Prologue to the Sumerian tablet of Ur about the exploits Gilgamesh, circa 2000 B.C. The Prologue recounts a creation legend:

> After heaven and earth had been separated and mankind and the underworld created, the sea ebbed and flowed in honor of its lord, but the south wind blew hard and uprooted a willow tree from its banks on the Euphrates. A goddess saw the poor tree and put it in Princess Inanna's garden in Uruk. Inanna tended the tree with great care, hoping some day to make a bed and throne from it. But alas, when the tree matured she found that a serpent who could not be charmed had made its nest in the roots, and a Zu-bird had made its nest in the branches, and the dark maid Lilith had built her home in the trunk.

In this tale we again find many of the symbols that appear around the ancient world: tree, serpent, and bird. In Yucatan, the Tree of Life is in the midst of the world, its roots descend into the Underworld and its branches upward to the Heavens. In this Sumerian tale we find the serpent nested in the roots and the bird in the branches, emblems of the greater story of the lower mind descending into the Underworld and the higher mind staying in the better perspective, the wiser knowing. Lilith, in this story, abides in between these two states of consciousness.

The second source for Lilith's legend is found in Jewish mysticism, notably "The Alphabet of Ben Sira," written sometime between 700 and 900 A.D. but recounting a tale that dates back to the time of the Babylonian king Nebuchadnezzar. In this account Lilith is Adam's first wife, before the more docile Eve. Lilith considered herself an equal of Adam's, made in the image of God. She would not subordinate herself to Adam's wishes, especially lying under him during sex. She insisted that if anyone was going under someone it was he not she. But Adam wanted her to be subservient to him. It all ended by Lilith invoking the name of the "Ineffable One" (a name that is so sacred, it is inexpressible), which was thought to be impossible since it was inexpressible; but she speaks it and thereby flies away. Adam, disheartened by her leaving, calls upon the Creator, "Sovereign of the Universe," to bring her back or give him another; for he had already looked among all the creatures of the Earth and found none to be his companion. A female godling was the only one who could be a true companion. The Creator then instructs three of his angels to go after Lilith and insist that she return. If she is determined to remain apart, then she must allow death to exist among her children. It may seem like a harsh demand but her children were immortals, immortals that had lost touch with God and the purpose for their existence. In order to ensure they did not live forever as terrestrial beings on this little blue planet, the Creator wanted them to experience death, an intermission from physical manifestation, in hopes that during this period they might recall their original state and seek to regain it. Lilith agrees. One hundred of her children will die every day. Returning to Adam was not an option for her. "Leave me!" she said to the angels. "I was created only to cause sickness to infants. If the infant is male, I have dominion over him for eight days after his birth, if female, for twenty days." The angels, still concerned for Lilith, told her that if she did not return with them, then she would die. Lilith, not one to be tricked, simply asked them how she could die since "God has ordered me to take charge of all newborn children: males up to eight days, females up to twenty days?" When their trick didn't work, the angels reverted to pleading with her. But she would not go. Yet, because of their concern, she swore to them by the name of the living and eternal God: "Whenever I see you or your names or your forms in an amulet, I will have no power over that infant." The names of these three angels became powerful shields on amulets worn around the necks of infants. Their names are: Snvi, Snsvi, and Smnglof; sometimes written as Senoy, Sansenoy, and Semangelof (the addition of vowels helps us pronounce them but ancient Hebrew used few to no vowels). Ben Sira recounts this legend to King Nebuchadnezzar when the king asks Ben Sira to heal his young son. Ben Sira writes the angels' names on an amulet and puts it around the boy's neck, who recovers his health.

Some Hebrew legends hold that because Lilith left Adam before the Fall in the Garden, having not eaten of the apple, she is immortal and has no part in the curse upon Adam and Eve. Nevertheless, most Hebrew tales portray her as a demon who seduces men in their dreams. It is said that she lives by the Red Sea where lascivious demons abide. (Hebrews have a tradition that water attracts demons.) If Lilith approached a child and fondled him, he would laugh in his sleep; striking the sleeping child's lips with one finger would cause her to vanish. After circumcision a male baby was permanently protected against Lilith. This leads one to ask how then did their men get seduced by her in their dreams?

Hebrews may have derived "Lilith" from "layil," which means "night." Some Hebrew traditions hold that she was incarnate as Queen of Sheba and seduced King Solomon. This mainly comes from an account which says that the Queen of Sheba had unshaven, hairy legs, a sure sign of Lilith because in both Hebrew and Arabian folklore, Lilith is a hairy night-monster. In Babylonian and Assyrian legend she is Lilitu, a wind-spirit, one of a triad.

The Bible passage is found in Isaiah 34:14-15 which describes the desolate ruins of the Edomite Desert where satyrs, reems (large, wild oxen), pelicans, owls, jackals, ostriches, arrow-snakes, and vultures (kites) keep Lilith company. It reads:

> Wildcats shall meet with hyenas,
>> goat-demons shall call to each other;
> there too Lilith shall repose,
>> and find a place to rest.
> There shall the owl nest
>> and lay and hatch and brood in its shadow.

In some translations of this passage the name "Lilith" is replaced with "night monster." The reference to an owl in this passage is significant because it too refers to Lilith. In a Sumerian relief Lilith is shown with owl's feet, standing on the backs of a pair of lions and holding in each hand the Sumerian version of the Ankh, the Egyptian symbol for Life. (See *figure 158*.) In Asia the owl is symbolic of wisdom, particularly wisdom received in the night. We find this pertinent passage in psalms 19:2: "Day unto day uttereth speech, And night unto night showeth knowledge." In the Roman Catholic edition of the Bible, the Book of Wisdom refers to wisdom using the feminine pronoun "she." An Asian proverb holds that the reason owls are usually seen alone, as is Lilith, is because "wisdom stands alone."

In the Hebrew *Targum Yerushalmi*, the priestly blessing in Biblical books of Numbers 6:26 becomes: " The Lord bless thee in all thy doings, and preserve thee from the Lilim!" Lilim are Lilith's children.

The Greek commentator Hieronymous identified Lilith with the Greek Lamia, a Libyan queen deserted by Zeus, whom his wife Hera robbed of her children. Lilith took revenge for this act by robbing other women of theirs.

In Cayce's reading of the Akasha there was not an evil, dark tale of Lilith, simply one of equality and feminine power. In fact, Cayce reads that these feminine and masculine portions of the incarnate Logos re-

turned to Earth as some very sacred people, always working together. He lists these incarnations as: Amilius and Lilith, Adam and Eve, Hermes and Maat, and Jesus and Mary. Each was an incarnation of the Logos, the Word, the Messiah: feminine and masculine aspects of them. According to Cayce, the Jewish sect called *Essenes* knew this and were actually looking among the woman of the time for the coming of the feminine Messiah, the feminine Christ, through whom the masculine Christ would be immaculately conceived. The Essenes simply read Genesis and determined

*Figure 158*
Lilith depicted on ancient Sumerian relief. From: Dover.

that when the Lord turned to Eve as she was leaving the Garden and said that out of her would come the redeemer, He meant a woman would come first, then the man. In their temple in Mt. Carmel the Essenes took in women of spiritual attunement and eventually they were rewarded by a young virgin who had actually been born in the temple of an immaculate conception of her mother Ann. But now let's return to Atlantis and our journey to Yucatan.

## Lilith and Amilius – A Golden Age

In Poseidia Lilith and Amilius attempted to establish a new order. They established principles to live by and developed a plan whereby all could be redeemed and realigned with the original purposes and consciousness. Among their plans was a five-point assault upon the dark forces influencing this world and tempting even the Children of One.

The plan called for five large groups of light bearers to incarnate in five different regions of the world and establish major centers of enlightened culture and education. Each group would assume responsibility for subduing the captivating influence of one of the five sensual influences: sight, sound, taste, smell, and touch. Each of the groups would assume some of the emotional and attitudinal characteristics of individualness represented by what we call today "racial characteristics." Atlantis would be the original place of the red race, accentuating the sense of touch. The Andes Mountains, especially the area near the Peruvian lands, would be the original place of the brown race, accentuating the sense of smell. The Gobi area (not a desert in those times) would be the original place of the yellow race, accentuating the sense of hearing. The Caucasus and Carpathian Mountains would be the original place of the white race, accentuating the sense of sight. Nubia, in the Sudan and southern Egypt, would be the original place of the black race, accentuating the sense of taste. These would setup a ring around the Earth of wisdom and light.

Amilius and Lilith firmly established principles that countered those of the Children of Darkness, who now had a new leader and a sexual preference for the masculine qualities. In Atlantis they became known as the Sons of Baal or Baaliel, or as Cayce so often called them, Sons of Beliel (a term that St. Paul and the poet Milton also used). But they were not the most dangerous problem. Among the Children of the One, jealousy over the varying degrees of beauty achieved began to infest their hearts. Those close to Lilith and Amilius began to argue over who was the more important. And those who were not as close to them as they would like began to envy those who were. The insidious way in which these little spites grow within hearts and minds was and remains today a serious danger to harmony and cooperation. Before long, factions developed among the Children of Oneness, factions that began to plot against one another's interests and influence. As bad as this was, there was an even worse development, one that even the Bible records in Genesis 6:1-4:

> And it came to pass, when men began to multiply on the face of the ground, and daughters were born unto them, that the Sons of God saw the daughters of men that they were fair; and they took them wives of all that they chose. And Jehovah said, 'My spirit shall not strive with man for ever, for that he also is flesh: yet shall his days be a hundred and twenty years.' The Nephilim (giants) were in the earth in those days, and also after that, when the Sons of God came unto the daughters of men, and they bare children to them: the same were the mighty men that were of old, the men of renown.

Up to this point in time there were three companies of beings: 1) the godlings who had pushed their way into matter for gratification and exaltation, using animals forms and later humanoid male and female forms to breed among themselves in the same manner as the animals; 2) the godlings who had come into the Earth — not for gratification or exaltation — but to help maintain enlightenment and a connection with the formless realms and were conceiving new forms within themselves into which came souls from out of the unseen realms of heaven; and, 3) the zombie-like "things" that were created by the minds of the godlings to serve them and had become a breeding group of their own, in the manner of the animals. Though Amilius and Lilith intended for males and females to come together to give comfort and oneness to each other and to conceive, it was more ideally done in subtle bodies and in accord with the Infinite One. They did not copulate in flesh bodies like the earthy Sons of Beliel, zombies, and animals. This is a difficult concept to convey today because we are so physical that coupling without copulation requires some imagination, and the difference between a child of God and a child of man is not as clear as it was back then. Cayce simply compares this type of conception with that of the lowly amoeba, who pushes out from within itself another separate body, splitting its own gene pool.

In those times the goal was to raise the consciousnesses, desires, and energies of the sons of man upward to the higher awarenesses, purposes, and energies of the sons of God, and eventually back into the Oneness of the formless realms of life and the cosmos. It didn't happen. The higher vibes and awarenesses of the sons of God began to descend further into physical matter and sensual experience.

In the sacred teachings, particularly in the Vedic ones, it was described as reversing the flow of the life force, energy, the mind, downward, often depicted as a serpent (representing the kundalini life force within each being) descending down a tree or staff. For example, in the Biblical Garden of Eden, the serpent descends from the Tree of the Knowledge of Good and Evil, eventually ending up crawling upon its belly among the dust of the Earth. This is often countered in mystical ceremonies in the ancient world by raising up the serpent energy, the mind, to higher levels of life and consciousness. This is the winged-serpent idea that we find in Central American and Egyptian art and mythology. It is even in some of our major texts today. Recall the teaching Jesus gave to Nicodemus during a secret nighttime visit (John 3:14). Nicodemus wanted to learn the secrets, seeking out this strange master who was becoming such a problem for the Sanhedrin, of which Nicodemus was a member. He received three key teachings from Jesus. The first is that we must be born again. We have been born physically but we need to also be born spiritually. The second teaching is that no one ascends to heaven but he or she who first descended from it, referring to the involution of mind into matter prior to our evolution up through matter. All of us, whether we remember it or not, have a soul within us that first descended from heaven. That part of us is familiar with the formless dimensions beyond the world. But the key to our study in this chapter is the third teaching: "As Moses raised the serpent in the desert, so must the son of man be raised up to eternal life."

Jesus is referring to the time when Moses left the kingdom of Pharaoh (so symbolic of the outer ego and worldly pursuits) to search for his true self and God in the desert. In his search he comes upon a deep well around which seven virgins are attempting to water their flocks. Seven virgins in the desert ... is there some deeper meaning here? Of course there is. These seven virgins, daughters of a high priest, are symbolic of the seven spiritual centers, the seven chakras, the seven lotuses within each being. Moses waters them and their flocks, ultimately marrying the eldest one. Afterwards, he meets God in a burning bush and, for the first time, is instructed how to transform his staff into a serpent and raise the serpent up again into a staff.[2] Later, when he has all the people out in the desert with him, Moses is instructed by God to place a fiery or brazen serpent upon a raised staff and anyone who looks upon

---

[2] Exodus 2, 3, and 4.

*Figure 159*
Gustav Doré's 1866 illustration of Moses raising the serpent on a staff.

it will be healed.[3]

The writer of Exodus is trying to convey more than a literal, physical story to us. We have to go back to the Garden of Eden to fully understand this, because Adam and Eve were not the only ones to fall in the Garden; the serpent fell also. The life force and consciousness within the descending godlings was falling to lower and lower levels. The life force can be harmful if misused, but raising it is a key to restoring the levels of energy and consciousness before the world was. In Patanjali's *Yoga Sutras* (circa 300 B.C.), the process of raising the energy begins with an understanding of where the energy is in the body, how it is raised, and the path it follows through the body. According to the *Yoga Sutras*, the energy is "coiled up" like a serpent (*kundalini*) in the lower part of the torso of the body, near

*Figure 160*
The Egyptians always depicted the cobra emerging from the forehead as in this illustration of Ramses II. From *Egyptian Motifs*, Dover.

[3] Numbers 21:8-9.

*Figure 161*
This huge sculpure at La Venta depicts how the Olmecs sought to receive Oneness via the forehead. Photo by Lora Little.

the base of the spine. It moves up the spinal column (*sushumna*) through the spiritual centers, *chakras* (wheels) or *padmes* (lotuses), to the base of the brain and over through the brain to the brow. The path of the kundalini through the body is represented by a cobra in the striking position or by pharaoh's crook or a shepherd's crook. (A crook is a staff with a hook on the upper end. The shepherd's crook is flared at the very tip.) Many books today teach that the kundalini culminates at the crown of the head, but the more ancient images and teachings as well as Cayce's always depict it culminating at the forehead, in the same place were pharaoh's brow cobra is positioned. This will cause some confusion among many who have studied and practiced for years using the crown chakra as the highest spiritual center in the body. Cayce insisted that the true path of the kundalini comes over through the crown chakra and into the third-eye chakra on the brow.

The seven spiritual centers are connected with the seven endocrine glands within the body: 1) testes or ovaries, 2) cells of Leydig (named after the doctor who discovered them), 3) adrenals, 4) thymus, 5) thyroid, 6) pineal, and 7) pituitary. They are also connected with major nerve ganglia or plexuses along the spine: pelvic or lumbar, hypogastric or abdominal, epigastric or solar, cardiopulmonary or heart and lung area, pharyngeal or throat, and the brain itself.

Though Amilius and Lilith's mission was successful in many ways, the declining awareness of the those in the Earth was evident. Salvation was not at hand, despite all efforts.

Amilius and Lilith withdrew to the deeper realms in the mind and spirit of God to prepare themselves for the next great effort. It was clear that the potential companions to the Creator were coming fully into selfishness and materiality. The plan to reverse this movement before it got out of hand had failed. Now spirit and mind were going to come fully into this world, experiencing every part of it until it no longer held any lure, and they could take it or leave it at will.

The ancient lands of Mu, Oz, Og, Ohum, Zu, Atlantis, and many others were coming to an end, forcing huge migrations to the lands of the new way. After the cleansing by flood (which Cayce dates at 22,800 B.C.), the lands of Yucatan, China, India, Persia, Egypt, Scandinavia, and others were beginning. Yucatan would rise from the ashes of Mu and Atlantis, and deep within her soil would be buried the records of the first three ages.

### 4th. Adam and Eve

According to Cayce's reading of the Akasha, the story of Adam and Eve that begins in the second chapter of Genesis is the creation of the fourth body-type, the fourth root race, for the godlings to use in their journey through this dimension. Let's look at some of the fascinating aspects of this story.

Genesis begins, "In the beginning God created the heavens and the earth." The word "God" is a translation of the original Hebrew word "Elohiym," which is a plural noun for the deity. The use of the plural form reflects the collective, holistic nature of the original aspect of God that began the creation. When Elohiym speak, "they" refer to themselves in the plural, as in Genesis 1:26: "Let *us* make him in *our* image, according to *our* likeness." Elohiym is clearly not a singular, supreme entity separate from the creation. God is the Collective, composed of the created ones while at the same time their source. We actually contribute to the composition of God. That is not to say that we compose all of God's being, but simply to say that a portion of God's being is us. In Cayce's reading 900-181 he encourages a person to come to know "that not only God is God but self is a portion of that Oneness."

Changing of the name of God is a way of conveying changes in our relationship with the Creator. Each movement further away from direct, conscious connection, changes the name. Therefore, the original creation is done by *Elohiym* in chapter 1 of Genesis. The second creation, which occurs in chapter 2, is done by the "Lord God," *Yahweh Elohiym.* But by Chapter 4, when Adam and Eve begin to conceive physically, the "Lord," *Yahweh* is the extent of our relationship. From being an integral portion of the Oneness to subordinate subject of the Lord, the godlings slipped into darkness and separation.

Originally, Elohiym (sometimes spelled *Elohim,* but is usually pronounced *El-o-heem*) creates us in Its own image, "Let *Us* make man [*adam*] in *Our* image, after *Our* likeness.... So Elohiym created man [*adam*] in His own image, in the image of God He created him; male and female He created them," (Gen. 1:26-27). In this passage the Hebrew word for man is *adam*, interpreted as meaning "reddish" or "ruddy," but also means "persons" or "people" collectively, and can mean an "indefinite someone."[4] Here adam is male and female – androgynous, hermaphroditic. It is not until the second chapter of Genesis that the "Lord God" creates adam "out of the dust of the earth," in other words, *in the flesh*, that these sexual parts are separated. When this occurs, the name "adam" takes on the meaning we most commonly associate with this word, "man," a male man with a capital "A." But "adam" was first made in the image of Elohiym, which is not flesh. Then, symbolized by the changing of the name of the creator from "God" to "Lord God" and, subsequently, to simply "Lord," we see the descent from direct God-consciousness to self-consciousness.

Another important point about this creation is that it is, according to Cayce's reading of the Akasha, a *group* creation, not just the creation of one famous person. At this stage of the creation "adam" is referring to an original group of souls created in Elohiym's image, and subsequently remade in spiritualized flesh by Yahweh Elohiym, then into mortal flesh by Yahweh. According to Cayce's readings, the souls, those godlings within the One God, entered the earth in five places, as five nations, and in five races; and one of these was "adam" ( 900-227, 364-9 & -13). The Bible is the story of those souls.

At this point in Genesis, God has created everything in *thought*, in God's mind, not physically — all existed in God's consciousness. This is symbolized in the passage that comes *after* the seven days of creation: "Now no shrub of the field was yet in the earth [physically], and no plant of the field had yet sprouted, for the Lord God [note the name change] had not sent rain upon the earth; and there was no man [in flesh] to cultivate the ground," (Gen. 2:4-15). The heaven, earth, and adam that had already been created in chapter one were only in the mind of God not yet in form or matter. This was our natural home before entering the flesh. It is what is spoken of in Jesus' prayer to God, "And now, glorify Thou me together with Thyself, Father, with the glory which I had with Thee *before the world was*."[5] And it is that realm spoken of when Jesus says to us, "I go to prepare a place for you ... that where I am there you may be also. And you know the way where I am going."[6]

Now, like many of us who are so much into physical consciousness, the disciple Thomas challenges this statement, "Lord, we do not

[4] The Hebrew-Greek Key Study Bible, Spiros Zodhiates, Th.D., AMG Publishers, 1990.

[5] John 17:5

[6] John 14:2-4

know where you are going. How do we know the way?" But we **do** know the way. Deep within us is our true nature. Deep within us we remember the original home, and we know the way. Each of us was there in the beginning. Each of us was originally created in the image and likeness of Elohiym. Within us that original nature lives and intuitively knows its way home. As Jesus said to Nicodemus, "No one ascends to heaven but he or she who has already descended from it, even the Son of Man."[7]

As we touched on earlier, ancient teachings hold that the One is composed of two qualities: that of the *dark* – meaning unseen, deep, and from out of which comes the other aspect, *light* – meaning seen, present, and active. In the Eastern philosophies the terms "yin" and "yang" are used to express these characteristics. Yin is a feminine, unseen, inner principle; yang a masculine, seen, projected principle. An objective observation of the physical bodies of the female and male, reflects these qualities. A female's sexual organs are deep *within* her torso, a male's outside his. A female body has more *inner* processes than a male, such as menstrual cycles, conception, gestation, and milk production. The female reflects the characteristics of the inner aspect of God. Thus she is a reflection of the dark, unknown, unseen, unmanifested God, the yin. She represents the unconscious, sleep, and "Night" in Genesis, thus, "the Moon and the Stars." This would also imply that the feminine is the wind, the spirit, especially since she is the conceiver, the "life-giver."[8] Eve is created by God casting a deep sleep over humanity (i.e. adam), and while in that deep state, the feminine is removed and separated into an individual form. (See *figure 162*.) The male reflects the characteristics of the outer, manifested God. Thus, he is a reflection of the active, changing, personal, present God. He represents the conscious, wakefulness; "Day" in Genesis, thus the Sun. He is the "tiller of the soil," the doer, the conqueror. This would also imply that he is then the reflection of the breath, the soul, especially since he is the changing, developing "doer." Our original nature was composed of both these forces in one being, but soon these were to be separated.

Our fall from the original place of being is allegorically presented as the separation of the sexes and the eating of the "Fruit of the Tree of the Knowledge of Good and Evil,"[9] which symbolizes consuming knowledge without understanding. The Cayce readings state it this way, "...seek not for knowledge alone. For, look – LOOK – what it brought Eve. Look rather for that wisdom which was eventually founded in she [Mary] that

[7] John 3:18

[8] "Chavvah," the Hebrew word first used to describe the Eve portion of the original adamic being.

[9] Gen. 2:17

*Figure 162*
Gustav Doré's 1866 illustration of Eve's split from Adam.

was addressed as 'the handmaid of the Lord'...."[10]

In the Genesis story, Yahweh Elohiym commanded adam not to eat from the Tree of the Knowledge of Good and Evil, saying "for in the day you eat from it, you shall surely die."[11] Up to this point, we were immortal beings, in the image of the immortal Elohiym. However, the further we moved from consciousness of our connectedness with the Eternal One, the more we lost connectedness to the source of life. Adam and Eve began to live too completely in the flesh, losing touch with the life-giving energy. They began to reverse the flow of the Life Force, the *élan vital*, bringing it further into self-consciousness. This became so acute that, according to the Cayce readings, we actually experienced a death of the spirit.[12] To put it another way, we died to the spiritual, life-giving influence. Another significant piece to this puzzling death was the growth of something *other than God*. The serpent in the Garden represents the mind and the life-force moving downward into only self, disconnected from the Collective. It is self without regard for the Whole or for other beings. It is the self that seeks self-gratification, self-glorification, self-aggrandizement, self-centeredness. But in order for the potential companions of God to be true companions, they had to have a strong sense of self. As the Cayce readings state it: we must come to know ourselves to be ourselves, yet one with the whole (the rest of creation and the Creator).[13] In order to achieve this goal, we had to develop a sense of self, who we are,

[10] #2072-10
[11] Gen. 2:17
[12] #281-33

individually. Then, we must choose to cooperate in oneness with the Whole. Therefore, despite the dangers inherent in the development of self-consciousness, it was allowed because it was and remains the way to full realization of our role as divine companions. Yet, it often becomes a stumbling block.

Adam, Eve, and the serpent (all aspects of ourselves) fall from grace and lose the comfort of the Garden. The Tree of Life, symbolizing immortality, is now protected from us, to keep us from becoming eternal *terrestrial* beings when we are meant to be eternal *celestial* beings. Now we enter the cycle of life and death. This is further symbolized in Eve's conception of the two beings we discussed earlier: Cain and Able. Cain literally means the "acquired" one (our forming egos). Abel means "a breath," or soul (our spiritually aware selves).[14] Of course, God favors the offerings of our souls more than our egos, as symbolized in Abel's offerings as opposed to Cain's. However, Cain (ego) is angered by this and kills Abel (soul). But the Lord, *Yahweh*, comes to Cain, and says, "Why are you angry, and why has your countenance fallen? If you do well, will you not be accepted? And if you do not do well, then sin is couching at the door [of your consciousness]; its desire is for you, but you must master it."[15]

The fourth creation was the one we have been living with for much of human history as we know it today. The bodies we use today are fourth-age bodies, adamic bodies, homo-sapien bodies. But, as the Mayan's prophetic calendar indicates, we are about to go through another change on December 22, 2012. The fifth age, the age of "movement," began with Noah, but the fifth body type begins to form in the first decades of the 2000s.

## 5th. Noah: The Age of Movement

This is the point in history that the Bible says God regretted making man and began to conceive of a way to start over. The legendary great flood that is recorded in all the world's ancient tales was about to begin. A Biblical reference is on the next page:

"And Jehovah [notice the name change once again] saw that the wickedness of man was great in the earth, and that every imagination of the thoughts of his heart was only evil continually. And it repented Jehovah that he had made man on

[13] #815-7
[14] Gen. 4
[15] Gen. 4:6-7

the earth, and it grieved him at his heart. And Jehovah said, 'I will destroy man whom I have created from the face of the ground; both man, and beast, and creeping things, and birds of the heavens; for it repents me that I have made them.'" (Genesis 6:5-7)

There is a fascinating past-life reading for a woman who Cayce said was on Noah's ark. In the reading Cayce gives some insights into the coming changes in the new age that we are expecting, the Aquarian Age, and their relationship to the changes that occurred during Noah's time. You'll recall, even Jesus references Noah's time when his disciples asked him about the so called "End Times" (see Matthew 25). The reading begins with Cayce's mind looking over this woman's "Book of Life," her records on the skein of time and space, the Akasha:

> What an unusual record - and one of those who might be termed as physically 'the mothers of the world!' Because the entity was one of those in Noah's ark. The entity has appeared when there were new revelations to be given. And again it appears when there are new revelations to be made.
>
> May the entity so conduct its mind, its body and its purposes, then, as to be a channel through which such messages may come that are needed for the awakenings in the minds of men as to the necessity for returning to the search for their relationship with the Creative Forces or God.
>
> For as has been given from the beginning, the deluge [Noah's flood] was not a myth (as many would have you believe) but a period when man had so belittled himself with the cares of the world, with the deceitfulness of his own knowledge and power, as to require that there be a return to his dependence wholly - physically and mentally - upon the Creative Forces.
>
> Will this entity see such again occur in the earth? Will it be among those who may be given directions as to how, where, the elect may be preserved for the replenishing again of the earth?
>
> Remember, not by water - for it is the mother of life in the earth - but rather by the element, fire. (Cayce reading #3653-1)

This is a disturbing reading. It seems to be saying that there will be a new destruction, like the one that occurred during Noah's period, only this time it will be by fire — not water. And it also seems to be saying that the destruction will be of such a magnitude that we will be "given directions as to how, where, the elect may be preserved for the replenishing again of the earth!"

I know many of us are tired of these doom prophecies which are so awesome. It seems impossible to go on living our daily lives with them hanging over our heads. One thing in Cayce's comments that is important to realize is that this reading does clearly indicate that life does go on, even as it did after Noah.

The fire mentioned in this reading could possibly come from the increase in solar radiation rather than combustion. There are many ways this could happen, from increasing "greenhouse" effect to a breakdown in the protective Van Allen belts during a planetary pole shift.

## A Shifting of the Earth's Poles

One significant event we should keep an eye on is the shifting of the Earth's poles – no small event! Cayce was asked, "What great change or the beginning of what change, if any, is to take place in the Earth in the year 2,000 to 2,001 A.D.?" Edgar Cayce answered: "When there is a shifting of the poles; or a new cycle begins," (826-8). We have to be careful with this reading because Cayce's trance mind is under the influence of the question, and here the question is rather open-ended, allowing for a "great change" to begin or take place in the year 2000 to the year 2001! Therefore, Cayce's answer could be about 2001 and simply the "beginning" of the pole shift. But other Cayce readings help us get a better understanding of what he was seeing. For example, in reading 378-16 he says the testing period "begins in '58 and ends with the changes wrought in the upheavals and the shifting of the poles, as begins then the reign in '98 (as time is counted in the present)." This seems to mean that the shifting poles begins in 1998 and therefore we might assume that his answer about the years 2000 to 2001 was the actual shifting becoming evident to us all. In reading 3976-15 he says, "There will be shifting then of the poles - so that where there has been those of a frigid or the semi-tropical will become the more tropical, and moss and fern will grow. And these will begin in those periods in '58 to '98, when these will be proclaimed as the periods when His light will be seen again in the clouds. As to times, as to seasons, as to places, ALONE is it given to those who have named the name - and who bear the mark of those of His calling and His election in their bodies. To them it shall be given." Again, Cayce seems to be saying that the shifting of the poles begins in the latter year of this forty-year period from '58 to '98, culminating in the actual or noticeable shift in 2000 to 2001.

Those who study paleomagnetics have found that in the last 70 million years the Earth's magnetic field has reversed "abruptly" more than 100 times. This refers to the magnetic north and south poles that affect our compasses and by which we navigate. The other poles are the north and south tips of the axis upon which our planet spins. Like a top, our planet spins around a central axis line. Has this ever shifted?

According to scientists, in the last 4 million years the axis around which the Earth spins has reversed its poles at least 9 times. That's an axis shift about every 444,444 years, while the magnetic poles have shifted about every 700,000 years. However, scientists disagree on the magnetic poles shifts. Some find evidence that the magnetic poles reverse every 100,000 years, some have found evidence of shifts every 50,000 years. Is Cayce talking about a magnetic shift or an axis shift? He certainly is talking about climate changes, so unless magnetic shifts would affect weather patterns, one would be inclined to believe that Cayce is seeing an axis shift. However, an exact reversal of the axis poles would not result in the type of weather changes that he describes: "frigid or the semi-tropical will become the more tropical, and moss and fern will grow." This would only require the axis to move enough to direct cooler portions of the planet toward the sun. Let's examine these two types of pole shifts.

The magnetic poles were first recognized by modern generations in the 16th Century as the direction to which compass needles point. But magnetic north continuously shifts position. It is now located at sea, about 93 miles north of Bathurst Island's May Inlet. This is a shift of about 530 miles north-northwest since 1831, when it was first reliably fixed. Magnetic north also fluctuates daily, effected by activity on the Sun. Solar flares create magnetic storms that travel through space and strike Earth's magnetic field, disturbing it like a stone on a pond. These disturbances to the magnetosphere surrounding Earth cause the magnetic poles, north and south, to move back and forth over the land and sea. Therefore, Canadian government scientists can only state the "average location" of the magnetic north pole for any given period.

In addition to the fluctuations of compasses, the magnetic poles are affecting biological life on the planet. Researchers in a relatively young science called *geomagnetbiology* have no doubt that the Earth's magnetic fields have profound effects on living organisms, even causing psychotic behavior and heart attacks in humans. Magnetic fields may also have played a major role in determining the course of evolution. If Cayce is speaking of a magnetic shift, then it has been going on since at least 1831, and is now some 530 miles from where it used to be.

Scientists also have evidence that the Earth's axis poles shifted before. William Sager of Texas A&M and well-known Anthony K.P. Koppers of Scripps Institution in San Diego reported in the January 21, 2000 edition of *Science* their findings of an axis pole shift 84 million years ago. In 1998 another scientific team of geologists at the California Institute of Technology reported that they found evidence of an axis pole shift, but their evidence dated a shift occurring around a half a billion years ago — a 90° shift! They believe that that pole shift touched off the great "Cambrian Explosion" of multicellular life – a period that saw all the major groupings of plants and animals begin their slow evolutionary march to where we are today. Definitely a new cycle began at that pole shift. Sager and Koppers say that the shift they detected was about 16 to 21°, which, if it happened today, would move Washington, D.C. to about where Cuba is presently located. San Francisco would be about where Baja California is. Obviously, North America would warm up. During the Sager-Koppers shift, volcanoes produced three massive plateaus, one around the Kerguelen Islands near Antarctica, another in the region of Jave, Indonesia, and the third in the Caribbean, near Columbia, South America. You might know, the Columbian-Caribbean area is where the massive asteroid struck the Earth, ending the age of the Dinosaurs. These shifts seem to be caused by magnetic changes combined with tectonic plates shifts. Both teams point out the pole shifts took a long time to be completed. The Sager-Koppers' shift took 2 million years to be completed. The California Institute of Technology's shift took 15 million years to be completed.

In Cayce's timeline (see chart at end of this chapter), the age of the Earth began some 4.6 billion years ago, with Mu (Lemuria) beginning about 12 million years ago, Atlantis beginning about 212,000 years ago (lasting about 200,000 years), Amilius entered Atlantis about 108,000 years ago, and the Adam-Eve human form we use today began about 14,000 years ago. Scientists say that the body-type we are currently using can be traced back to about 400,000 years ago, but you have to remember that Cayce said we were making many modifications to this homo-sapien body. He described how during the time of Hermes, Ra, and Isis in Egypt, we actually performed operations in the Temple Sacrifice to remove a low, animalistic chakra from the thighs of these bodies. Therefore, homo sapien could have had several versions or editions.

Cayce predicts that our bodies will make another change around the time of this coming pole shift. The first was with the entering into Mu, 12 million years ago. The second was about 10 millions ago, still in Mu. The third root race was made by Amilius and Lilith in Atlantis about 106,000 years ago. And the fourth root race body, which we are using a form of today, was created about 14,000 years ago. Time for a new, improved version, don't you agree?

Earth's poles have been wobbling for some time now. This may be a sign that the poles are going to shift again soon. This motion is like a top when it is about to fall over. It spins tightly around its axis poles, then, as it is about to fall over, it begins to wobble. The gravitational attraction of the Sun and Moon on the non-spherical Earth cause the rotational axis of the Earth to precess in space similar to the action of a top. In addition to this motion, the axis undergoes a small "nodding" motion called nutation. Both these motions can be described theoretically to a high degree of accuracy. Forces within the Earth also affect its rotation. Many organizations are watching this: The National Earth Orientation Service (NEOS), the sub-bureau for rapid service and prediction of the International Earth Rotation Service (IERS), both located at the U.S. Naval Observatory (NSNO), and International Astronomical Union (IAU), and countless independent teams around the world.

In looking at the scientific data, we learn that a shifting of the Earth's axis poles has happened and can happen again; that shifting occurs over long periods of time; that wobbling tends to precede shifting; and that shifts result in major changes to life on the planet. The Aztec/Maya Age of Movement may well end in a big movement of the whole planet.

## After the Fifth Age

According to Cayce's reading of the Akasha, following the end of the Fifth Age is a return back through the earlier Ages, but at a faster pace. We will regain our godling powers, reunite our sexual qualities into one body type, and begin to move into cosmic consciousness again. Our Earthly, material needs will change because our new body-type will not be so needy or so vulnerable to the dangers of this world. Those needs that remain will be fulfilled easily because we will regain the powers we had as godlings in the early millennia in this world, able to control and guide the forces of Nature. He warns that we will once again be challenged to see how we use these powers, reminding us that in Atlantis they brought destruction. What will they bring in the new age? Just as the Sun and Venus did, the mind and heart also went through many cycles of trials and tests facing the challenges of evil and darkness. So too in the next era will we recycle through another period of testing to see if we really have subdued the Earthy influences and selfish urges; to see if we recognize ourselves to be a part of that about us in oneness again. If not, then the Forces of Life will cleanse themselves and this planet and it will begin again. But if we have caught a glimpse of our inner godly nature, of our potential companionship with the Universal Creator, of the oneness of all life, then an age of enlightenment will begin. The Logos will come again among us. Spitefulness, contention, hatred, bloodshed, vengeance, envy, will subside. Patience, understanding, kindness, gentleness, forgiveness, love, healing, will rise and transform everyone. This will not be in an airy, fairy manner, for we have all seen the shadow side of human nature, and are wiser for it. It will be in a deep contentment that will never be moved by urges of selfishness and separateness again. The rebel in all of us will be tempered. The use of free will without consideration of its affect on others and the Whole will not be done again. Cooperation will be the spirit that pervades relationships; first within individuals, then classes, then the masses, until the whole of humanity is imbued with a renewed sense of oneness, with a peacefulness that passes all understanding.

As Cayce saw it, we are close:

> Yet, as time draws nigh when changes are to come about, there may be the opening of those three places where the records are one, to those that are the initiates in the knowledge of the One God:
>
> The temple by Iltar will then rise again. Also there will be the opening of the temple or hall of records in Egypt, and those records that were put into the heart of the Atlantean land may also be found there - that have been kept, for those that are of that group.
>
> The RECORDS are ONE.[16]

---

[16] 5750-1

## EDGAR CAYCE'S PREHISTORIC TIMELINE

| YEAR | EVENT |
|------|-------|
| 4.6 Billion Years before the present | **Beginning of the Earth Experience.** "When the morning stars sang together and all the sons and daughters of God shouted for joy announcing the advent of man into material existence." |
| 12 Million years before the present | **1st Root Race**: The first soul influx into the ancient Pacific Ocean continent of Mu, or Lemuria. The records found in a cave in China referred to this ancient land as the Motherland Mu. |
| 10 Million Years before the present | **2nd Root Race**: The second soul influx into improved bodies began in Mu, or Lemuria. |
| 210,000 B.C. | **Atlantean Civilization begins** with influx of souls into the ancient Atlantic Ocean continent of Atlantis. |
| 106,000 B.C. | **3rd Root Race:** The third improvement upon a physical form for the souls to inhabit begins. The Logos, Son of God, enters to help all souls. Up to this point bodies have been female and male in one. The Logos divides its two united genders into separate beings, Amilius and Lilith. Lilith is dominant, as are all females at this time. Feminine rule begins around the planet and lasts until the Great Flood. After the Great Flood, the masculine begins to dominant and rule. |
| 50,700 B.C. | **First breakup of Atlantis** into islands. |
| 28,000 B.C. | **Second breakup of Atlantis.** Five islands now compose Atlantis. |
| 22,800 B.C | **The Great Flood begins.** God decides to wash the slate clean and begin again. |

# EDGAR CAYCE'S PREHISTORIC TIMELINE

| YEAR | EVENT |
| --- | --- |

**12,000 B.C.** — **4th Root Race**: A new an improved body is developed to help souls better evolve through this entrapment in matter. It is the Adamic body. The Logos again enters and separates its genders into Adam and Eve. This pattern occurs in five places on the planet at once.

The White Race in the Caucus. The Black in the Sudan, Nubia. The Yellow in the Gobi. The Brown in the eastern portions of the remnant of Mu, the Andes mountain range. The Red in the remnant of Atlantis.

**10,500 B.C.** — **The new centers are being built.** Most notable are the Giza plateau in Egypt, the Golden Temple in the Gobi, temples and pyramids in Yucatan, Mounds in North America, even temples that evidentially sink are built in Atlantis and Mu. The Giza monuments, especially the Sphinx and the Great Pyramid, are constructed during this period. The Great Pyramid takes 100 years to complete.

**10, 014 B.C.** — **The Final Destruction of Atlantis.** The only remaining island of Poseidia sinks. All remnant groups from Atlantis have migrated to the shores of North America (today these are the Iroquois), to the Pyrenees Mountains, (today these are the Basque), to the Yucatan Peninsula, and to Egypt. Only tiny little islands remain from Mu's destruction. Many of the Lemurians migrated to Asia, South and North America, some to as far away as India.

**SPECIAL NOTE:** Our fall from original grace and direct contact with God occurred in the spirit, long before our involution into matter.

# Afterword

# Confirming Cayce's Timeline

*by Gregory L. Little, Ed.D.*

Since the 1930s, academic archaeologists have promoted the view that humans were not in the Americas until about 11,000 years ago. According to the academics, rather suddenly large tribes of nomadic hunters from Siberian Asia entered the Americas across the ice sheets then covering the Bering Straits. They followed an ice-free corridor into Canada and America and, within a few thousand years, had populated all of the Americas. Their unique type of spear point — termed Clovis for the area where the points were first uncovered — has been found everywhere in the Americas at the same archaeological dating level. Because of this, the academics claim, there was no reason to dig deeper since additional layers of human artifacts could not be there.

From time to time excavations have turned up evidence of human occupation in the Americas prior to Clovis. However, all such finds were systematically attacked and ridiculed, so few archaeologists risked the damage to job and reputation to report their findings. However, in 1997, a panel of archaeologists certified that the Monte Verde site in southern Chile was occupied at least 1,000 years prior to Clovis. Additional evidence showed that Monte Verde could have levels of human occupation reaching back 33,000 years. Evidence in Brazil then showed occupation traces as long ago as 50,000 years. With this, the Clovis-First barrier was officially broken and a mass of additional excavation reports were made showing that America was, indeed, an ancient melting pot. Further evidence indicates that the Clovis culture itself may not be Asian in origin, but rather a result of an European influence.

## Ancient America Was A Mosaic of People

The emerging picture of ancient America is now, as Edgar Cayce put it nearly 70 years ago, apparently the result of a mosaic of influences. Evidence shows that mummies in the Andes have a genetic viral link shared only by a unique group of Japanese islanders. Other genetic evidence shows that the Americas were settled at least 30,000 years ago by several large waves of immigrants. Ancient visitors from Polynesia, Australia, China, Japan, Siberia, and Europe all came to the Americas. In addition, linguistic analysis shows that three separate, distinct and large migrations of people to the Americas occurred.

One of the arguments put forth against pre-Columbian visits to the Americas is that the people of A.D. 1492 barely had the capability to arrive here from Europe. How then, it is asked, could more primitive peoples have possibly come here? Yet archaeologists have known that Australia was populated from Indonesia beginning 60,000 years ago and an article in *Science* (March 9, 2000) reported the astonishing find of an 800,000 year-old boat made of Indonesian bamboo on an Australian Island. There really isn't any doubt that small boats carrying bands of migrants could have come to ancient America.

Elsewhere in the world, archaeologists are finding ruins of ancient civilizations lying on the bottom of ocean floors. Japan, the Mediterranean area, and other regions of earth have yielded enigmatic underwater evidence of a cataclysm sometime in the remote past. Graham Hancock is following these clues in an attempt to link them to a massive catastrophe around 10,500 B.C.

# Taking Cayce Literally

Until 1997, Edgar Cayce's readings linking Atlantis, Mu, the Yucatan, and the Hall of Records could not have been taken literally by scholars. The simple reason is that the 9,000 B.C. Clovis Barrier precluded Cayce's time frame. Cayce indicated that Atlantis began to break up in 50,700 B.C. with a second, more violent breakup in 28,000 B.C. Some time prior to this, the island of Mu began to sink creating a pattern of islands. With each of these cataclysms, several groups of people left their island homes migrating to numerous locations including both North and South America. Prior to the final destruction of Atlantis in about 10,000 B.C., Cayce indicates that small groups of enlightened ones built temples near Bimini (Atlan) and in the Yucatan (Iltar). The new archaeological evidence in the Americas supports Cayce's conclusion that a mosaic of peoples did, in fact, migrate here in waves probably centering around 50,000 B.C., 30,000 B.C., and 10,000 B.C.

Few people in America are aware that a Mu museum exists in Japan and that many foreign scholars take the existence of Mu seriously. Artifacts probably referring to Mu have been recovered in underwater excavations off the islands of Japan. In addition, with the discovery of stone ruins in the same area, the myth of a submerged civilization somewhere in the Pacific is confirmed. The myth of Atlantis is more problematical in that the very name "Atlantis" brings to mind images unrelated to Cayce's readings on the ancient island. In archaeology, Atlantis is a "dirty" and taboo word and the mere mention of it elicits incredulous looks and derision. Yet it is wise to remember that at one time the earth was believed to be flat by scientists and that archaeologists asserted that the stories of Troy were just that — stories.

The evidence of Atlantis at Bimini is, thus far, unconvincing — yet promising. Edgar Evans Cayce explained our failure to uncover the massive island civilization rather rationally during an Atlantis special shown on the *Discovery Channel*. He asks how easy would it be to find ruins of an island shaken apart by violent earthquakes after 12,000 years of being submerged under the ocean depths?

One thing is clear. As the Cayce readings related to us, both genetic and archaeological evidence confirm that several groups of visitors from the "east" and "west" did arrive in ancient America. Genetic research on modern Native Americans shows a small but highly distinctive mDNA haplotype labeled haplogroup X by geneticists. Haplogroup X is a Caucasian European who appears to have arrived in the Americas first in 10,000 B.C. This date is, of course, the date given by Cayce for the arrival of Iltar's group in the Yucatan. Cayce also related that some Atlanteans migrated north to merge with the people already there eventually becoming the Moundbuilders. Of importance to this finding is the sudden emergence of the "Clovis" point spreading all over the Americas at the same time. The Clovis culture is nearly identical to the Solutrean culture of Spain and southwestern France beginning about 16,000 years ago. It is certainly possible that both the Solutrean Culture in Europe and the Clovis Culture in America resulted from a simultaneous migration from a third area — possibly from an area centered between Europe and America.

## Lost Tribes

Cayce's readings indicating that small groups of ancient Israelites (known as remnants of the Lost Tribes) arrived in the Americas in 3,000 B.C. have also had strong recent support from archaeological finds.

In 1889 an expedition by the Smithsonian uncovered a small stone tablet from a small, undisturbed mound in Tennessee along with a variety of other artifacts. The tablet was inscribed with characters that were immediately interpreted as "Cherokee," however, it was also found that the characters appeared to bear an uncanny resemblance to paleo-Hebrew. In 1988, an article appeared in a mainstream archaeology journal showing that the characters were paleo-Hebrew and that artifacts found with the tablet were of a leaded brass produced only in the ancient middle-east. In addition, an ancient, massive earthwork in Ohio, called the Hanukkiah Earthworks for its uncanny resemblance to a Jewish menorah encircled by an oil lamp, was first reported in the 1700s. Early Smithsonian reports included surveys of the site, but farming gradually obliterated it. Because the earthworks clearly pointed to a Hebrew origin, archaeologists have long asserted that it simply didn't exist. In the mid-1990s it was discovered that the US Army Corp of Engineers had surveyed the site in 1823. Their original signed survey map was found — and still remains — in the National Archives in Alexandria, Virginia. Finally, one additional bit of evidence on the possibility of Lost Tribes arriving in the Americas in 3,000 B.C. is relevant. Prior to 1997, the beginning of moundbuilding in North America was dated to 2,000 B.C. at Poverty Point, Louisiana. In 1997 and 1999, carbon dating of a newly excavated mound site near Monroe, Louisiana showed that it was constructed around 3,000 B.C. The site, known as Watson Brake, is a gigantic, circular embankment enclosing 22 acres. Eleven mounds are constructed on the circular embankment. The site is easily reached from the Mississippi River.

Cayce indicated that the first arrivals of the Lost Tribes entered the southernmost portions of America on boats in 3,000 B.C. and then moved on to the Yucatan. Watson Brake may be the remains of the first Lost Tribe's migrants.

## The Yucatan & The Hall of Records

With archaeological evidence now supporting Cayce's previously impossible time frame, a consideration of the validity of his readings on the Yucatan is possible. In this book, the authors have done a meticulous job of correlating Cayce's statements with the archaeological record. What emerges is an astonishing validation of Cayce. The "mosaic" of influences by different cultures is apparent in the Yucatan as well as all of the Americas. Piedras Negras does appear to be the specific site Cayce indicated as holding the Hall of Records. But why Piedras Negras?

Piedras Negras — to this very day — is nearly inaccessible. It cannot be reached by air or even by a small boat. Traveling by foot through the dense jungle is nearly impossible. One has to arrive at Piedras Negras by paddling small canoes and occasionally carrying the boats through the jungle around several rapids. Iltar placed the Hall of Records in an inaccessible spot to keep them safe and undiscovered — until the time was right.

At Piedras Negras the exact location of the Hall of Records appears to be hinted at in several areas. The Acropolis, the South Group Ballcourt, Altar 1, the caves, and the pyramids of the South Group are all possibilities. The incredible pyramid alignments with Orion's rise in 3114 B.C. and its setting in A.D. 2012 show a relationship to other ancient cultures — especially Egyptian — that hints of an Atlantean influence. An intriguing possibility is that a part — or all — of the Hall of Records have already been found there. Although none of the archaeological reports have indicated such a find, it is well established that everything found at the site has not been reported.

Perhaps the most astonishing aspect of this book is Cayce's readings of the Akasha telling us what is actually recorded in the Hall of Records. It relates the history of humanity. It confirms our link with spirit and our fall from grace. It tells of the ongoing struggle between the forces of light with the forces of darkness and the personal battle all of us have within ourselves. Similar records have been passed on from generation to generation. The Bible tells of the same struggle but centers on the history of Israel. So it is with other religious texts including those of the Maya and Aztec.

All cultures and societies — both ancient and modern — have taken great pains to leave a written record of their history, knowledge, ideals, and purpose. We shouldn't be surprised if a culture entering the Yucatan 12,000 years ago in a time of crisis took great pains to ensure that their knowledge wasn't lost. We should only be surprised if they didn't.

# Index

# About The Authors

John Van Auken is the Director of the Edgar Cayce Foundation and author of numerous books including *Mayan, Toltec, and Aztec Visions of Our Soul Life* and *Ancient Egyptian Visions of Our Soul Life*.

Lora Little holds a master's degree and doctorate in Counseling and Health Care Administration from the University of Memphis. She is a long-time student of the Edgar Cayce readings with a particular focus on both spiritual development and archaeology. This interest has led her to travel extensively to historical sites throughout North and Central America and Europe since the 1980s, as well as serve as a member of the A.R.E. Atlantis Research Team doing active research and exploration in Guatemala and the Bahamas since 2003 with Greg Little. A former co-editor of the A.R.E. *Ancient Mysteries Newsletter*, Lora has spoken both nationally and internationally and is coauthor of six books relating the Edgar Cayce readings to various archaeological and historical topics including *The Lost Hall of Records* (2000) with John Van Auken; *The A.R.E.'s Search for Atlantis* (2003) with Greg Little; *Mound Builders* (2001), *Ancient South America* (2002), *Secrets of the Ancient World* (2003) and *Edgar Cayce's Atlantis* (2006), all with Greg Little and John Van Auken.

*Epilogue*

# Piedras Negras Update

Since this book was written nearly 20 years ago there have been several amazing new discoveries that provide additional corroboration not only for Cayce's ancient timeline, but also for the 17 clues regarding the location of the Yucatan Hall of Records outlined in Chapter 3 of this book.

Evidence continues to mount indicating that a major catastrophic event occurred across North America and the Caribbean around the time of Cayce's final destruction of Atlantis. The 10,000 B.C. Younger Dryas geological ash line found all over the world may explain the readings' assertion that a "record in the rock still remains ... OF those peoples ... that did escape during the periods of destruction."

Progress in the decipherment of the Maya hieroglyphs has uncovered mysterious stories carved into monuments that date back many thousands of years prior to the Classic era. Scientists were shocked to discover a Pre-classic mural in a tomb in Guatemala containing the earliest known painting of the Maya origins story. A similar image of the emergence of "first father" Itzamna can be found at Piedras Negras strangely carved almost 3 stories high on the side of a cliff in a remote area just outside the central complex. Its age is still undetermined.

But the most interesting decipherment comes from the enigmatic Altar 1 located in a place of honor in front of the palatial Acropolis complex. It contains a memorial to an important event witnessed by a "Holy Piedras Negras Lord" in the year 4691 B.C.! The event involves the paddler gods who traveled by canoe to "the first 3-stone place," near "the edge of the sky" and the mythical "five flower place." Scholars consider it yet another account of the Maya creation legend. It is tempting to wonder whether it was inspired by a distant memory of the transfer of the Yucatan records from a location near the coast to their current resting place at Piedras Negras.

At the recently discovered El Mirador ruins, mainstream archaeologists are finding greater sophistication at older levels of the site that contradict the long held dogma that the first millennia Classic Maya were the apex of that civilization. The entire field of Maya archaeology is undergoing a massive transformation through aerial laser mapping of ancient sites previously hidden beneath dense jungle cover throughout Central America. The data is revealing a society startlingly larger and more interconnected than ever imagined. Many now believe that the Classic Maya period may actually represent the final decline of a much older and more highly complex empire.

The discovery of ritual artifacts and burials in underwater Central American cave systems, believed to have been flooded since at least 10,000 B.C, provide further support for an earlier advanced culture. Artifacts identified by divers are in places that could only have been utilized at the time these caves were above sea level.

## 2004 Visit to Piedras Negras

In 2004, Greg Little and I had the opportunity to explore Piedras Negras spending several days camping on the banks of the Usumacinta River. It was an awe inspiring experience to view first-hand the mysterious pyramids, bathhouses, enigmatic rock carvings, stelae, altars, and other monuments I had studied so intensely while writing this book.

Above: Our camp as seen from the Usumasinta river. Left: Our tent at the campsite. Photos: Lora Little.

Above: The boat we took on the Usumasinta river to reach Piedras Negras.

Above: Lora next to altar top shaped as a Jaguar paw. Bottom: Lora and Greg Little stand next to the Sacrificial Stone at site entrance.

Above: Lora beneath the Turtle/Itzamna Emergence Cliff carving.

The remains of Altar 1 at Piedras Negras.

Lora stands on the top of the Sweat Bath at Piedras Negras.

Toward the end of our visit, while winding through the East Group, the Guatemalan park rangers drew my attention to a small opening within a pile of stones at the base of Pyramid O-13 that is built into the side of a cliff. This was the place, they told me, where Brigham Young University had recently attempted unsuccessfully to excavate a suspected royal tomb. They encouraged me to insert my hand into the gap. Amidst the stifling jungle heat and humidity I felt cold air that had to be emanating from a large cavity deep underground.

As has been confirmed at many other classic Maya cities, the limestone bedrock at Piedras Negras is very likely riddled with a labyrinth of subterranean tunnels connecting its various temples and pyramids. Although none have been identified at Piedras Negras so far, during our trip we had been allowed to peer over the edge of the largest cenote (sinkhole) in Guatemala located not far from Pyramid O-13. Interestingly, it is now known that the original Maya name for Piedras Negras is "Yokibi" which means "great entrance," although no one is clear why it would have been given that name.

In light of this new evidence, and much more than I can cover here, I remain convinced that Piedras Negras hides a long forgotten passageway that leads to Cayce's Yucatan Hall of Records. The mystery deepens and we will continue to watch with anticipation as the true story continues to unfold.

- Lora Little, Ed.D. May 2020

Guatemalan Park Ranger inserting his hand into the opening where cold air emanates from the base of Pyramid O-13.

Composite Picture (3 photos) of Pyramid O-13 Rubble and opening.

Printed in Great Britain
by Amazon

18600571R00169